THE COMPLETE BOOK OF
GOLF

Acknowledgments

Tom Lehman

Laura Davies

Marie-Laure de Lorenzi

Malcolm Campbell; editor, author and category 'A' golfer

Peter McKay and Michael McDonnell of the *Daily Mail*

Allan Hall

Alan Fine; Tour psychologist, president of Inside Out Inc. and author of *Mind Over Golf* (BBC Books)

David White; author and golf historian

Mike Wood of *Golf Monthly*

Bill Robertson of *Today's Golfer*, swing analyst

Alan and Margaret Ashworth

Simon Cainey

Kevin Brown

Sarah Fabbien Baddiel

Golfiana at Grays in the Mews, B24 Davies Mews, London, Tel: 0171 408 1239

Michael Hobbs

Generation Associates Ltd and Mary Killingworth

DC Publications Ltd

Extracts by kind permission of the *Daily Mail Centenary CD-Rom*

Editor: Steve Lynas

Project Manager: Gaynor Edwards

Picture Research: Ricky Leaver

Designers: Paula O'Brien, Angus Elton-Miller, Edwin Donald, Lucy Bryant

Special thanks to:

David Crowe

THE COMPLETE BOOK OF

GOLF

An unrivalled collection of writing and photography

on the world's fastest growing sport

ANDRE
DEUTSCH

First published in Great Britain in 1997 by André Deutsch

an imprint of André Deutsch Ltd

106 Great Russell Street

London WC1B 3LJ

www.vci.co.uk

André Deutsch Ltd is a subsidiary of VCI plc

Printed and bound in Great Britain by Butler and Tanner, Frome, Somerset

Design and Project Management: Jupiter 7 Graphics Ltd

A catalogue record for this book is available from the British Library

ISBN 0 233 99090 9

'IT IS ONE OF THE IRREFUTABLE TRUTHS OF GOLF THAT YOUR GAME IS SIGNIFICANTLY HAMPERED BY

STANDING TOO NEAR TO THE BALL... THIS IS ESPECIALLY TRUE AFTER YOU HAVE HIT IT.'

Anon

Contents

'The golfer who hit an air shot on the first tee at St Andrews' by H.M. Bateman.

A FIERCELY ADDICTIVE PURSUIT

by Peter McKay

GOLF, '… a game played by individual competitors, whose object is to drive a small, hard ball with one of a set of clubs towards and into a series of holes …'. *Encyclopaedia Britannica* is admirably concise, but its description of golf requires amplification. Golf is a 'game' only in the limited sense that, when we've failed at it, we may console ourselves by saying: 'It's only a game.' We know it's never merely a game, far less 'only' a game. Rather it's a cruel test of human endurance and character – like life itself but a little more complicated. 'Game' suggests a beginning, middle and end – a pastime, a recreation, an amusement. But true golfers hunt the rolling green fairways as Captain Ahab pursued the great white whale Moby Dick. Once started, there is no proper end.

'Individual competitors' may sound accurate enough. But no golfer ever stood on a tee thinking of himself or herself as an individual competitor. They stand there, squinting into the horizon and fussily arranging grip, stance and knee-flexibility, as complete, evolved masterful human beings at the peak of their attention span, pitting themselves against every contradictory force in life and in aerodynamics. Everything they've learned and thought is focused on the moment they swing that club. No matter how dire the result, or grievously bad their performance, no true golfer thinks of himself as an 'individual competitor'.

We do not 'drive' a small, hard ball with one of a set of clubs towards and into a series of holes. We drive cars. In golf we 'address' a small, hard, infinitely capricious sphere with the club we have judged perfect for the purpose after a period of calm reflection. Prior to the critical moment of address, studies will have been made of the terrain, the wind conditions and the desired final destination of the ball.

There are endless arguments about this but the case is now well proven that golf began in fifteenth-century Scotland. It was established in America in 1888 when two Scots – John Reid and Robert Lockhart – organized the St Andrews Golf Club in Yonkers, New York. Accordingly, the rules of golf are now governed by the Royal and Ancient Golf Club at St Andrews, Scotland, and the US Golf Association. The Americans and the British have studied each other's methods, sometimes with success, at other times unhappily. The late humorist Patrick Campbell developed what he called the Hogan Crouch, first exhibited by the US champion Ben Hogan.

'In the Crouch the knees are bent throughout the duration of the performance. The back is bent and the buttocks are thrust out in the sitting position... If the knees should suddenly straighten, owing to centrifugal force, the clubhead passes over the ball, resulting in a clean miss (Wentworth, April 1951; Stoke Poges, April 1951; Walton Heath, April 1951; Sunningdale, April 1951, etc.).'

The ancient Scottish connection lends importance to the character of golf. Its pitiless disciplines delight the mordant Presbyterian character. One of the oldest golf stories is of four Scotsmen preparing to tee off one day when, about to begin his swing, the 'first-off' player sees out of the corner of his eye a funeral procession approaching on a nearby street. He pauses, rests his clubhead on the tee and bows his head patiently until the cortége has passed. One of the 'individual competitors' turns to another and says:

'I didna ken Jock was religious.' His friend gazes at the retreating mourners and replies: 'Och well, she was a good wife to him for forty years.'

Golfers enjoy black humour, especially if it is topical. I heard recently of the player who, depressed by his inability to hit the ball farther than 80 yards, took advice from his club pro. After studying his swing for a few moments, the pro said the problem was very simple. He wasn't keeping his head down and very still while swinging through. He demonstrated what he meant, hitting the ball 280 yards down the middle of the fairway.

His student stepped up to the tee, and kept his head down until the ball was well on its way. A beautiful shot. He repeated the exercise several times with the same result. He told the pro: 'This is marvellous. There's only one problem. My sight's not great and I don't know where the ball's landed.' Easy, said the pro. Hire a caddie to keep an eye out. Next morning, he was joined on the tee by an elderly, white-haired man who said he was the caddie. The golfer groaned: 'I was expecting someone younger, with good sight.' The old man assured him his sight was fine. So off they went. Keeping his head down all the way through, our hero drove the ball 250 yards down the middle. He knew he had hit a good shot. It felt right. He turned to his caddie. 'Did you see where that landed?' 'Yes, sir,' said the caddie. 'Where is it, then?' asked the golfer. 'I've forgotten,' replied the caddie.

My own golf experience began in northern Scotland when I was around ten. With two boyhood friends, I positioned myself on a hillside and tried to catch damaged golf balls our older siblings hit there during their pre-season practice. This was only slightly less hazardous than catching flaming arrows or cannonballs, but we came to no harm. Later we spent drowsy summer days hunting lost balls and selling them back for pennies to those who'd lost them. (Years later I heard of the Irishman who appeared outside a posh club near London and approached a departing member. Did he want to buy a golf ball? A golf ball? He had hundreds of golf balls. The Irishman persisted: 'Sir, this is a special ball. Hit it into the deep rough and a wee aerial comes up and transmits a bleeping noise. If it lands in the water, this little propeller comes out and drives it up to the surface.' The golfer was intrigued. 'Where'd you get it?' he enquired. The Irishman replied: 'Oi found it!')

I've played for about twenty years now, and never got my handicap lower than 14. Sometimes I've played well, but never brilliantly. At other times I've played badly, but not spectacularly so. So I've never been in any position to boast about my golf but, on the other hand, neither has it driven me to despair. Certainly I have never experienced the horrors suffered by my occasional partner, whom I shall identify simply as the Captain.

The son of a famous diplomat, the Captain was once a gifted actor in the Royal Shakespeare Company. In his time he acted alongside the likes of Diana Rigg and Julie Christie. Although he was talented and could have gone far, he gave it up to become a journalist. He became a success at that and now lives in an imposing Cotswold residence with its own lake. He has had three hobbies – playing the French horn, fishing and aerobatic flying.

His horn playing might bring a tear to the eye of a hardened Marseilles brothel madam. Fish of all kinds queued to swallow the flies he cleverly fashioned. In the skies, at the controls of an aerobatic trainer, he was Monarch of the Heavens. The Captain never gloated about his mastery of these pursuits. He merely radiated a modest satisfaction.

It is entirely possible that he could have flown his trainer upside down twenty feet off the ground while playing the French horn, or fashioning a new trout fly. Had he done so there would have been no boasting. The Captain is not that kind of man. He believed that any intelligent human being can master most pursuits with patience and diligence. The day he took up golf brought this world of cosy certainty to a terrible close.

The Captain does nothing by halves. He bought expensive equipment and a library of golf videos, and signed up for lessons with one of the country's top pros. A month or so later, he joined me for a round. The pro had said he possessed one of the finest natural swings he'd ever seen, he remarked modestly. He didn't think personally that he was anything special, but the pro thought otherwise. He had 'the fundamentals'. Now for the fine-tuning.

The following weeks were a nightmare for the Captain, and for myself. When a friend plays a shot badly, it is permissible to chuckle. When every single shot over an entire round is a dud, there can be no mirth. The Captain would miss the ball completely on the tee – several times. Then it might skitter forward on to the ladies' tee. Often it went sharp right, or left. Twice his ball hit me, standing at right angles to him. Or rocketed back at us off a tree.

His mood ranged from incredulity to blind rage. Sometimes both, simultaneously. His trudge from tee to green – often via rough, deep rough, trees, meadows, public roads and ploughed fields – was a personal trail of tears. A golf partner in this situation has to observe certain rules. Sympathy can be expressed but it must not be laid on too heavily. To do so is to invite the suspicion that you're trying to make matters worse. Mild regret is the tone to seek. As if to say: 'Oh dear, never mind, isn't it a fine day, anyway?'

At one point – having impoverished my vocabulary searching for new, mild ways of saying the same soothing thing – I merely said: 'No, sir!' after he had shanked a shot into the brambles. He put down his club, his face a throbbing mask of suffering and barely contained fury. 'I think that is possibly the most annoying thing you could say in the circumstances,' he informed me through clenched teeth. 'It is an infuriating mixture of insincere respect and unnecessary admonition.'

The Captain persevered for ten years, to no avail. He will never play golf satisfactorily. Some mysterious malfunction in his body's co-ordination system has rendered him unable to play a golf shot. For a long time, he admits, he refused to acknowledge this. Now he has accepted it. And why not? As he says, it is not a real tragedy. He doesn't have to play golf. He can fish, fly and play the French horn. So, I said one recent day, did he want me to buy his fine, now unwanted, clubs? The Captain looked thoughtful for a moment. A slight narrowing of his eyes suggested embarrassment. He shifted awkwardly. 'Well, no, actually. I'll hang on to them … to tell the truth, I've been practising again on my own, in the field behind the house, and I've been striking the ball really well …' The awful truth is that golf, a fiercely addictive pursuit, has the Captain in its thrall. Being bad at it lights his fire more than performing well at other things.

For me, the true power of golf is its ability to remain above the human capacity for wrecking a good thing. I can think of no other sport which has more successfully resisted the great changes in human social behaviour over the past century.

Those who make monkeys out of themselves by wearing ludicrous clothes, or devising ever more stuffy golf club rules, are harmless boobies when compared with the modern followers of other sports. Some see golf as another means of importuning customers for double-glazing products, or replicating the kind of life they enjoyed in the armed services. They, too, can always be avoided. Others seek in its scoring system the success which has eluded them elsewhere. They can be left in their private agonies.

No blame attaches to golf itself. It neither encourages nor discourages foolish behaviour. Like the ocean, it neither likes nor dislikes us. It's there. It'll always be there. We may devise better equipment, or design ingenious new courses, but golf itself can never really change.

Peter McKay is a columnist for the *Daily Mail*

A DARK HISTORY

Since the days when wild gangs of ill-bred fishermen spent their summer

evenings thrashing a home-made ball across sand dunes, the game has

attracted its fair share of ruffians, incidents and outrages.

For a game that is accepted as representing all that is correct in sporting morality, golf has a surprisingly dark side to its history.

Since the days when wild gangs of ill-bred fishermen spent their summer evenings thrashing a home-made ball across sand dunes, the game has attracted its fair share of ruffians, incidents and outrages.

Many of the early societies which helped build the foundations of our modern game were little more than wild gaming clubs where betting was the norm and heavy drinking was essential.

Churches have excommunicated worshippers over golf. Queens have been reprimanded for their unseemly love of the game and kings have appointed clubmakers before they have created judges and generals.

Governments have banned the game for fear that their armies were so obsessed that they would abandon military training. Men have been murdered on the course, others have seen their powers usurped, and fortunes have been won and lost.

Some of its most powerful fans have been racist, isolationist, bigoted and intolerant. The rich have abused its qualities to exclude the poor and even now there are golf club committees where smug self-importance seems to be the main criterion for executive rank.

Spawning an industry that is worth billions every year, golf is addictive and obsessive, and its adherents spread like wildfire across the globe.

Sometimes it is hard to believe it is legal.

And yet, and yet …

BEGINNINGS

Nobody knows who invented golf. The chances are nobody ever will know for sure. Library floors groan under the weight of more than 5,000 books written on the game. They are full of scholarship, hypothesis and quite a few wild deductions made by studying ancient pictures.

Most books give an interpretation of the history, or make a guess at it. All historians suggest early links with the Dutch – all bar the most zealous of Scots, that is. Sometimes new theories are put together from an odd fact or two, but none point to golf's real beginnings.

Adam may have played in the Garden of Eden, with Eve the first golf widow – we shall never know. There are claims that the Romans, Persians, Egyptians and Greeks played a version of the game, though these may be discarded as distantly related forerunners of hockey, polo or lacrosse.

Just to add to the confusion, the Chinese have staked a claim that they played golf two thousand years before the Scots first wielded clubs. Beijing University professor Ling Hongling says the modern game originated during the Song Dynasty (960–1279), alleging it was refined out of an ancient game involving hitting a ball with a club. Clearly, the Chinese have studied ancient western tomes, for an amusing People's Party propaganda leaflet describes golf thus: 'When shepherds got their cows wandering around they played a game with wood clubs. They threw stones or rocks into rabbit holes. The winter was dreadfully cold, and the shepherds took one mouthful of wine with the cap of their bottle while they hit the ball. When they hit 18 balls with the clubs the liquor was gone. This resulted in the rule of 18 holes for the game. This made the British Royal House interested very much. The word golf is a combination of the initial letters of the four English words, Green, Oxygen, Light and Foot. The charm of the game is hidden behind.' Complete nonsense really.

We can divide the evolution of golf into three categories: the old long game, played in the Low Countries from about AD 1300–1700, known as colf; the short game, which developed from colf after 1700, and which is still played, called kolf; and finally the game that began in Scotland around 1450,

By definition, golf is a game in which a player, taking stance astride the direction of play, strikes a ball with a club for the lowest number of strokes from one point to another. Colf, in the beginning, was played with wooden balls and these were used well into the seventeenth century.

There is no doubt that colf was an early form of golf, while a similar ball-and-club game existed in England. Fute-ball, club-ball (like hockey) and cambuc, most closely related to golf, were all banned by Edward III in an edict dated 1363. So much time was devoted to the playing of these sports that the English archers began to ignore weapons practice, and their officers genuinely believed that the country's defences were suffering as a result.

There is also a stained-glass window in Gloucester Cathedral, dating from around 1350, depicting what is clearly an early golfer at the top of his swing. Equally, in northern Germany there was a similar game called Kolbe. Even in America, when New York was New Amsterdam, kolf was banned in 1659 because of damage to property.

Though no records exist of golf in Scotland before 1457, in an Act of King James II it is made clear that golf had so captured the imagination that it interfered with the practice of archery – so the king banned it. Before this Act ... nothing at all.

It seems likely that golf evolved on parallel lines along the east coast of Scotland, from Dornoch to Musselburgh, as a direct result of trade across the North Sea with the Dutch. There were of course some inland courses, Perth for example, the seat of the Stuart kings of Scotland, but golf did not reach the west of Scotland until the 1850s.

As a result of Scottish enthusiasm for the game, there was an enormous trade in wooden golf balls; a few Dutch villages lived almost solely on their manufacture, first of wood and then of leather stuffed with cow hair. One sale alone was for an amazing 40,000 balls in the year 1500 (lost balls were

The stained-glass window in Gloucester Cathedral depicting an early (headless) golfer.

which developed into the modern game of golf.

Though documentation is scant, proof does exist in the Low Countries of damage being caused by the flight of wooden and leather balls, with broken windows and injuries being a cause for concern. By the beginning of the fourteenth century, when the game seems to have first attracted artistic attention, sporting paintings have helped greatly in the assembly of the jigsaw.

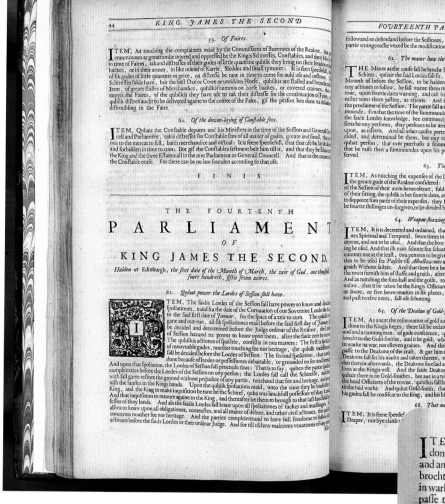

a greater hazard in those days). Multiple barrels of balls were sold to Scotland

but there was a reciprocal trade in wooden clubs from Scotland in the 1650s,

back to the Netherlands and France.

In the Netherlands, colf was an autumn-to-spring game played either on

ice, or where grass was short. For the same reason golf was initially a winter

game in Scotland. However, it was made possible over a longer season

Kolven, a seventeenth century Dutch form of winter golf as seen by artist Aert van der Neer.

because of Mother Nature's gift: fine turf found naturally where the receding sea left sandy wastes, linked with the more fertile soil inland. At least one could find the ball, even if putting surfaces left something to be desired by today's standards.

The name 'links' – areas that 'link' the land and the sea – originally had no connection with golf. Often, such land was common, open for all games, drying clothes or fishing nets, and other diverse purposes. Cattle-grazing concessions were sometimes granted, but secondary to the use by inhabitants. As one of the early writers on golf puts it: 'Links are too barren for cultivation, but sheep, rabbits, geese, and professionals pick up a precarious livelihood on them.'

At first the courses were very narrow and preparation was simple. A flattish area, reasonably free from rabbit holes, with a hole cut by a knife, was the green. Places where sheep had found shelter in hollows were soon converted by wind into pits of sand and became bunkers. A few holes placed at proper intervals around the barren soil constituted the golf course. Thrifty Scots often made the holes do double duty: playing out from the starting point to the finish, then reversing the procedure. There was no set number of holes: Leith had five; Crail and Bruntsfield had six; Glasgow, North Berwick and Aberdeen, seven.

At St Andrews they played 12 greens, many doubling up to make two holes, totalling 22 holes. In 1764 two double greens were discarded, dropping the number to 18. When St Andrews became the arbiter in golfing matters, this number was adopted as the standard. The smallest golf course is the three-hole links on the Isle of May in the Firth of Forth.

Golf was played in Scotland by all, irrespective of class; it was as popular with the monarchy as it was with its subjects. Every reigning monarch from 1502 to 1688 played golf, two kings and one queen of Scotland and the four

Golf in Scotland was popular with all classes. This portrait depicts one of the children of the MacDonald clan getting to grips with the great game.

kings of the United Kingdom. The line was broken with the end of the Stuarts; William of Orange soon put a stop to that south of the border.

It was, in fact, more than a hundred years before golf became popular again in England and, for years, there were more courses in the east of Scotland than in the whole of the rest of the United Kingdom.

Around 1830, Edwin Budding, an engineer employed in the weaving industry, devised a machine with a cutting cylinder to shear the nap of woven cloth to produce a smooth surface. Budding adapted this concept and applied it to mowing grass, and its potential was discerned by Ransomes of Ipswich, who produced the first lawn mowers in 1832. By 1858 they had sold 1,500 machines and, though fairly primitive and heavy, the machines caught on. Ransomes then switched to their own design, with an enclosed gear case, which was so successful they sold a thousand in the first season.

Boom time in the 1890s. Players enjoying the great links at Lahinch on the west coast of Ireland.

Certainly it was not until the mower became a feasible way of imposing the golfers' ideas of playing conditions on the turf – and in so doing, defining the expressions 'fairway' and 'rough' – that it was possible to build and maintain courses away from naturally occurring fine turf areas. Before the mowing machine, the player was 'through the green', in a hazard, or in the cup; there were no other divisions.

There were, in the later years of the nineteenth century, alternative ways of keeping grass short, chiefly scything. Even in living memory greenkeepers mowed tees by scythe, the only mower being kept strictly for greens use. Others could mow out clover on a green with a really sharp scythe.

A boom in golf followed in the 1890s. Assessing the number of golf courses in Britain has always been fraught with problems. Early records indicate that, in 1857, there were 17 courses in Scotland, but by 1888 there were 73, though only 57 in England, six in Ireland and two in Wales. Most of these courses, outside Scotland, were started by Scottish garrison troops or expatriate Scottish professional men. The oldest links course in England, Royal North Devon Golf Club at Westward Ho!, which opened in 1864, owed much to the support and advice given by a visitor from St Andrews,

Greenkeepers scything the 18th green on the old course at St Andrews. Notice the grass cuttings at the back of the green.

ABOVE: A postcard of the Royal North Devon golf club at Westward Ho!, the oldest links course in England.
RIGHT: Willie Park Jnr pictured at Huntercombe in Oxfordshire. The course was his first attempt at golf
course design and is now considered a classic.

General Moncrieff. Even earlier, (Royal) Blackheath, dating from 1603, owed its existence to the demand from the largely Scottish Royal Court of King James VI (James I of England) for a golf course.

The earliest golf course architects were, generally, leading amateurs, or the best golf professionals. Old Willie Dunn laid out the London Scottish course in 1865 while he was a greenkeeper at Royal Blackheath. Even in those days there was a thriving export business in golf greenkeepers from Scotland.

While it is perhaps invidious to single out one man, Willie Park Jnr deserves the title of the first full-time golf course architect. He was a man of education and ambition, far more intelligent than the earlier type of golf professionals, who had risen from the ranks of caddies.

Willie was Open Champion in 1887 and 1889, but, more significantly, he

Golf at Blackheath as seen by painter Francis Powell Hopkins in 1875. Built in 1603, Blackheath is the oldest course in England.

was the first to decry the old method of designing courses by siting greens on 'good-looking' sites, often unrelated to the overall layout. He developed, if not invented, the concept of strategic, as opposed to penal, design, which obliged anyone with ambitions on winning to plan his tee shots thoughtfully, rather than just firing at random.

It is worth noting that one of Willie's most famous memorials is the Old Course at Sunningdale, laid out in 1900. It seems extraordinary that, in those days when mechanisation meant the use of horse-drawn earth scoops and everything done by hand, it took only a year for the course, which was seeded throughout, to be ready for play.

The popularity of the game suddenly blossomed. From only 57 English courses in 1888, by 1890 there were 90 and by 1894 the number had doubled to 182, with a dramatic extension to no fewer than 655 by 1914. This means that 473 new courses were built in England in those two decades alone, an average of nearly 25 a year. Similar expansion took place in Scotland, with 223 new courses between 1890 and 1909. Most of these clubs are still in existence, though not all are still playing on their original courses.

THE GOLFERS ORGANIZE

Throughout the reign of the Stuarts golf had a precarious existence. Indeed, it is a wonder the game survived. There were no formal golf clubs, in the modern sense, before then, and the development of the game is to the credit of the Scottish golfing societies.

There are no records of any clubs in existence until Scotland settled again after the bloody suppression in the Highlands by the English, though there seems little doubt that the Honourable Company of Edinburgh Golfers, first known as the Company of Gentlemen Golfers and founded in 1744, was the father of them all.

It was the Honourable Company that promoted the first competition, the Town Council presenting a silver club, the winner designated as captain. Club championships meant something in those days. It was the beginning of a tradition, for not only did the winner fix a silver ball, bearing his name, to the society's silver club, but he automatically became captain.

Other eighteenth-century clubs, which fostered and preserved golfing traditions, while protecting the links, were St Andrews (1754), Edinburgh Burgess (which claimed 1735, but was minuted 1773), Bruntsfield (1790), Royal Musselburgh (1774), Royal Aberdeen (1780) and the Glasgow Club (1787).

These clubs were little more than groups of friends banded together. They had no clubhouses, the nearest tavern being thought sufficient for their needs of wine and victuals. They wore red coats to distinguish themselves from others of low estate who played upon the same links. They met to talk 'business', a euphemism for throwing out challenges to play, which were duly recorded in the match book. Each challenge would attract huge wagers on either side. While match-play bets were most common, the books contain a diversity of wagers, covering subjects from politics to the sex of a coming child. At least once a year they would stage a banquet, with the members wearing the club uniform and with the newly chosen captain escorted by pipers to his seat of honour.

The same society might play on several links, for few could lay claim to their own course. At one time the links at Musselburgh was home to four Scottish societies, dividing the cost of upkeep.

From the standpoint of golf, the principal influence of these societies was to standardize the rules and protect the links. The Honourable Company was the first group to formalize rules, in 1744, while each society laid down its own rules of play. Standardization was reached by the middle 1790s, when most of them adhered to the St Andrews rules. When golf crossed the

Atlantic, the St Andrews rules followed, and, except for minor variations, Americans looked to the Royal and Ancient for guidance. Today, the R & A and the United States Golf Association work hand in hand.

The early clubs, being organized, gradually assumed a measure of control over the links. From helping to pay for the repair or improvement of the links, they moved to hiring caddies or clubmakers for such work. Finally, many groups built their own courses, and the modern golf club is the result.

This may all have been serious business, but their principal activity remained social. Golf, gambling and eating and drinking with friends have always blended together, and in these old societies conviviality was the canon for membership. The members were men of high social standing, often members of the professions. The black ball and the golf clique, prevalent then, remain the most ancient of golf club institutions.

Food was cheap, and the monthly dinners were frequently paid for by a levy against all members, whether present or not. In 1766, the novelist Tobias Smollett, describing one gathering of elderly golfers, stated: 'They were all gentlemen of independent fortunes, who had amused themselves with this pastime for the best part of a century, without having ever felt the least alarm from sickness or disgust; and they never went to bed without having each the best part of a gallon of Claret in his belly.'

'Drunk as a lord' was no empty phrase. For example, at one dinner of the Honourable Company in 1801, the liquor bill, apparently for a dozen members, included 16 bottles of claret and seven bottles of port and sherry, besides quantities of gin, brandy, porter and ale.

Old club records are full of references to golfers' exploits at their dinners, with many ingenious methods of securing liquor. Fines of a gallon of claret were levied for even petty offences. The captain might be fined for failing to wear his uniform on the links; another for hosting a dinner on the night of the club meeting, with an additional gallon for each club member who was his guest.

At Crail, in 1789, they were particularly hard on temperance and resolved that 'no member, in particular the secretary, shall absent himself from the bowl, on pretence of tea-drinking.' Later, they fined a member one-half mutchkin of punch (about half a pint) 'for being about drinking tea – convicted on his own confession.'

These early socializers were, in the end, doomed by prosperity. As the popularity of golf expanded, so they dwindled, their membership too large for the closeness that had so distinguished them. The modern golf club was their downfall.

CADDIES, EARLY PROS AND GREENKEEPERS

Sir Walter Simpson, author of *The Art of Golf*, knew only too well that caddies were a poor lot, given to drinking away what little they earned. From the earliest times they had worn several bonnets, some being rough clubmakers, others labouring on the links, while a few purported to be mentors of the game. Yet he loved them.

He wrote: ' "The caddies will only drink the more if overpaid," you say. Indeed! and to what good purpose do you apply the money you grudge the poor? Is there something nobler in your gout and dyspepsia than in my caddy's red nose? Or no! I do not despise your gout (I feel a twitch myself), but your incapacity for taking pleasure in giving it (cheaply) to others is what I condemn. An Epicurean with the vices of a Stoic, and none of his virtues! I shall grossly overpay my caddy in future.'

Originally the term cadie or cawdie was applied to a loafer or hanger-on,

RIGHT: Young French caddie enjoying a bite of lunch, pictured at the turn of the twentieth century.

A collection of English child caddies at around the beginning of the twentieth century.

who frequented the streets of Edinburgh. He hired himself out as an errand boy. From earliest times, though the common man carried his own clubs, nobility hired 'cadies'– one as 'forecadie' to be ahead and watch for the ball, one to herd aside wayward cattle, yet another to carry the clubs. Golf bags did not show up until the 1880s, when they were introduced to protect clubs from the rain.

Early golfing societies would hire caddies, though members were reluctant to pay too much, 'because it is bad for them', and they would readily fine a caddie for being impertinent or late, while fixing miserly rates. The low point was reached when, in 1773, the Royal Burgess club ruled 'that no member pay the cadies more than one penny per round'. On the credit side, they often helped a young boy with elementary schooling.

As a caddie grew older he would reach a point where his advice would be sought, and he earned a measure of respect – the first teaching professionals were from this school – and good caddies would properly earn their badge of recognition.

From these modest beginnings came the playing caddies, men who acquired great ability in the game, and these were the forefathers of our present playing professional. From this they progressed to work as assistants, making clubs, or, occasionally, taken by a member as a partner in a match, often collecting

Willie Gunn, caddie to the Royal Burgess Society of Edinburgh at Bruntsfield Links, captured by C.H. Robertson in 1839.

a substantial bonus if they won.

The more ambitious aspired towards becoming clubmakers or greenkeepers, while run-of-the-mill types were content to drink away what little they earned. Many went on to become famous, while some emigrated and became professionals in America.

The pinnacle for many was to be appointed clubmaker and greenkeeper, the two vocations commonly related. He would make clubs, while the concession for greenkeeping was an extra duty, a proud assignment exercising general care of the course.

What these duties entailed may be seen in the minutes of the Dunbar Club (1859), which provided: 'The putting greens shall be swept and sorted every Wednesday and Saturday – the molehills on the course shall be kept down as much as possible – and that he shall be in attendance on medal days, and when the tent is required to be out.'

Many believe that the dominance of St Andrews stems from the long line of clubmakers and professionals who worked there. They were consulted on links construction and as arbiters in contentious issues. Though the R & A today is very much the fount of all knowledge, rule and lore, it is interesting to think back on its humble ancestry.

the Continent for a variety of games, and probably the Scottish makers followed Low Country methods of manufacture.

The feather ball was the standard missile of the game for at least five centuries, from early in the fourteenth century until 1848. Without much doubt, the 'feathery' when new was fine. In dry weather it appeared to fly quite well, though being hand-made it was often not perfectly round. In wet conditions it became sodden and liable to burst and 'moult' its feathers.

At first, the best balls were imported from Holland, though in 1618, James VI of Scotland granted a monopoly on making balls, for a period of 21 years, to a man named Melville. (What that would be worth today!) Ten years later an argument erupted between Melville and Dicksons at Leith, probably the first case of litigation in the golf industry, and the patent was held invalid. Thereafter, every clubmaker in Scotland was trying his hand at the new trade.

It took a single top hat full of feathers to make one ball. After the leather had been stuffed to capacity, it was stitched up, hammered until roughly spherical, and given three coats of whitening. At best it lasted two, perhaps three, rounds.

The feather-ball era lasted until about 1848, when the gutta-percha ball was introduced. Gutta-percha is a tough grey-black substance developed from the latex from Malayan trees, then a new importation largely used by dentists.

First attempts were unsuccessful, as the balls would not fly straight; but it was noticed that after they had been hacked a little by the iron clubs, they flew better. Thereafter the balls were marked by blows with a nicking hammer, into criss-cross patterns, before being painted. The gutta balls cost only one shilling, while feather balls cost three or four times more. That alone would have been conclusive for the Scots; but as they also were more accurate and lasted longer, the new gutta ball, even in its primitive stage,

Examples of early rubber-cored balls. Designers experimented with different patterns to improve aerodynamics.

BALLS, HISTORY, EVOLUTION AND DEVELOPMENT

In the pre-history of golf, what might be titled the pre-feather-ball era, early balls used for paganica, mail, chole, kolf, colf and, arguably, goff were made of wood, though even ivory and iron were also used experimentally.

None proved very accurate, but in the seventeenth and eighteenth centuries, trials saw the use of various materials, stuffed hard into a case of leather. Wool, straw, hemp, all sorts were used – but the best, which finally won universal favour, were stuffed with feathers. Such balls were used on

HASKELL ROYAL 2/- EACH

"I must have his name & address - he's driven beyond the limit."

quickly ousted the so-called feathery, which was consigned to antiquity.

The gutta passed through many stages, nicked, hand-hammered, roughened with a rasp, given fancy patterns by the score. By about 1900 the gutta had reached a high state of perfection, the finest balls being sold at 12 shillings per dozen. The balls were economical, in that the gutta could be melted and remoulded, and many professionals made their own golf balls, each claiming miraculous results from their individual pattern.

In 1901 the rubber-core ball was invented by Coburn Haskell, an American, and some of his new balls were tried in the British Amateur Championship at Hoylake in 1902. At first their performance was dismal, bursting readily, and they were considered far too lively when putting. When the Open Championship was played a few weeks later, improved examples of the rubber-core ball were available. Alex Herd became the professional guinea pig, and with this new wonder-ball he won the Open title. On the last day of the championship, demand exceeded supply, and a black market opened with ludicrous prices paid by professionals for a single specimen.

The gutta ball was quickly discarded and in 1903 use of the rubber-core ball became widespread. The average score per round of the Open Championship winners for the years 1902–26 was 75.1, compared with that of 78.5 for the ten years prior to the introduction of the rubber-core ball.

Gradually, responding to a perceived need, championship courses were increased in length until they became about 500 yards longer than in the days of the gutta. From 1927 to 1949 the average winning score per round was 72.2, underlining, if nothing else, the priceless contribution that Haskell and his wonder ball had made to the game.

During World War II there was a shortage of the rubber-core balls, and wooden balls were once more called into play. A Wooden Golf Ball Championship was held in South Africa, the winner scoring 90. Then it was found that a thin insert of balata or rubber added to wooden clubheads increased the life of the ball.

CLUB EVOLUTION AND DEVELOPMENT

Winston Churchill, no devotee of the game, described golf as 'putting little balls into little holes with instruments ill-adapted for the purpose'.

'Follow the Ball' might be our catchphrase, for club development is very closely integrated with the ball, evolving gradually over the three eras of feather ball, gutta and modern rubber-core. Though changes in clubs have occurred, they have been less dramatic than those of the ball, while attracting far less controversy.

The full, free style which became known as the 'St Andrews swing' developed out of the feathery period. The clubs, at first crude, tended later to be long and elegant; and the feathery was swept from the turf with a full swing which was attenuated and graceful. The shafts were whippy and the calfskin grips chunky. As early as 1503, the cash books of James II show him purchasing clubs, while later, James VI paid for his 'play clubis', 'bonker clubis' and 'irone club' to be repaired. The clubmaker has always been a

Winston Churchill and Lloyd George take to the links in Wales in 1910.

respected member of the golfing fraternity, with the foremost of these, Hugh Philp and Douglas McEwan, the golfing equivalent of Chippendale and Hepplewhite.

The basic implement was the driver or 'play club', made of hedge thorn, pear or apple, and used off the tee and any reasonable fairway. If its loft was noticeably angled, it was said to be 'grassed'.

In contrast with today, the head was long, narrow and shallow. Strips of cowhorn were often inserted to the face to protect it. For poor lies, or shorter shots, a variety of spoons (lofted, or backward-sloped, at various angles) might be used, while the baffy (equivalent to a seven wood) was a favourite for approaching the green.

Shafts were originally of ash, later of hickory. At first shafts were spliced to the head, with the neck and shaft bevelled, mated and bound together with whipping. The socket joint, bore to bore, came into vogue about 1900, along with the gutta.

While the introduction of the gutta did not change the clubmakers, it made them more inventive. In 1890 came the first real innovation, the bulger, which

PREVIOUS PAGE: The tools for Jeu de Mail, an Italian and French form of golf popular in the seventeenth century.
LEFT: A seventeenth century Scottish 'play' club.
RIGHT: A model of Walter Travis's notorious Schenectady putter.

had a convex face and was short and squat. Its theory was that the bulge would tend to straighten out shots. The first anti-slice club, perhaps, though the hypothesis was dubious from the start and players argued that it was just sales talk. They were probably right, but to this day the bulge remains.

Irons at first were nasty-looking weapons, trouble clubs used only in dire emergencies. There were sand irons for bunkers, and track irons designed to be used when the ball lay in cart ruts. Around 1850 the cleek came into being, a straight-faced iron of various lofts which could be used for driving, approaching or even putting. Then came the lofting iron with a concave face, later fabricated as the lofting mashie, and regarded with some misgiving. The niblick followed, with its large round head for chipping, and somewhat later, the mashie niblick.

In feather-ball times a set might contain a driver, three spoons, a trouble iron, a cleek and a wooden putter. Any more would be considered frivolous. Harry Vardon, five times Open Champion, in 1905 carried just two woods, six irons and a putting cleek. By the thirties, tournament players were carrying 18 or 20 clubs, while in 1934, Lawson Little, playing in the Amateur Championship, had so many clubs in his bag that his long-suffering caddie

demanded extra money. In desperation, in 1936, the ruling bodies finally limited the number to 14.

Early in the 1920s steel shafts came into vogue, certainly in America, though they were looked on with disfavour and it was not until 1929 that they were approved by the Royal and Ancient.

In 1904 a centre-shafted putter became the focus of a huge controversy. Someone in America had attached a shaft to the centre of a thick wooden putter, though it attracted zero attention until Walter Travis won the British Amateur with it that same year. Being off his putting, he tinkered with a Schenectady, for that is what it was called, and it worked like magic. His exceptional putting won the tournament, and overnight the centre-shafted putter became famous.

Castigated by the British, who thought the putter unfair, Travis was given short shrift, while in the window of the clubhouse a bulletin appeared – it was to be banned. In the event, it took five years for St Andrews to outlaw these new-fangled instruments.

David White

THE MIND GAME

PROBABLY THE MOST IMPORTANT QUALITY OF A GREAT GOLFER ON OR

OFF THE TOUR IS THE ABILITY TO PERFORM CONSISTENTLY UNDER

INCREDIBLE PRESSURE — PRESSURE THAT CAN WILT ALL THE REST.

Much has been speculated about what makes a golfer great, and no doubt the pondering will continue.

Considering the millions who play the game, not to mention the countless hours and vast sums we spend to get better at it, one would think, simply from a statistical point of view, there must be thousands of great players out there somewhere.

Alas, golf can be such a humbling experience that few golfers can classify their games as consistently 'good'. And as for 'great' – well, aside from the occasional round that surprises those of us who play, great is a title reserved for such a small number of players that when we see them in action, we stand in awe with our heads uncovered. Then we tell ourselves: 'Maybe I could make that shot', and end up heading back to the practice tee or the putting green to spend a little more time and a lot more money.

Look at a professional golfer and you will see a picture of extraordinary technical competence, most noticeable in a reliable, smooth and consistent swing – the kind of swing many of us would give a month's salary to call our own. This is not surprising, given the amount of attention devoted to hitting the golf ball. Professional golfers have honed their physical skills through thousands of hours of practice and millions of shots.

Line up a hundred professional golfers and analyse their swings, and you would see that they display superb fundamentals. But not all professional golfers are great – some manifest tremendous talent in practice but then never rank among the leaders, while other players have wonderful early rounds only for them to falter.

What keeps many of these talented and technically superb golfers from becoming great is not the physical side of the game. It is their inability consistently to control the mental side of golf, particularly on the big occasion when victory is in the balance.

So the question remains – what makes a golfer great? Are great golfers born or are they made? Are the qualities that comprise greatness definable and learnable? And, speaking for the millions who toil in the world of 'averagedom', can we really get up there from here?

With only an occasional exception, when we think of great golfers we think of the PGA or pro tours – those who are good enough to make their living playing golf. And with touring pros, most people agree on some general standards of greatness. Consistent success is one; number of wins in a major is another. Also included are the length of career and the amount of money earned. But probably the most important quality of a great golfer on or off the tour is the ability to perform consistently under incredible pressure – pressure that can wilt all the rest.

Looking for examples? For number of wins and career length,

Tiger Woods seems to revel in the pressure of tournament golf.

there is Jack Nicklaus. For the amount of money earned look at Greg Norman. Laura Davies and Nancy Lopez, on the women's tour, are models of consistency, and who can match the toughness under pressure displayed by Nick Faldo and now the young Masters-winning Tiger Woods?

GREATNESS

Given all the criteria to consider and the examples to watch, it has been my observation that great golfers exhibit the following key attributes: passion for the game, vision of what they can become, and a willingness to take action. Together, passion, vision and action create the mental toughness that keeps great players focused on their goals.

Passion could be described as a burning, almost overwhelming desire to win. It produces the commitment (and often, the sacrifice) to do whatever it takes – physical, emotional, financial – to get there. It is the fuel needed to power one to greatness.

Colin Montgomerie displays this passion. His determination to be the best probably has no equal. Sometimes it is so strong that it seems to create a lot of frustration for him, but it has been an enormous powerhouse of energy that has brought him four European championships so far.

Colin Montgomerie: another good walk spoiled?

Vision is the combination of the dream and the plan of execution. It contains a clear concept of what the dream is – the goals (which are defined in ways that are meaningful, challenging and energizing) and the steps necessary to reach them – the plan. Phillip Price said after winning the Portuguese Open that he identifies how much money he wants to earn, what he will do with it (perhaps buy a house or a car) and what ranking he wants to finish with.

Action is the consistent execution of the plan and a willingness to change quickly, often with significant risks attached, when results are less than you would have expected.

Two out of three is not enough. Those who lack passion quickly drop by the wayside. Those without a plan don't know where to focus their energy. And those who do not take action will always say to themselves: 'If only I had done this ...' or 'I didn't because ...'

Nick Faldo epitomizes a player with all three attributes. He leaves no stone unturned in his quest for greatness. Nick's passion is so great that in

Team Faldo: under the close eye of coach David Leadbetter.

addition to his technical coach, David Leadbetter, he has consulted nutritionists, physiologists and optometrists in his quest to be the best he can. He creates a plan of what he wants to do and takes action on it relentlessly. He spent three years remodelling his swing, enduring much criticism in the process.

The combination of all three is often described as mental toughness. Every great player has displayed phenomenal mental toughness. One way to understand mental toughness is to look at what goes on in those of us that don't display it.

The Californian Timothy Gallwey, in his book *The Inner Game of Golf*, described the noise and activity that goes on inside our minds, particularly when we are under pressure, as 'mental interference'.

Caddie Fanny Sunesson lends a guiding hand.

And the result is another perfect shot.

No one is immune from mental interference. Anyone who has choked on a two-foot putt or thought, 'I hope I don't hit it into the water', only to land the ball right in the middle of a pond, knows what I am talking about.

Interference can be brought on by any number of reasons: the pressure to do well, a loss of belief or confidence brought on by an injury or a significant change or emotional event − even wanting something too much. It will manifest itself in any number of ways: fear, doubt, inability to concentrate. What is common is the negative effect interference has on performance.

A painful but all too real example of interference was the world-stage mental meltdown Greg Norman experienced in the 1996 Masters at Augusta. Heading into the last round, the world's top money-earner had a five-stroke lead, and seemed on course to win his first major. However, one bad shot led to another and soon the mental interference took one of the most technically gifted players on the planet right out of the match, and he ended up in second place behind Nick Faldo.

Interference is invasive, in that it gets in the way of what we normally do very well. As a result it negatively impacts our skills and blocks or dilutes our passion, blurs our vision, and prevents us from taking action on what we know. Typically, the more we think about what is causing us interference, the worse our performance gets until we get into a state of trying too hard, as with Norman, where suddenly nothing seems to work.

Great players seem able to manage this phenomenon of interference on the important occasions. They use their passion, vision and action to concentrate in a way the rest of us can find very difficult to do.

They are exceptional at what we call focusing attention. By focusing their attention on something other than what is causing interference, they manage

LEFT: The agony of losing the Masters. Greg Norman went through mental meltdown in 1996.

the mental side of their performance. Focused attention reduces the negative effects of interference while helping to knit together the attributes of passion, vision and action into a state of relaxed concentration.

By way of example, the world record for the lowest round of golf in a PGA tournament – 59 – was equalled by a Welshman, David Llewellyn. David (nicknamed the Happy Buddha) was so focused during this round that he had no idea what he had done. When he walked off the course, he was asked how he felt, and his reply was: 'About what?' He had been so intent on the playing of his round he had lost track of everything other than playing shots. There was no score, no crowd and certainly no world record in his mind.

Most psychologists talk about the quiet mind and using one's ability to focus on 'the here and now' – on what is actually happening.

Some years ago Richard Boxall was playing in Portugal in the last tournament of the season. (Richard has since become bizarrely famous for breaking his leg in the very process of striking the ball while playing in the British Open with Colin Montgomerie.) It had not been a great year and he was left with an eight-foot putt on the last hole of the last round of the tournament. It was an entirely critical moment for him, for he had to sink this putt to keep his playing card and avoid going back to the qualifying school.

His way of quietening his mind was to visualize the colour blue as he was stroking the putt (blue symbolized quiet to him). He thought blue, controlled his nervousness, sank the putt and kept his card.

When great players focus attention, several things happen at the same time. First, they manage and limit the interference inside themselves by learning to concentrate on external stimuli, particularly the critical success factors (CSFs).

These are the elements of the task they are doing that are easy to pay attention to and about which it is important to have up-to-date feedback. As they concentrate on these CSFs the mental interference is reduced because they simply cannot attend to the interference and the CSFs at the same time.

Second, when they concentrate or focus attention on these CSFs, their awareness of what they are doing increases, and the quality of what they are experiencing, the specific stimuli entering the brain, is higher and much more intense.

When they are engaged in this way, their learning rate speeds up and their level of performance using the skills that they already possess increases in a very natural, seemingly effortless way.

SELF-HELP

The effect that 'focused attention' has on performance has been so profound that most world class athletes practise some sort of focusing regime – so one of the easiest ways we can help ourselves to a little greatness is to do the same for ourselves. To do this we harness something that we are all born with – curiosity. The essence of curiosity, and a great focusing exercise in golf, is to ask ourselves to notice some detail about what we are doing. In order to notice that thing, we have to focus even more of our attention on it. By engaging the mind in this way, we free the body to do what it does naturally.

Phillip Price used a trick devised by Timothy Gallwey to harness his curiosity to help win his Portugese Open title. He tried to observe the impact of the club on the ball and say 'hit' out loud at that moment. Because it wasn't an easy task, it made him curious about how to do it and prevented his mind from wandering.

Great golfers have experienced the overwhelming pressure of playing in front of thousands of people for hundreds of thousands of dollars and the interference it can cause. To help them perform, most golfers practise focused attention by targeting some relevant aspect of their game to concentrate on, thus avoiding the interference that can block their performance. They overcome the interference by setting clear goals that are connected to the heart, and concentrating and being objective about their current reality: 'being in the moment'.

Back in the early 1980s David Feherty, the Irish Ryder Cup golfer, was having great trouble staying committed throughout his downswing. He would pull out at the last moment and this would open the blade of the club and send the ball out to the right – enough to cost him a couple of shots a round. He would try each week to remedy this but without success. His next tournament was to be the Italian Open and we badly needed to find a way to keep his attention in the here and now. We had a conversation that went like this:

'David, if I came with you next week and threatened to blow your head off if you don't commit on each shot, would you do it?'

'Of course I would. I wouldn't care about where the ball went.'

'So if you had to, you could commit?'

'Yes, I suppose so.'

'And if I offered you a hundred thousand pounds to commit on each shot would you do it?'

'Yes, of course I would. That's more money than I would get for wining the tournament. So I wouldn't care where where the ball went.'

I checked again.

'Yes, I suppose so.'

'How much money can you afford to lose?'

'A thousand pounds ... five hundred pounds.'

'Then write a cheque for a thousand pounds to your favourite charity. Leave it with me. If you commit on every shot I'll give it back to you. If you don't commit on any one shot I will send the cheque off. And I will be the sole judge of whether you did or not. Do you want to do this?'

David saw the point and said OK. He made out a cheque to the RSPCA, left it with me and went off to play in the Italian Open, which he duly won.

As effective as focused attention can be in helping improve performance and making great golfers out of good golfers, it is hard to stay focused continuously. In fact some researchers including James Loehr, author of *Mental Toughness Training Techniques* and a coach to many world-class athletes, suggests that focusing attention is cyclical in nature. Loehr believes that we need periods of regeneration or rest to prepare for the times we need to focus our attention.

The great Walter Hagen said: 'Don't forget to stop and smell the flowers along the way'. When you are not focused on your shot, relax.

The secret to greatness is being able to align the ability to focus our attention with the time when we need to perform. Great golfers seem to be able to muster the concentration when they need it most, and to be able to relax when the pressure is off.

Given the fact that the Number One and Number Fifty golfers in the world are often separated by only about one stroke for every round, the ability to stay focused long enough to make one fewer shot for every four hours on the course would seem like a worthy and achievable goal. And it is a goal that most average golfers might consider.

Shakespeare wrote: 'Some people are born great, some achieve greatness and some have greatness thrust upon them.' That leads to the last quality of any great performer – commitment.

Ultimately, when it comes to golf, greatness is not, as some might argue,

A cash incentive helped David Feherty win the Italian Open.

achieved through birth, but rather through scratching, clawing and willing yourself there. Nothing significant happens without commitment, and change will not take place without action.

Here's to the passion, vision, and action within all who play the game of golf – from the good to the great, from the average to the truly dreadful.

May you experience greatness for even a few moments, however you define it.

Alan Fine

THE ONLY REAL SECRET OF GOLF

'GOLF IS DECEPTIVELY SIMPLE, ENDLESSLY COMPLICATED. A CHILD
CAN PLAY IT WELL AND A GROWN MAN CAN NEVER MASTER IT.
IT IS ALMOST A SCIENCE, YET IT IS A PUZZLE WITH NO ANSWER.'

Arnold Palmer

Until the last few years of his life, Sir Henry Cotton followed an inflexible daily routine and worked on the practice ground to maintain his golf swing even though there were no more worlds to conquer. At the time he was almost 80.

The explanation was simple enough. To him, the act of striking a golf ball had become so much part of his existence that even though the purpose no longer mattered, the procedure had to be followed so that he could judge the quality – albeit diminished – of his skill.

It is this inescapable obsession with excellence that drives all the great players throughout their lives and never leaves them even when it should no longer matter.

The American champion Ben Hogan, a contemporary of Cotton, was arguably the greatest worker the royal and ancient game has ever seen, and pushed himself to quite extraordinary areas of self-discovery and control to find a degree of mechanical perfection and consistency in his technique.

He once noticed that a fault developed in a certain stroke when he felt tired; so he decided to hit practice shots until he was exhausted enough to re-create the state of fatigue that caused the problem. Only then could he first study, and then cure it.

Such towering diligence earned Hogan an impressive collection of major titles, including three in one season during 1953, but his standards were so high that he claimed that in his best rounds of golf he hit perhaps only one stroke that was truly satisfactory and would never be content until every stroke was flawless.

Practice, practice and more practice was the motto of Henry Cotton.

IRON

WOOD

The act of hitting a golf ball is one of basic
geometry. The ball on the ground lies on the
circumference of a circle, the radius of which is
made up of the player's arms and golf club. As a
wooden club is longer than an iron, a golfer has
to address the ball further from the body.
Consequently, the swing with a wooden club is
flat and wide, while the swing with
an iron is shorter and steeper.

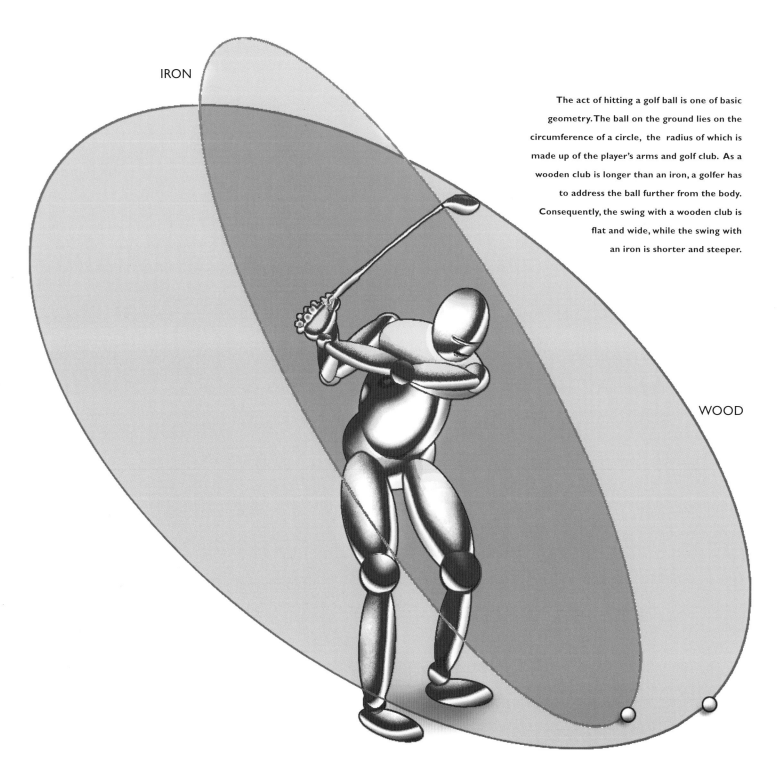

An impossible dream, of course. Indeed the art of golf – and certainly winning at it – is to negotiate a golf ball over a stretch of countryside by whatever legitimate means possible to bring in the best score. Technique, therefore, is only the means to that end and other important factors such as will-power, concentration and focus also play crucial roles in the process.

The act of hitting a golf ball is basic geometry. The ball on the ground lies on the circumference of a circle whose radius is made up of the player's arms and golf club and therefore the arc so described should bring the clubhead into contact with the ball, which means the immediate purpose of practice is to perfect that particular action.

And yet there is a theory that the great players have discovered a more compelling dimension to practice which goes beyond technique and takes them into the realms of spirituality in which they acquire, quite unintentionally, an ability to control their own minds and in so doing reduce the psychological fears and pressures involved in the sport.

Quite simply they have learned the art of self-hypnosis, and the ritual of practice is the means by which they reach that state, which is then triggered whenever they take a club in their hands to hit a golf ball. The great American champion Billy Casper admitted that in mental terms his golf swing really began at the precise moment he removed the club from the bag. If the procedure was interrupted in any way, the club had to be replaced so that he could start the ritual all over again. The self-hypnosis hypothesis is confirmed by the legendary Sam Snead, who revealed that he was not really aware of any conscious thought as he swung the club.

Certainly the practised ritual of hitting a golf ball reduces the element of failure as well as the fear of it, and also accounts for the huge difference in playing ability between great champions and lesser mortals. An eminent specialist in human movement, Moshe Feldenkrais, concluded that the pause

between the creation of a thought pattern for any particular act and the execution of the action is the physical basis of awareness. In golf, however, it is the moment when negative thoughts creep in so that essential focus and confidence is dissipated unless protected by routine.

A test. Place a plank on the floor and walk along it. No problem. Place the same plank one hundred feet in the air and try again. Same plank. Same task. But a totally different penalty for error. In such circumstances the awareness of the penalty inhibits what is really a simple act. In golf, the best players have learned to focus on the task to the exclusion of all else. Tony Jacklin put it succinctly when he said: 'I don't worry what's going to happen to the ball at the other end. I just concentrate on hitting it this end.'

David Canova, a respected hypnotherapist, worked in hospitals throughout East Anglia then turned his attention to golf. He came to the conclusion that there were five elements to success in the game: Equipment, Course Knowledge, Physique, Skill and State of Mind.

No golfer has ever possessed these ingredients in greater measure than Jack Nicklaus, who is acknowledged to be the most successful player in the history of the game. He was so meticulous about his equipment that he once bought a golf club factory to ensure the items satisfied his high

Ross MacFarlane's personalised yardage chart for the Dubai Classic in 1997.

RIGHT: Ross MacFarlane's notes for the 18th hole at Dubai. They indicate that he was to take a driver off the tee to leave 279 yards to the green; take a three iron to lay up short of the water and then hit a nine iron 111 yards (96 + 15) to the flag. Below are the pin placements for each of the four days of the tournament.

LEFT: A map of the same 18th hole pinpointing hazards such as bunkers, water and trees and displaying other features such as the shape of the fairway and various humps and hollows. The numbers indicate distances in yards to the green or from the tee.

His precise knowledge of the golf courses he plays worldwide is phenomenal and unquestionably the result of hard work and scrupulous study. He was one of the first golfers to adopt the system of charting courses by mapping out the features on every hole and selecting landmarks by which to judge distances. For such a globe-trotter with limited time at his disposal to become accustomed to a course and conditions it is an essential exercise and means he can refer to his records whenever he returns to a venue.

His research and preparation go much deeper and in fact have a major influence on his state of mind, too. For example he is the dominant figure of the US Masters, having won the title six times, and played the Augusta National course in Georgia for more than 30 years. Yet each year he approaches the championship as though he were playing the course for the first time and makes a private weekend visit a month before the event to reacquaint himself with the terrain.

It is a fundamentalist approach which makes no assumptions and is very much part of the Nicklaus attitude to playing competitive golf. He may well be the most successful player that has ever lived but for many years he would return to his old teacher at the start of the season and say: 'Teach me how to play golf again from the beginning.' This back-to-basics attitude in which grip, stance and so on were relearned meant that any flaws that had crept in unnoticed could be eliminated.

In one practice session at Augusta National, he suspected that a new texture of sand had been placed in the bunkers around the short 12th green and tackled the greenkeeper, who confirmed that inevitably Jack was right – the sand had been changed.

Throughout that practice round, Nicklaus deliberately placed the ball in the most awkward and frightening lies, then played the strokes and explained afterwards: 'I have now been everywhere on the course where I shouldn't

standards. Even now, when handed a box of golf balls before he goes out to play, Nicklaus tests each one of them with a special device to determine whether they are the correct compression for his swing to fly on the exact trajectory he desires.

be so there will be no surprises.'

When he prepared for one Open championship at Muirfield, he seemed to be having an erratic time with his tee shots and constantly missed the fairways but said: 'I did it deliberately. I just wanted to see what liberties I could take with the rough because of the narrow fairways.'

Such an attitude leaves nothing to chance and follows the precedent set by Ben Hogan when he travelled from the United States in 1953 for his only attempt on the British Open championship. He arrived a week before the event, played and practised every day, then walked the course in the evenings from green to tee to establish a different perspective on the location of bunkers and other hazards. The effort paid off handsomely because he won the title and managed to improve his score progressively through all four rounds.

In modern golf, there is now a greater awareness that physique really does matter and that while all shapes and sizes may play the game, the correctly proportioned body is a more efficient mechanism with which to propel the ball. Statistical research on the top players has revealed a blueprint of the ideal male golfer, which shows him to be six foot tall and have wide shoulders, slim waist and powerful legs.

Moreover the ideal body should be long and the legs comparatively short so that a powerful blow can be delivered from a solid base, which is less prone to error. Sandy Lyle, the former US Masters and Open champion, is the perfect shape (6ft and 29in inside seam) while Nick Faldo (6ft 3in and 33in inside seam) is by his own admission too tall and susceptible to various problems of positioning and synchronization in the swing. This is one reason he can often be seen painstakingly rehearsing parts of the swing before he

LEFT: The masterly Ben Hogan rifles another iron at the flag during his British Open triumph at Carnoustie in 1953.

interlocking version so that he could hold on more firmly while allowing his body to generate the power.

An obvious equation therefore emerges in which the first four factors of Canova's Doctrine – Equipment, Course Knowledge, Physique and Skill – combine to produce the fifth aspect, State of Mind, which can be influenced in so many seemingly trivial ways.

Nick Faldo does not trim his fingernails before a tournament because he thinks his hands lose some of their sensitivity, affecting his putting touch. A seemingly pedantic point, perhaps, but one that threatens the peace of mind of the player and so can undermine confidence.

There is no documented evidence that any successful golfer has resorted to the use of drugs to improve performance although some have found ways of calming themselves – but not always with the desired effect. One young professional found the use of tranquillizers extremely counterproductive and explained: 'I still hit bad shots but because of the pills I didn't really care!'

Seve Ballesteros at one time tried tranquillizers but found they left him feeling sluggish and less alert. However, after taking an aspirin to cure a headache he felt calm and quite sharp, so the aspirin dosage became part of his pre-match routine when he was at the height of his career.

Inevitably this desire for the proper state of mind leads into areas of superstitious ritual and other practices that produce a feel-good factor. Most of the top players have a special preference for the number on their golf ball. Ballesteros will never play with a number '3' ball because he feels he might three-putt. Nor, when he has surveyed a putt from all aspects, will he walk back to the ball on the right-hand side because he fears this will make him miss.

The one thing that prevents most players using a so-called lucky charm is their fear that they might lose it before a game and then be distracted from the task of playing. The American professional Doug Sanders held the

Jack Nicklaus has surprisingly small hands for a big man, so uses the interlocking grip.

plays the shot as if 'reminding' his muscles where they ought to be.

In terms of physique, Jack Nicklaus also might have been regarded as ill-equipped because his hands are relatively small and bear no comparison to the banana-proportioned digits of most champions. Nicklaus abandoned the more orthodox overlapping grip on the club and adopted the unconventional conviction that white tee pegs were unlucky and in an unthinking moment used one at the last hole at St Andrews during the 1970 Open championship. He lost the title by a stroke, to confirm his belief.

Other players prefer to play mind games with themselves to overcome fears and boost confidence rather then rely on superstition. The great Marley Harris, who twice won the British Ladies' championship, had an infallible ruse when faced with a difficult stroke. She simply imagined herself to be back at her home course playing at her favourite hole. Thus all fear was removed and her golf swing could function perfectly.

Arnold Palmer achieved similar success without the need for such self-deception and once explained the secret of his famous last-round winning charges thus: 'I just see what I have to do and I just make up my mind to do it. If I face a long putt I think about making the putt and shut out all thoughts of missing from my mind.' A complete refusal even to countenance failure leads to absolute faith in yourself and hugely increases your chances of making the shot.

Indeed the experiences of all these great champions suggest that successful golf is based on profound self-knowledge and sustained by a ferocious mental strength that probably cannot be acquired but is God-given. They follow a lonely pursuit in which their own imperfections have to be contained while they tackle the wider task of beating their rivals.

Whatever natural flair they bring to the game, the ultimate achievement is based on the measure of work they put into their preparation. There is no short cut to greatness, only hard and constant work which becomes a way of life even when it is no longer required. It is a lesson and legacy that Henry Cotton and other great players pass on. It is the only secret of golf worth possessing.

Michael McDonnell

Positive thinking: Arnie Palmer always charged the hole with his putts and never worried about going three or four feet past.

IT ISN'T ALWAYS
JUST A GAME

'IN TWO OR THREE YEARS IT IS GOING TO BE

COMPLETELY DIFFERENT. WE SHALL SEE BLACK MEMBERS

IN ALL OF THESE ELITE CLUBS.'

Arthur Ashe, 1990

From clubhouse to fairway, from sea to shining sea, the game of golf, across the world and particularly in America, has long been a lily-white affair.

Although technically all racism is illegal in the 50 United States, in the big-money, elite world of private clubs and courses a certain code still prevails.

It is the code whereby any and all are allegedly welcomed ... but where a black face is never seen, where a Jewish name is not written on a scorecard.

The exclusivity of golf clubs, their elitist image as self-styled 'country clubs', their association with wealth – all have perpetuated attitudes that belong to a different century. When European nations, particularly Britain, dominated much of the globe, the status of non-whites was so low that consideration of any kind of equality was never given serious thought – never mind the prospect that they wouldn't be allowed to socialize on equal terms with the ruling white classes.

Across the globe 'natives' have been issued with walking sticks, clubs and other useless implements to pose for stunted and nonsensical greetings cards. From the earliest days of the game the role of caddie – the game's beast of burden – was always carried out by the poorest in society. The faces of long-dead children smiling bravely while carrying clubs for the white player have such poignancy because they sum up attitudes that still scar the sport; they underline the truth that for a diminishing yet still powerful sector of society in many countries, golf is more than just a game. It is symbol of an outdated and unpleasant social fortress.

And while many countries still harbour the same prejudices, the United States is a high-profile example that bears examination.

Golf has exploded across America, with an estimated 26 million people pumping the sport up into a £23-billion-a-year industry. Yet minorities often find that they remain outsiders unable to get inside the bastions of a ruling class.

The decision by the Professional Golfers' Association to stage the 1990 PGA championship at the all-white Shoal Creek golf club near Birmingham, Alabama, led to a defining moment in the history of golf in America.

This erstwhile citadel of confederate values actually prided itself on its apartheid policies, which closed the door to any and all blacks, regardless of their wealth, status or playing skills.

The outcry was spontaneous, prolonged and loud – forcing a national spotlight upon an unwelcome issue that had generally been treated by authorities like a mad old aunt in the attic: always there, but largely ignored.

Outrage at the Shoal Creek policy forced an immediate climbdown. The 400-strong club instantly admitted two black members – a move blasted as tokenism by critics, but hailed by others as a big step forward for the game.

'Golf up-to-date' – a postcard dating from 1905 sent from
Pietermaritzburg, South Africa.

The PGA tour championship went ahead as the body itself imposed anti-bias rules, probably more out of practicality than deep conviction. Image-sensitive corporations and TV networks provide most of golf's cash prizes and the controversy prompted sponsors like IBM to yank a promised two million dollars in advertising from ABC's PGA telecast. The events inspired Arthur Ashe, icon to black athletes the world over, to declare: 'In two or three years it is going to be completely different. We shall see black members in all of these elite clubs.'

But Ashe did not live to see that vision realized. Calvin Peete, one of the nation's foremost black pros, said: 'Shoal Creek really did not have much impact,' and the verdict of the athletics historian David Weddel is: 'The nation's private golf clubs – symbols of power and privilege at play, manicured enclaves of racial, religious and sexual discrimination – show few signs of more than token reform.'

Calvin Peete – one of the first black tournament professionals.

There are approximately 15,500 golf courses in America, some 64 per cent of them public. For many blacks, these are the ones that they have to play on by dint of their race.

At least eight of the courses that the PGA considered playing following the Shoal Creek showdown actually ruled themselves out from the honour of hosting the tournament, preferring to remain all-white.

The St Louis Country Club in Ladue, Missouri, ceded the 1992 Women's Amateur Championships, ostensibly because it was 'renovating the greens', although many regarded this to be a convenient excuse. The Chicago Golf Club felt no need to search for excuses. It relinquished the 1993 Walker Cup to remain a 'white bread' club.

Others opted for tokenism that was soon exposed as such. Aronimink Golf Club in Newtown Square, Pennsylvania, took in a few blacks as junior members in the early 1990s – but withdrew from the 1993 PGA championship because it could not guarantee that such members would move up to full voting status by then.

Aronimink tried to take the moral high ground by saying that it did not exclude blacks per se – just that none had sought admission. Yet the flaw in this argument is easily detected. New members are always proposed by old members. They naturally choose friends, relatives, business associates and neighbours, a process which simply reinforces the circle of privilege that already exists.

It was a similar story with the Merion Golf Club in Ardmore, Pennsylvania, which pulled out of the 1994 US Women's Open because it could not guarantee integration by then.

Today, the underlying racism continues. Experts say that two-thirds or perhaps even three-quarters of America's private golf and country clubs have no black members. 'Whatever,' said the Los Angeles civil rights activist James Standish, 'it is a shameful figure.'

And it is not only blacks that are discriminated against. Many 'Wasp' (white, Anglo-Saxon, Protestant) clubs, particularly in New England and the Mid-West, have a code by which no Jews are admitted. Consequently, Jewish golfers build their own courses, thereby making a further mockery of the great 'melting-pot' myth of the United States. Washington's rich Jews congregate at the Woodmont Country Club, and no gentiles need apply.

The veteran pro Tom Watson knows all about the 'code' which works against Jews. The player, whose wife and children are Jewish, resigned from

The Zulu Golf Club.

A typical example of 'natives' being issued with walking sticks to pose for
nonsensical greeting cards. Henry Cotton changed the sticks to clubs in his
book *Thanks for the Game!*

A Ceylonese caddie around the end of the nineteenth century.

the Kansas City Country Club in 1990 after it blackballed the Jewish accountancy mogul Henry Bloch.

With Bloch's high-profile case threatening to drag the club into an unwelcome media spotlight, the burghers in charge went back on their decision and said he could stay. But the incident revolted Watson, who declined to rejoin. In a public statement he decried the 'hypocrisy' of the club he once loved, adding: 'Let's discriminate right now, each one of us, privately, between what is right and what is wrong.'

Watson's case was by no means unique, although it is mostly blacks who continue to feel the bitter sting of racism. In the moneyed Westchester County suburbs of New York, for instance, only 11 of the 39 clubs have black members while in metropolitan Detroit the tally is 11 out of 38. In Chicago the ratio is even worse – only 10 out of 74 private clubs admit to having black members.

Discrimination is also rearing its ugly head against Hispanic people – ironic in a country that, by all demographic studies, will have Hispanics as the majority of its citizens by the year 2050.

In one survey of 20 courses on the pro circuit, nine said they had 'a few' Hispanic members, 10 refused to respond – although private inquiries found they had none – and one only declared it had none. Rudy Berumen, a member of the Mexican-American Golf Association in Tempe, Arizona, said: 'It is not that easy for an Hispanic to join some clubs around here. It would, admittedly, be tougher for a black man, unless he was governor or a senator.

'But many rich white people feel uncomfortable on a course with people they traditionally see as house-painters, waiters, gardeners and tradespeople. That is a mindset that is unfortunate but difficult to change.

'The wrongs seem obvious. The highly visible act of excluding people from prominent community institutions based on skin colour serves as a powerful and disturbing symbol that racism is considered tolerable in the nation's elite social echelons.

'It is the same message that says sexism and anti-semitism should also be considered permissible. In addition, in almost all cases, the private clubs bring together a community of business, professional and personal elites that continue to perpetuate patterns of unequal opportunity.'

Dan Ridder, a black golfer in California who was excluded from 20 clubs before finding one to accept him, said: 'The clubs make the excuse that it is the very essence of freedom for them to choose who to associate with. There is a small amount of validity in that, of course. But while most Americans accept that discrimination in any form is wrong – when it comes to work, or schooling, or government services – they turn a blind eye when it comes to social issues. People who think they are the biggest liberals in the world see nothing wrong in playing on all-white courses.'

Another major factor enmeshed in the snobbery/elitism/exclusion trinity is money. Playing even one round of golf is an expensive business, requiring the use of specialist – and pricey – equipment, on greens that are manicured to perfection. Most of the major clubs require massive bonds – at private Baltusrol new members put up £20,000 as an initiation fee, a £3,500 bond and annual dues of £3,000 – which also serve as a deterrent for minorities, even though the door at this Springfield, New Jersey, institution is technically open to them.

The median income for a white US household is around $37,000 (about £22,000). Black households are a full 30 per cent behind this figure. For the Denver Urban League president Tom Jenkins, these sums alone are enough to keep blacks off of the fairways. 'I don't personally know of any racial problems at the golf clubs,' he said, 'but it is an economic barrier at this point. With 35,000 to 75,000 dollars for memberships, I don't know of too many blacks who can put up that kind of money.'

SINGHALESE GOLF CADDIE.

A young Singhalese caddie. The callous inscription reads: 'This little kid would make a good caddie for you for he is very slow and does not care how long the player takes to go around.'

Young caddies have always been seen as the game's beasts of burden. Here young
Japanese bag-carriers pose with white colonial golfers at Yokohama in 1920.

A golfing divide: the player – a young **Bobby Locke** – and the spectators in the 1934

Transvaal Open are all white; only the caddie is black.

There is no single agency or group that tracks minority memberships of golf and country clubs across the USA, but plenty of newspapers and civil rights organizations have completed their own surveys. One report in the *Democrat and Chronicle* of Rochester, New York, showed in a survey that of 17 private clubs, there were only 16 blacks among 6,061 members – 0.3 per cent – which is a figure that, experts concur, may hold true nationally. Clarence Jackson, a member of the national board of directors for the Congress of Racial Equality, said: 'Black folks have to understand that racism is alive and well in America. For those who think we have done so much to get rid of it, we have not. We have just begun the real fight.

'It is not just public facilities we are dealing with from this point on. It is those things which sustain our livelihoods and our lives. Golf clubs should simply not be allowed to get away with the brand of racism they practise. Sport is a microcosm of total life – just as we advocate equal opportunities in the business world, we need to do that in the places where we practise recreation. Otherwise, we send the totally wrong messages to everybody, particularly our youth.'

Exclusions on the grounds of skin colour, or on the grounds of lack of wealth, which often has exactly the same effect, is a global issue. Keeping out 'the wrong sort' is rife from Australia to Zimbabwe, and is by no means just a North American issue.

While the picture may be bleak, there are chinks of light shining through the gloom. In states like California – despite the problems experienced by Dan Ridder – the integration of minorities, albeit wealthy ones, on courses has been a real success story. At the Riviera Country Club in Los Angeles, where the initiation fee is a staggering £40,000, one-fifth of the 1,500 members are black, Hispanic, Asian or Middle Eastern.

The admission procedures are as rigorous and ancient as any of the 'white bread' clubs, with applicants requiring sponsorship from members who have known them for three or more years. Bill Masse, general manager, said: 'We are proud to have admitted our first black member in the 1940s. We are known as non-discriminatory and relish that fact.'

Black-built and black-owned golf courses are in the minority, but also a way for minorities to enjoy the game. They may not help promote racial harmony, but they give ordinary people a chance to break into a mostly white world.

William Powell, 79, is unique in America as the only black person to design, build and own a golf course, according to the National Golf Foundation.

His course in East Canton, Ohio, was born out of the overt, rather than insidious, racism of the 1940s. He had loved golf ever since he caddied for a white doctor at the age of nine and, when he returned home safe from World War Two, promised himself that he would play the game at every opportunity. Except there were no opportunities – not for a black man on Canton's all-white courses.

'It hurt – I had fought for this country and this flag, but I was told to my face that I was not allowed to golf alongside my fellow Americans.

'It is distasteful when you get turned down. You have a little pride. You say: "The hell with them." You say: "I am not going to badger them, I am not going to beg them." What I did was build my own course.'

Working the night shift as a security guard at a steel company, he used some of the daylight hours not spent sleeping pulling up picket fences and clearing stones from an old dairy farm. Clearview became the golf course and it stands as the epitome of what sport should be all about: open to all and enjoying as many white members as it does black.

'I couldn't run this course if it wasn't for the white people,' said Powell, who hasn't a racist bone in his body. 'I couldn't run it without *good* white people – and I don't give a tinker's cuss about the bad ones.'

Postcard titled 'The Black Tee' issued by Detroit Publishing Co. in 1905.

So, although it wasn't until 1962 that the PGA dropped its 'Caucasians Only' clause – fully 101 years from the start of the American Civil War, which was fought against slavery – people of all colours were playing golf side by side in Canton as they had since the course was completed in 1950.

'We just wanted somewhere where we wouldn't be humiliated,' said Powell. 'When we opened some rednecks rode over the course and stole flag sticks, dug up the greens, yelled racist slurs. But it wasn't long before blacks played alongside whites and the only thing that mattered was your scorecard.'

Yet the fairway Utopia achieved by Powell is, sadly, the exception, not the rule. And as clubs continue to bar blacks, so the number of minority pros in country clubs and touring with the PGA remains minuscule.

Bill Crossman of ARISE – Against Racism in Sports Events – said: 'It has always been this way in golf. Although a black man invented the tee [in 1899 Dr George F. Grant, a Boston dentist, patented the first tee], blacks traditionally have been denied full and fair access to the greens.

'If it isn't out-and-out racism, it is money, and if it isn't money, it is waiting lists. Take the case of the prestigious Cypress Point golf club in Pebble Beach, California. In September 1990 it withdrew from the PGA-sponsored pro-amateur tournament that it had been host to since 1947. Cypress Point insists it has no ban on blacks – although it had no black members and none on the waiting list where the delay is seven years.

'Former vice-president Dan Quayle belongs to Maryland's male-only Burning Tree Country Club, which played at Cypress Point. When he was tackled about the racism issue he said confidently that the club "does not discriminate" and, technically, he may be right. But he is morally wrong, as is anyone who genuinely believes such nonsense.

'It is this lack of entrée to the bastions of racism which accounts for the astonishingly low number of black role models in the game.'

Which is why the brilliant Tiger Woods, the first black player to win a major title, is so important to the minority communities and why the race issue and his game are inextricably linked. Part black, part Chinese, part Thai, part American Indian, Tiger is perhaps the biggest hope of accelerating the inevitable victory over the diehards.

Tiger Woods' Masters victory will inspire more minority youngsters to get involved in golf.

His phenomenal talent and inherent charm will speed the change simply because everyone wants to follow the best – and all the signs point to Tiger Woods becoming the best by a country mile. The physical performance of his stunning Masters victory was brilliantly enhanced by its significance for black golfers. No black player was allowed to compete in the Masters until Lee Elder qualified as a tournament winner in 1975. Elder returned to Augusta to watch Tiger's victory. 'I came,' he said, ' because I wanted to see some history being made. I always knew I would return to see this happen one day.

'I am so proud. Now we have a black champion and that is going to be of major significance. It will open doors for more blacks to become members of clubs and it will inspire more minority kids to get involved in golf.'

His Atlanta breakthrough came almost 50 years to the day since Jackie Robinson ran out with the Brooklyn Dodgers as the first black man to play major league baseball. Robinson was greeted by racist abuse and death threats. Tiger's PR company hired ten bodyguards to protect him from similar outbursts, but with luck such madness will be further reduced as this one young man's expertise pushes further back the barriers of intolerance.

'I have been kicked off courses just for the colour of my skin,' says Woods, who believes golf deserves a kick in the pants. 'I've had hate mail and death threats, but if you are a leader you take the initiative and do what's right and I feel I am doing what's right.'

A two-part report in the magazine *Golf Digest* said private and country clubs had come under legal attack in recent years and had almost always lost when it got to court. But litigation is expensive and time-consuming, leaving only those with the will and the financial might opting to use the justice system as a lever for equality.

Yet the fight goes on, and not just for racial minorities, but for women too, many of whom find themselves being treated as lesser citizens. At Washington's Burning Tree Country Club, where President Eisenhower used to play, women are still banned from the course. The men even had to change their tax status to keep women out.

The former Women's Sports Foundation president Deborah Anderson chronicled many places where clubs retain separate dining areas for men, where divorced or widowed women are not allowed to renew memberships and where tee-times are always slanted in favour of men.

She said: 'There are a lot of discriminatory golf courses out there, not just against blacks. The fight is on every level of discrimination, to make this game what it should be – enjoyable. All the rest is baggage that should be left at the clubhouse door.'

Allan Hall

CADDIES OF GREAT SOUTHERN HOTEL, GULFPORT, MISS. THE OLD DARKY IN CENTER, WAS JEFFERSON DAVIS' PRIVATE BODY-GUARD DURING THE CIVIL WAR.

THE CLICKING OF CUTHBERT

A STORY BY P.G. WODEHOUSE

The young man came into the smoking-room of the club-house, and flung his bag with a clatter on the floor. He sank moodily into an armchair and pressed the bell.

'Waiter!'

'Sir?'

The young man pointed at the bag with every evidence of distaste.

'You may have these clubs,' he said. 'Take them away. If you don't want them yourself, give them to one of the caddies.'

Across the room the Oldest Member gazed at him with a grave sadness through the smoke of his pipe. His eye was deep and dreamy – the eye of a man who, as the poet says, has seen Golf steadily and seen it whole.

'You are giving up golf?' he said.

He was not altogether unprepared for such an attitude on the young man's part: for from his eyrie on the terrace above the ninth green he had observed him start out on the afternoon's round and had seen him lose a couple of balls in the lake at the second hole after taking seven strokes at the first.

'Yes!' cried the young man fiercely. 'For ever, dammit! Footling game! Blanked infernal fat-headed silly ass of a game! Nothing but a waste of time.'

The Sage winced.

'Don't say that, my boy.'

'But I do say it. What earthly good is golf? Life is stern and life is earnest. We live in a practical age. All round us we see foreign competition making itself unpleasant. And we spend our time playing golf! What do we get out of it? Is golf any use? That's what I'm asking you. Can you name me a single case where devotion to this pestilential pastime had done a man any practical good?'

The Sage smiled gently.

'I could name a thousand.'

'One will do.'

'I will select,' said the Sage, 'from the innumerable memories that rush to my mind, the story of Cuthbert Banks.'

'Never heard of him.'

'Be of good cheer,' said the Oldest Member. 'You are going to hear of him now.'

It was in the picturesque little settlement of Wood Hills (said the Oldest Member) that the incidents occurred which I am about to relate. Even if you have never been in Wood Hills, that suburban paradise is probably familiar to you by name. Situated at a convenient distance from the city, it combines in a notable manner the advantages of town life with the pleasant surroundings and healthful air of the country. Its inhabitants live in commodious houses, standing in their own grounds, and enjoy so many luxuries – such as gravel soil, main drainage, electric light, telephone, baths (h and c), and company's own water, that you might be pardoned for imagining life to be so ideal for them that no possible improvement could be added to their lot. Mrs Willoughby Smethurst was under no such delusion. What Wood Hills needed to make it perfect, she realized, was Culture. Material comforts are all very well, but if the *summum bonum* is to be achieved, the Soul also demands a look in, and it was Mrs Smethurst's unfaltering resolve that never while she had her strength should the Soul be handed the loser's end. It was her intention to make Wood Hills a centre of all that was most cultivated and refined, and, golly! how she had succeeded. Under her presidency the Wood Hills Literary and Debating Society had tripled its membership.

But there is always a fly in the ointment, a caterpillar in the salad. The local golf club, an institution to which Mrs Smethurst strongly objected, had also tripled its membership; and the division of the community into two rival camps, the Golfers and the Cultured, had become more marked than ever. This division, always acute, had attained now to the dimensions of a Schism. The rival sects treated one another with a cold hostility.

Unfortunate episodes came to widen the breach. Mrs Smethurst's house adjoined the links, standing to the right of the fourth tee: and, as the Literary Society was in the habit of entertaining visiting lecturers, many a golfer had foozled his drive owing to sudden loud outbursts of applause, coinciding with his down-swing. And not long before this story opens a sliced ball, whizzing in at the open window, had come within an ace of incapacitating Raymond Parsloe Devine, the rising young novelist (who rose at that moment a clear foot and a half) from any further exercise of his art. Two inches, indeed, to the right and Raymond must inevitably have handed in his dinner-pail.

To make matters worse, a ring at the front-door bell followed almost immediately, and the maid ushered in a young man of pleasing appearance in a sweater and baggy knickerbockers who apologetically but firmly insisted on playing his ball where it lay, and, what with the shock of the lecturer's narrow escape and the spectacle of the intruder standing on the table and working away with a niblick, the afternoon's session had to be classed as a complete frost. Mr Devine's determination, from which no argument could swerve him, to deliver the rest of his lecture in the coal-cellar gave the meeting a jolt from which it never recovered.

I have dwelt upon this incident, because it was the means of introducing Cuthbert Banks to Mrs Smethurst's niece, Adeline. As Cuthbert, for it was he who had so nearly reduced the muster-roll of rising novelists by one, hopped down from the table after his stroke, he was suddenly aware that a beautiful girl was looking at him intently. As a matter of fact, everyone in the room was looking at him intently, none more so than Raymond Parsloe Devine, but none of the others were beautiful girls. Long as the members of Wood Hills Literary Society were on brain, they were short on looks, and, to Cuthbert's excited eye, Adeline Smethurst stood out like a jewel in a pile of coke.

He had never seen her before, for she had only arrived at her aunt's house on the previous day, but he was perfectly certain that life, even when lived in the midst of gravel soil, main drainage, and company's own water, was going to be a pretty poor affair if he did not see her again. Yes, Cuthbert was in love: and it is interesting to record, as showing the effect of the tender emotion on a man's game, that twenty minutes after he had met Adeline he did the short eleventh in one, and as near as a toucher got a three on the four-hundred-yard twelfth.

I will skip lightly over the intermediate stages of Cuthbert's courtship and come to the moment when – at the annual ball in aid of the local Cottage Hospital, the only occasion during the year on which the lion, so to speak, lay down with the lamb, and the Golfers and the Cultured met on terms of easy comradeship, their differences temporarily laid aside – he proposed to Adeline and was badly stymied.

That fair, soulful girl could not see him with a spy-glass.

'Mr Banks,' she said, 'I will speak frankly.'

'Charge right ahead,' assented Cuthbert.

'Deeply sensible as I am of –'

'I know. Of the honour and the compliment and all that. But, passing lightly over all that guff, what seems to be the trouble? I love you to distraction –'

'Love is not everything.'

'You're wrong,' said Cuthbert earnestly. 'You're right off it. Love –' And he was about to dilate on the theme when she interrupted him.

'I am a girl of ambition.'

'And very nice, too,' said Cuthbert.

'I am a girl of ambition,' repeated Adeline, 'and I realize that the fulfilment of my ambitions must come through my husband. I am very ordinary myself –'

'What!' cried Cuthbert. 'You ordinary? Why, you are a pearl among women, the queen of your sex. You can't have been looking in a glass lately. You stand alone. Simply alone. You make the rest look like battered repaints.'

'Well,' said Adeline, softening a trifle, 'I believe I am fairly good-looking –'

'Anybody who was content to call you fairly good-looking would describe the Taj Mahal as a pretty nifty tomb.'

'But that is not the point. What I mean is, if I marry a nonentity I shall be a nonentity myself for ever. And I would sooner die than be a nonentity.'

'And, if I follow your reasoning, you think that that lets me out?'

'Well, really, Mr Banks, have you done anything, or are you likely ever to do anything worth while?'

Cuthbert hesitated.

'It's true,' he said, 'I didn't finish in the first ten in the Open, and I was knocked out in the semi-final of the Amateur, but I won the French Open last year.'

'The – what?'

'The French Open Championship. Golf, you know.'

'Golf! You waste all your time playing golf. I admire a man who is more spiritual, more intellectual.'

A pang of jealousy rent Cuthbert's bosom.

'Like What's-his-name Devine?' he said sullenly.

'Mr Devine,' replied Adeline, blushing faintly, 'is going to be a great man. Already he has achieved much. The critics say that he is more Russian than any other young English writer.'

'And is that good?'

'Of course it's good.'

'I should have thought the wheeze would be to be more English than any other young English writer.'

'Nonsense! Who wants an English writer to be English? You've got to be Russian or Spanish or something to be a real success. The mantle of the great Russians has descended on Mr Devine.'

'From what I've heard of Russians, I should hate to have that happen to me.'

'There is no danger of that,' said Adeline scornfully.

'Oh! Well, let me tell you that there is a lot more in me than you think.'

'That might easily be so.'

'You think I'm not spiritual and intellectual,' said Cuthbert, deeply moved. 'Very well. Tomorrow I join the Literary Society.'

Even as he spoke the words his leg was itching to kick himself for being such a chump, but the sudden expression of pleasure on Adeline's face soothed him; and he went home that night with the feeling that he had taken on something rather attractive. It was only in the cold grey light of the morning that he realized what he had let himself in for.

I do not know if you have had any experience of suburban literary societies, but the one that flourished under the eye of Mrs Willoughby Smethurst at Wood Hills was rather more so than the average. With my feeble powers of narrative, I cannot hope to make clear to you all that Cuthbert Banks endured in the next few weeks. And, even if I could, I doubt if I should do so. It is all very well to excite pity and terror, as Aristotle recommends, but there are limits. In the ancient Greek tragedies it was an ironclad rule that all the real rough stuff should take place off-stage, and I shall follow this admirable principle. It will suffice if I say merely that J. Cuthbert Banks had a thin time. After attending eleven debates and fourteen lectures on *vers libre* Poetry, the Seventeenth-Century Essayists, the Neo-Scandinavian

Movement in Portuguese Literature, and other subjects of a similar nature, he grew so enfeebled that, on the rare occasions when he had time for a visit to the links, he had to take a full iron for his mashie shots.

It was not simply the oppressive nature of the debates and lectures that sapped his vitality. What really got right in amongst him was the torture of seeing Adeline's adoration of Raymond Parsloe Devine. The man seemed to have made the deepest possible impression upon her plastic emotions. When he spoke, she leaned forward with parted lips and looked at him. When he was not speaking – which was seldom – she leaned back and looked at him. And when he happened to take the next seat to her, she leaned sideways and looked at him. One glance at Mr Devine would have been more than enough for Cuthbert; but Adeline found him a spectacle that never palled. She could not have gazed at him with a more rapturous intensity if she had been a small child and he a saucer of ice-cream. All this Cuthbert had to witness while still endeavouring to retain the possession of his faculties sufficiently to enable him to duck and back away if somebody suddenly asked him what he thought of the sombre realism of Vladimir Brusiloff. It is little wonder that he tossed in bed, picking at the coverlet, through sleepless nights, and had to have all his waistcoats taken in three inches to keep them from sagging.

This Vladimir Brusiloff to whom I have referred was the famous Russian novelist, and, owing to the fact of his being in the country on a lecturing tour at the moment, there had been something of a boom in his works. The Wood Hills Literary Society had been studying them for weeks, and never since his first entrance into intellectual circles had Cuthbert Banks come nearer to throwing in the towel. Vladimir specialized in grey studies of hopeless misery, where nothing happened till page three hundred and eighty, when the moujik decided to commit suicide. It was tough going for a man

whose deepest reading hitherto had been Vardon on the Push-Shot, and there can be no greater proof of the magic of love than the fact that Cuthbert stuck it without a cry. But the strain was terrible and I am inclined to think that he must have cracked, had it not been for the daily reports in the papers of the internecine strife which was proceeding so briskly in Russia. Cuthbert was an optimist at heart, and it seemed to him that, at the rate at which the inhabitants of that interesting country were murdering one another, the supply of Russian novelists must eventually give out.

One morning, as he tottered down the road for the short walk which was now almost the only exercise to which he was equal, Cuthbert met Adeline. A spasm of anguish flitted through all his nerve-centres as he saw that she was accompanied by Raymond Parsloe Devine.

'Good morning, Mr Banks,' said Adeline.

'Good morning,' said Cuthbert hollowly.

'Such good news about Vladimir Brusiloff.'

'Dead?' said Cuthbert, with a touch of hope.

'Dead? Of course not. Why should he be? No, Aunt Emily met his manager after his lecture at Queen's Hall yesterday, and he has promised that Mr Brusiloff shall come to her next Wednesday reception.'

'Oh ah!' said Cuthbert dully.

'I don't know how she managed it. I think she must have told him that Mr Devine would be there to meet him.'

'But you said he was coming,' agreed Cuthbert.

'I shall be very glad,' said Raymond Devine, 'of the opportunity of meeting Brusiloff.'

'I'm sure,' said Adeline, 'he will be very glad of the opportunity of meeting you.'

'Possibly,' said Mr Devine. 'Possibly. Competent critics have said that my work closely resembles that of the great Russian Masters.'

'Your psychology is so deep.'

'Yes, yes.'

'And your atmosphere.'

'Quite.'

Cuthbert, in a perfect agony of spirit, prepared to withdraw from this love-feast. The sun was shining brightly, but the world was black to him. Birds sang in the tree-tops, but he did not hear them. He might have been a moujik for all the pleasure he found in life.

'You will be there Mr Banks?' said Adeline, as he turned away.

'Oh, all right,' said Cuthbert.

When Cuthbert had entered the drawing-room on the following Wednesday and had taken his usual place in a distant corner where, while able to feast his gaze on Adeline, he had a sporting chance of being overlooked or mistaken for a piece of furniture, he perceived the great Russian thinker seated in the midst of a circle of admiring females. Raymond Parsloe Devine had not yet arrived.

His first glance at the novelist surprised Cuthbert. Doubtless with the best motives, Vladimir Brusiloff had permitted his face to become almost entirely concealed behind a dense zareba of hair, but his eyes were visible through the undergrowth, and it seemed to Cuthbert that there was an expression in them not unlike that of a cat in a strange backyard surrounded by small boys. The man looked forlorn and hopeless, and Cuthbert wondered whether he had had bad news from home.

This was not the case. The latest news which Vladimir Brusiloff had had from Russia had been particularly cheering. Three of his principal creditors had perished in the last massacre of the bourgeoisie, and a man whom he owed for five years for a samovar and a pair of overshoes had fled the country, and had not been heard of since. It was not bad news from home that was depressing Vladimir. What was wrong with him was the fact that this was the eighty-second suburban literary reception he had been compelled to attend since he had landed in the country on his lecturing tour, and he was sick to death of it. When his agent had first suggested the trip, he had signed on the dotted line without an instant's hesitation. Worked out in roubles, the fees offered had seemed just about right. But now, as he peered through the brushwood at the faces round him, and realized that eight out of ten of those present had manuscripts of some sort concealed on their persons, and were only waiting for an opportunity to whip them out and start reading, he wished that he had stayed at his quiet home in Ninji-Novgorod, where the worst thing that could happen to a fellow was a brace of bombs coming in through the window and mixing themselves up with his breakfast egg.

At this point in his meditations he was aware that his hostess was looming up before him with a pale young man in horn-rimmed spectacles at her side. There was in Mrs Smethurst's demeanour something of the unction of the master-of-ceremonies at the big fight who introduces the earnest gentleman who wishes to challenge the winner.

'Oh, Mr Brusiloff,' said Mrs Smethurst, 'I do so want you to meet Mr Raymond Parsloe Devine, whose work I expect you know. He is one of our younger novelists.'

The distinguished visitor peered in a wary and defensive manner through the shrubbery, but did not speak. Inwardly he was thinking how exactly like Mr Devine was to the eighty-one other younger novelists to whom he had been introduced at various hamlets throughout the country. Raymond Parsloe Devine bowed courteously, while Cuthbert, wedged into his corner, glowered at him.

'The critics,' said Mr Devine, 'have been kind enough to say that my poor efforts contain a good deal of the Russian spirit. I owe much to the great Russians. I have been greatly influenced by Sovietski.'

Down in the forest something stirred. It was Vladimir Brusiloff's mouth opening, as he prepared to speak. He was not a man who prattled readily, especially in a foreign tongue. He gave the impression that each word was excavated from his interior by some up-to-date process of mining. He glared bleakly at Mr Devine, and allowed three words to drop out of him.

'Sovietski no good!'

He paused for a moment, set the machinery working again, and delivered five more at the pithead.

'I spit me of Sovietski!'

There was a painful sensation. The lot of a popular idol is in many ways an enviable one, but it has the drawback of uncertainty. Here today and gone tomorrow. Until this moment Raymond Parsloe Devine's stock had stood at something considerably over par in Wood Hills intellectual circles, but now there was a rapid slump. Hitherto he had been greatly admired for being influenced by Sovietski, but it appeared now that this was not a good thing to be. It was evidently a rotten thing to be. The law could not touch you for being influenced by Sovietski, but there is an ethical as well as a legal code, and this it was obvious that Raymond Parsloe Devine had transgressed. Women drew away from him slightly, holding their skirts. Men looked at him censoriously. Adeline Smethurst started violently, and dropped a tea-cup. And Cuthbert Banks, doing his popular imitation of a sardine in his corner, felt for the first time that life held something of sunshine.

Raymond Parsloe Devine was plainly shaken, but he made an adroit attempt to recover his lost prestige.

'When I say I have been influenced by Sovietski, I mean, of course, that I was once under his spell. A young writer commits many follies. I have long since passed through that phase. The false glamour of Sovietski has ceased to dazzle me. I now belong whole-heartedly to the school of Nastikoff.'

There was a reaction. People nodded at one another sympathetically. After all, we cannot expect old heads on young shoulders, and a lapse at the outset of one's career should not be held against one who has eventually seen the light.

'Nastikoff no good,' said Vladimir Brusiloff, coldly. He paused, listening to the machinery.

'Nastikoff worse than Sovietski.'

He paused again.

'I spit me of Nastikoff!' he said.

This time there was no doubt about it. The bottom had dropped out of the market, and Raymond Parsloe Devine Preferred were down in the cellar with no takers. It was clear to the entire assembled company that they had been all wrong about Raymond Parsloe Devine. They had allowed him to play on their innocence and sell them a pup. They had taken him at his own valuation, and had been cheated into admiring him as a man who amounted to something, and all the while he had belonged to the school of Nastikoff. You never can tell. Mrs Smethurst's guests were well-bred, and there was consequently no violent demonstration, but you could see by their faces what they felt. Those nearest Raymond Parsloe Devine jostled to get further away. Mrs Smethurst eyed him stonily through a raised lorgnette. One or two low hisses were heard, and over at the other end of the room somebody opened the window in a marked manner.

Raymond Parsloe Devine hesitated for a moment, then, realizing his situation, turned and slunk to the door. There was an audible sigh of relief as it closed behind him.

Vladimir Brusiloff proceeded to sum up.

'No novelists any good except me. Sovietski – yah! Nastikoff – bah! I spit me of zem all. No novelists anywhere any good except me. P. G. Wodehouse and Tolstoi not bad. Not good, but not bad. No novelists any good except me.'

And, having uttered this dictum, he removed a slab of cake from a nearby plate, steered it through the jungle, and began to champ.

It is too much to say that there was a dead silence. There could never be that in any room in which Vladimir Brusiloff was eating cake. But certainly what you might call the general chit-chat was pretty well down and out. Nobody liked to be the first to speak. The members of the Wood Hills Literary Society looked at one another timidly. Cuthbert, for his part, gazed at Adeline; and Adeline gazed into space. It was plain that the girl was deeply stirred. Her eyes were opened wide, a faint flush crimsoned her cheeks, and her breath was coming quickly.

Adeline's mind was in a whirl. She felt as if she had been walking gaily along a pleasant path and had stopped suddenly on the very brink of a precipice. It would be idle to deny that Raymond Parsloe Devine had attracted her extraordinarily. She had taken him at his own valuation as an extremely hot potato, and her hero-worship had gradually been turning into love. And now her hero had been shown to have feet of clay. It was hard, I consider, on Raymond Parsloe Devine, but that is how it goes in this world. You get a following as a celebrity and your admirers desert you. One could moralize on this at considerable length, but better not, perhaps. Enough to say that the glamour of Raymond Devine ceased abruptly in that moment for Adeline, and her most coherent thought at this juncture was the resolve, as soon as she got up to her room, to burn the three signed photographs he had sent her and to give the autographed presentation set of his books to the grocer's boy.

Mrs Smethurst, meanwhile, having rallied somewhat, was endeavouring to set the feast of reason and flow of soul going again.

'And how do you like England, Mr Brusiloff?' she asked.

The celebrity paused in the act of lowering another segment of cake.

'Dam good,' he replied, cordially.

'I suppose you have travelled all over the country by this time?'

'You said it,' agreed the Thinker.

'Have you met many of our great public men?'

'Yais – Yais – Quite a few of the nibs – Lloyd Gorge, I meet him. But ...'

Beneath the matting a discontented expression came into his face, and his voice took on a peevish note. 'But I not meet your real great men – your Arbmishel, your Arreevadon – I not meet them. That's what gives me the pipovitch. Have you ever met Arbmishel and Arreevadon?'

A strained, anguished look came into Mrs Smethurst's face and was reflected in the faces of the other members of the circle. The eminent Russian had sprung two entirely new ones on them, and they felt that their ignorance was about to be exposed. What would Vladimir Brusiloff think of the Wood Hills Literary Society? The reputation of the Wood Hills Literary Society was at stake, trembling in the balance, and coming up for the third time. In dumb agony Mrs Smethurst rolled her eyes about the room searching for someone capable of coming to the rescue. She drew blank.

And then, from a distant corner, there sounded a deprecating cough, and those nearest Cuthbert Banks saw that he had stopped twisting his right foot round his left ankle and his left foot round his right ankle and was sitting up with a light of almost human intelligence in his eyes.

'Er–' said Cuthbert, blushing as every eye in the room seemed to fix itself on him, 'I think he means Abe Mitchell and Harry Vardon.'

'Abe Mitchell and Harry Vardon?' repeated Mrs Smethurst, blankly. 'I never heard of–'

'Yais! Yais! Most! Very!' shouted Vladimir Brusiloff, enthusiastically.

'Arbmishel and Arreevadon. You know them, yes, what, no, perhaps?'

'I've played with Abe Mitchell often, and I was partnered with Harry Vardon in last year's Open.'

The great Russian uttered a cry that shook the chandelier.

'You play in ze Open? Why,' he demanded reproachfully of Mrs Smethurst, 'was I not been introduced to this young man who play in opens?'

'Well, really,' faltered Mrs Smethurst. 'Well, the fact is, Mr Brusiloff–'

She broke off. She was unequal to the task of explaining, without hurting anyone's feelings, that she had always regarded Cuthbert as a piece of cheese and a blot on the landscape.

'Introduce me!' thundered the Celebrity.

'Why, certainly, certainly of course. This is Mr–'. She looked appealingly at Cuthbert.

'Banks,' prompted Cuthbert.

'Banks!' cried Vladimir Brusiloff. 'Not Cootaboot Banks?'

'Is your name Cootaboot?' asked Mrs Smethurst, faintly.

'Well, it's Cuthbert.'

'Yais! Yais! Cootaboot!' There was a rush and swirl, as the effervescent Muscovite burst his way through the throng and rushed to where Cuthbert sat. He stood for a moment eyeing him excitedly, then, stooping swiftly, kissed him on both cheeks before Cuthbert could get his guard up. 'My dear young man, I saw you win ze French Open. Great! Great! Grand! Superb! Hot stuff, and you can say I said so! Will you permit one who is but eighteen at Nijni-Novgorod to salute you once more?'

And he kissed Cuthbert again. Then, brushing aside one or two intellectuals who were in the way, he dragged up a chair and sat down.

'You are a great man!' he said.

'Oh, no,' said Cuthbert modestly.

'Yais! Great. Most! Very! The way you lay your approach-putts dead from anywhere!'

'Oh, I don't know.'

Mr Brusiloff drew his chair closer.

'Let me tell you one vairy funny story about putting. It was one day I play at Nijni-Novgorod with the pro against Lenin and Trotsky, and Trotsky had a two-inch putt for the hole. But, just as he addresses the ball, someone in the crowd he tries to assassinate Lenin with a rewolwer – you know that is our great national sport, trying to assassinate Lenin with rewolwers – and the bang puts Trotsky off his stroke and he goes five yards past the hole, and then Lenin, who is rather shaken, you understand, he misses again himself, and we win the hole and match and I clean up three hundred and ninety-six thousand roubles, or fifteen shillings in your money. Some gameovitch! And now let me tell you one other vairy funny story–'

Desultory conversation had begun in murmurs over the rest of the room, as the Wood Hills intellectuals politely endeavoured to conceal the fact that they realized that they were about as much out of it at this reunion of twin souls as cats at a dog show. From time to time they started as Vladimir Brusiloff's laugh boomed out. Perhaps it was a consolation to them to know that he was enjoying himself.

As for Adeline, how shall I describe her emotions? She was stunned. Before her very eyes the stone which the builders had rejected had become the main thing, the hundred-to-one shot had walked away with the race. A rush of tender admiration for Cuthbert Banks flooded her heart. She saw that she had been all wrong. Cuthbert, whom she had always treated with a patronizing superiority, was really a man to be looked up to and worshipped. A deep, dreamy sigh shook Adeline's fragile form.

Half an hour later Vladimir and Cuthbert Banks rose.

'Goot-a-bye, Mrs Smet-thirst,' said the Celebrity. 'Zank you for a most charming visit. My friend Cootaboot and me we go now to shoot a few holes. You will lend me clobs, friend Cootaboot?'

'Any you want.'

'The niblicksky is what I use most. Goot-a-bye, Mrs Smet-thirst.'

They were moving to the door, when Cuthbert felt a light touch on his arm. Adeline was looking up at him tenderly.

'May I come, too, and walk round with you?'

Cuthbert's bosom heaved.

'Oh,' he said, with a tremor in his voice, 'that you would walk round with me for life!'

Her eyes met his.

'Perhaps,' she whispered, softly, 'it could be arranged.'

'And so' (concluded the Oldest Member), 'you see that golf can be of the greatest practical assistance to a man in Life's struggle. Raymond Parsloe Devine, who was no player, had to move out of the neighbourhood immediately, and is now, I believe, writing scenarios out in California for the Flicker Film Company. Adeline is married to Cuthbert, and it was only his earnest pleading which prevented her from having their eldest son christened Abe Mitchell Ribbed-Faced Mashie Banks, for she is now as keen a devotee of the great game as her husband. Those who know them say that theirs is a union so devoted, so—'

The Sage broke off abruptly, for the young man had rushed to the door and out into the passage. Through the open door he could hear him crying passionately to the waiter to bring back his clubs.

MAGNIFICENT MEN

'GOLF IS A FICKLE GAME, AND MUST

BE WOOED TO BE WON.'

Willie Park Jnr

Tom Morris: the Grand Old Man of Golf.

TOM MORRIS

Tom Morris, the Grand Old Man of golf, was born in St Andrews and started playing as 'a toddler with a putter under his arm'.

He became a club and-ballmaker under Allan Robertson, who was regarded as the finest player of that period, and with the encouragement of Robertson he was soon a high-ranking player.

Morris and Robertson became an invincible team. Their first important match as a pair came in 1849 against the prominent golfing brothers, the Dunns of Musselburgh, for a purse of £400 – this at a time when average wages were about £10 a year. Three matches, 36 holes each, were to be played at Musselburgh, St Andrews and North Berwick, the winners to be decided by match play. The Musselburgh round saw Allan and Tom crushed by a huge margin, 13 down and 11 to play. However, with their local knowledge they came to St Andrews for the second leg, confident that the defeat could be reversed. It was, but by a much narrower margin.

Betting odds were high against them at North Berwick, but they recovered from four down with eight to play, to win by a single hole. The win of £400 plus additional wagers proved to be a great confidence booster to Tom and thereafter he and Allan were impossible to defeat.

After a successful partnership, they parted company through a disagreement over the new gutta-percha balls. Robertson hated them, since they would make the feather ball obsolete, while Morris recognized their importance and was all in favour of the change. Both believed they were right.

Tom became 'custodian of the links' at Prestwick in 1851 and held this post for 12 years. He was already 39 when the first Open was played in 1860. He was beaten, by a single stroke, by Willie Park, a long-driving man and a magician with the putter. The following year Tom carried off the Champion's Belt and, after repeating his brilliant performance in 1862, he won again in 1864 and 1867. He was prevented from continuing his successes by his son, Young Tom taking the title from him in 1868. Between them, the Morrises young and old won the championship eight times.

From 1863 Tom was the custodian of the Royal and Ancient Golf Club of St Andrews, an appointment that lasted 30 years. As well as being greenkeeper, he ran a thriving club and ball making business, and played golf every day, except on the sabbath.

On his 64th birthday Tom accomplished the remarkable performance of playing St Andrews Old in 81 strokes, this with a gutta-percha ball and wooden play clubs. In later years he never missed his birthday round. When he retired, the R & A appointed him 'honorary advising greenkeeper' and he discharged his duty as starter on competition days, almost to the last.

He died, after a fall, in 1908. He was 86. Andrew Kirkcaldy in his book *Fifty Years at St Andrews* recalls the funeral: 'Maybe a man is known by the funeral he gets. Tom's was the biggest funeral I ever saw in St Andrews. The whole town was a cloud of people and there were many wet eyes amongst us, for Tom was beloved by everybody. Flags flew at half-mast, the greens were deserted and not a ball was struck on the links that day. Tom was buried beside his son, Young Tommy, and close to the grave of Allan Robertson, the feather ball champion of Scotland.'

Tom Morris, born St Andrews 1821. Died 1908. British Open Champion 1861, 1862, 1864, 1867. Honorary professional to the Royal and Ancient Golf Club. Elected World Golf Hall of Fame 1976.

YOUNG TOM MORRIS

What might have been! What greatness there was. In a career lasting just ten years, Young Tom Morris wore the coveted Open Championship Belt three times in succession, in 1868, 1869 and 1870, when it became his

property. After the belt had been won outright, an elegant claret jug was substituted, the same trophy as is played for today. Young Tom was the first winner in 1872.

The son of Old Tom Morris, who was himself four times the Open

Young Tom Morris wearing the Belt which he kept outright after winning the British Open three times in succession.

Champion, Tom Junior was gifted with immensely strong hands, and brought flamboyance to the game, along with power controlled to perfection, and delicacy on the greens. With such attributes he was winning professional cash prizes at the tender age of thirteen.

In 1868 he entered and won the Open Championship with the then marvellous score of 154 for the 36 holes. Prestwick was a severe test, and to follow up his victory of 68 with an even more convincing win the following year, 11 strokes ahead of the nearest rival, was heralded as magnificent. His third triumph, however, was his most brilliant, for his record score of 149 was 12 strokes ahead of the nearest opponent.

That he was head and shoulders above all others was beyond argument, and it was 34 years before his average score in retaining the Belt – 74.5 strokes – was to be bettered. But in those 34 years fairways were widened, greens became keener, clubs were improved, and the rubber-cored Haskell ball came into general use in 1902. There was to be no competition for the Open in 1871, but it came as no surprise when Young Tommy was again the winner of the 1872 contest. In winning for the fourth successive time he set a record that remains unbroken.

His last match took place in 1875, when he and his father played Willie and Mungo Park at North Berwick. When the game was over he returned to the clubhouse to be told that his beloved young wife, soon to give birth to their first child, was critically ill. By the time he got home he found his wife and the baby were both dead.

He never recovered and died shortly afterwards at the age of 24. The autopsy said it was a haemorrhage – those who knew him said it was a broken heart. What great heights he may have reached we shall never know.

At St Andrews there is a fine monument that was erected on his death. It reads: 'Deeply regretted by numerous friends and all golfers, he thrice in succession won the Championship Belt, and held it without rivalry and yet without envy, his many amiable qualities being no less acknowledged than his golfing achievements.'

Tom Morris Jnr, born 1851. Died 1875. Open Champion 1868, 1869, 1870, 1872. Elected World Golf Hall of fame 1975.

JOHN BALL

With a consistency that these days seems hard to comprehend, John Ball won the British Amateur title an astounding eight times, and was the first player to win the Amateur and Open titles in the same year.

When he took the Open in 1890 he was the first amateur so to do and the first Englishman to wrest the title from the Scots, who had come to regard it rather as their birthright.

Even though competition was not so intense, or indeed worldwide, in those days, Ball's dominance was nevertheless remarkable in spanning two stages in golfing history – the gutta-percha period, during which he won his Open title and five Amateur crowns, followed by the introduction of the Haskell ball, to which he adapted so readily, winning three more Amateur titles.

John Ball, the first amateur to win the British Open.

In a golfing career of enviable longevity, Ball last played in the Amateur in 1912, when he was 50. Certainly he bowed out on a note of glory, for he took with him the scalp of Abe Mitchell, a talented professional who to this day is heralded as 'the best man never to have won the Open'.

Ball was a natural swinging player with apparently no obvious theories. In turning from the old style of closed stance and playing the ball well forward – the established Scottish method that produced low running shots – Ball adopted an open stance that enabled him to lob the ball high with remarkable accuracy, his irons peppering the flag from every direction.

He scorned the niblick and refused to carry one, once describing it as 'a bloody spade'. Nobody could keep the ball down better against a breeze, but he had an uncanny ability for getting the ball up, so that a mashie could be a decided menace to him. In playing from sand he would lay the blade of his mid-iron open, hit the sand an inch or so behind the ball and float it out with smooth follow-through. His contemporaries were in awe, though some were critical of such new-fangled modernity, and it took the likes of Taylor and Vardon several years to bring what was essentially John Ball's method into universal acceptance.

Modern golfers would do well to heed Ball's other great attribute – his ability to get on with the job. Not for him the pacing, prancing, dawdling or hesitating; no dropping on haunches to study a line. Though he often appeared in a hurry, he knew what he was doing and was relentless in his criticism of 'modern' golfers – their alibis and their fuss. His style was simple – he just played.

That his style and manner were so admired goes without saying, drawing supreme compliments time and again from the finest writer and swing analyst of his day, Bernard Darwin: 'I can only rejoice that I saw him, when perhaps some of the dash and ferocity had gone, but when he was still magnificent beyond words. I would rather watch Mr Ball play than any other man, and that of all beautiful styles his had for me a beauty apart.'

John Ball was a great golfer, yet the trappings of fame meant little to him. A colleague, John Harris, wrote to him in the 1930s asking if he would lend his nine gold championship medals for a grand exhibition of sporting trophies about to take place in London, Ball replied: 'I'm sorry, I don't know where they are. I think I've given them away to friends.'

John Ball, born Hoylake 1861. Died North Wales 1940. British Amateur Champion 1888, 1890, 1892, 1894, 1897, 1907, 1910, 1912. British Open Champion 1890.

WILLIE PARK JNR

Willie Park Jnr: player, architect and inventor.

Willie Park Jnr, a Musselburgh man, was the great Scottish professional for two decades at the end of last century. He was a natural ball player and inherited his love of the game from his father, Willie, who won the first Open in 1860, and won it again three more times.

He won his own laurels twice, taking the Open Championships of 1887 and 1889, and he may well have won a third title, but at Prestwick in 1898 he decided to play safe at the last hole, aiming for the four he needed to tie with Harry Vardon, only to discover – this before scoreboards and field telephones – that Vardon had in fact birdied the hole.

Willie was also an exceptional businessman. He was the first to travel south to England, and though golf occupied some of his time, it was as a golfing entrepreneur that he became famous. Park's initial and most successful business enterprise was to enter the heady world of golf course architecture. His first course at Huntercombe in Oxfordshire is regarded as a classic and fortunate golfers still enjoy this example of his genius, while Sunningdale Old is enshrined as his finest design and is quite possibly one of the greatest courses ever.

In all he designed around 170 courses, wrote three books of instruction and was the inventor and manufacturer of several exceptional new golf clubs.

His greatest golfing skill was in the use of Old Pawky, a putter which became something of a legend. A Willie Park goose-neck putter is something collectors now cherish, a much-valued instrument with which Willie was known at times to inflict considerable torture.

He was a great challenge match player and his most famous encounter – a two-course affair against Harry Vardon staged at Ganton and North Berwick – attracted huge crowds. Willie lost by a mile.

Willie Park Jnr, born Musselburgh, Scotland, 1864. Died England, 1925. British Open Champion 1887, 1889.

HAROLD HILTON

One of England's greatest amateurs of the period before the World War I, Harold Hilton won four British Amateurs, in 1900, 1901, 1911, 1913, and two Open titles, in 1892 and 1897.

Although a fine match player who won his amateur laurels in the approved method of man-to-man combat, he was also an excellent medal player. He travelled to the United States in 1911 and won the USGA Amateur on the 37th hole, defeating Fred Herreshoff in an exciting final.

MR. H. H. HILTON.

CHAMPION GOLFER, 1892.

By virtue of his stature, short, sturdy and powerfully physical, Hilton's method of play was described as that of juggler as well as golfer. He had a fast swing and literally came up on his toes at impact on a full drive. His cap

would fall off at the end of such exertion and though some thought he was unduly forceful, it was rare that his enthusiasm and effort contributed to a series of poor strokes. He was a perky man with a cigarette constantly dangling between pursed lips – even while driving – and the second-greatest thrill for spectators was to see him charge off down the fairway after his shot, as though a pack of wolves was after him.

Hilton, a great student of the game, had a most analytical golfing mind and he wrote several learned books on the subject. He was the first of only three men to hold the British and American Amateur Championships at the same time, the others being Bobby Jones and Lawson Little. He was also the first editor of *Golf Monthly*.

Bernard Darwin wrote that Hilton had such astonishing accuracy with his woods, his spoon in particular, that his shots sometimes finished so close to the hole that opponents were thoroughly demoralized.

Harold Horsfall Hilton, born West Kirby, Merseyside, 1869. Died Westcote, Gloucestershire, 1942. British Open Champion 1892, 1897. Irish Amateur 1897, 1900, 1901, 1902. British Amateur Champion 1900, 1901, 1911, 1913. US Amateur Champion 1911.

FREDDIE TAIT

A heroic soldier as well as an exceptional golfer, Lieutenant Freddie Tait was killed while leading men of the Black Watch into battle at Koodesberg Drift, one of so many victims in the cruel Boer War. He was barely 30, and in the very prime of his golfing life.

Freddie was no ordinary golfer; indeed in his short life he became something of a national treasure in his native Scotland, and was perhaps the

Freddie Tait who was a prodigious hitter and was the first man to score a par 72 on St Andrews Old Course.

first player to be idolized; a legendary figure in every sense.

Players young and old were saddened by his passing, many believing that the game would never be the same again without him. All had tales to tell of his exceptional prowess, for he'd taken to the links at the tender age of five, and completed the Old Course at St Andrews in under 100 whilst not yet in his teens, an exceptional achievement in those days of gutta-percha and whippy hickory.

Here was a man who had golf in his veins, a powerful six-footer with rippling muscles, honed in the army gymnasium, where for two or three years he was an instructor. Yet his style was unorthodox and many thought of him as a wild and dashing hitter with an old-fashioned St Andrews swing; wonderful to behold, prodigious of length, yet suspect in an emergency.

But he was not that at all. With so much power to spare his was a singularly controlled swing and he appeared to hit the ball almost delicately, reserving his power and using it only when something quite exceptional was demanded. Though he was acclaimed during his short career as the greatest amateur golfer, no player ever tried to imitate his style.

Freddie's prowess is well related in golf records; wherever he played he sooner or later lowered the record score for the course. Twice before 1900 he cut the Old Course record, first to 77 in match play, four years later to 72.

He won a rich harvest of medals at St. Andrews, twice he won the Amateur Championship and twice the St George's Vase at Sandwich. His first and greatest Amateur Championship at St George's, Sandwich, was a triumph described in the records of the time as coming as near 'perfection's sacred heights' as was possible.

He was third to Vardon and Taylor in the Open Championship of 1896, third again to Braid and Hilton in 1897, and fifth in 1898, though he regarded medal play as a dull performance akin to rifle shooting.

Tait was the consummate match player; he loved the challenge of real combat – no quarter asked and none given. The stymie he regarded as nothing more than a hazard of the game, describing it as one of the most beautiful shots in golf.

Freddie Tait's memory does not rest with his golfing prowess: rather it made him known to a wider circle. His memory lives with the honour of the Black Watch.

Frederick Guthrie Tait, born Dalkeith 1870. Died South Africa 1900. British Amateur Champion 1896, 1898, runner-up 1899. Tied third British Open Championship 1896–97.

HARRY VARDON

Harry Vardon will forever be remembered as the only golfer to win the Open Championship six times. He was without question the golfer of his time, winning the Open in 1896, 1898, 1899, 1903, 1911 and 1914. He also won the US Open in 1910.

He had been, like so many greats, a caddie as a child, and had an elder brother who was a pro. Harry was first noticed in 1893 and within two years was very much the man to beat. In the winter of 1895 he was invited to take part in a series of matches at Pau and, suddenly, the whole Continent was buzzing with the name of Harry Vardon. The following spring, J.H. Taylor, already a double winner of the Open, played Vardon at Ganton and was defeated by such a huge margin that it left him shaking his head in wonder. J.H. declared that there was no player he feared more in the coming Open. It was to be prophetic. The two men tied, and Harry won the play-off.

By 1898 Vardon had come at the game with all barrels blazing and the next two years were to be his finest. If he entered, invariably he won, crushing all who came against him.

He beat Willie Park by one stroke to take the 1898 Open and in 1899 beat Jack White by five strokes. Vardon was later to contract tuberculosis, but such was his dedication that he often played against medical advice. 'If I make a promise, I must never let them down' was his unshakable philosophy.

In a letter written from hospital later in his life he acknowledged that it cost him his health, and although he was to win two further Open titles he was never again able to demonstrate the totally crushing superiority of former days, days which the great Scottish player Andrew Kirkaldy said 'would break the heart of an iron ox'.

From 1910 until the beginning of the World War I he remained one of a handful of the best, but was never again in a class of his own. After finishing runner-up in the Opens of 1900, 1901 and 1902 he was to win again at Prestwick in 1903 in what he regarded as his finest achievement ever. Under medical supervision, and told to guard against undue exertion, he was warned that to take part would be foolish. Again declaring that a promise was a promise, he decided to compete despite feeling weak and unwell, and completed the event by taking a glass of stout and a nap before embarking on the afternoon rounds. In the finishing round he felt so faint it was doubted if could finish. That he was able to last until the final putt showed how great a competitor he was and the applause that greeted his victory could never have been more richly deserved.

Such was the man's dedication that on the following day he played again,

Harry Vardon: No one has matched his six Open titles.

this time at Western Gailes. In his book *My Golfing Life* he wrote: 'I would not have played, save that I had already promised to compete.' He won, breaking the course record, but the exertions of the two contests consigned him to months in a sanatorium.

In 1911 Harry was to win his fifth Open, this time against the Frenchman Arnauld Massy, who retired, beaten and demoralized, on the 17th green. Vardon had just one more Open to contest, in 1914, and now, at the age of 44, he returned to Prestwick, scene of former triumph, to defeat J. H. Taylor. It was a hand-to-hand fight, the ordeal a trying one. At lunch Taylor had a two-stroke advantage. After nine holes the order was reversed, Vardon three strokes ahead, and Harry was to finish with this same advantage. On the following day, he took part in an exhibition tournament at Turnberry!

Harry Vardon is thought of today not only as a golfer of genius but also one who produced a swing of elegance, ease and grace. Professionals annually vie for the Vardon Trophy, one of the most elegant statues ever to be sculpted, and golfers the world over use the so-called Vardon V grip — invented and first used by J. E. Laidlay but adopted and made popular by one of golf's greatest old masters.

Harry Vardon, born Jersey 1870. Died 1937. British Open Champion six times (a record). US Open Champion 1900. PGA matchplay Champion 1912. Elected World Golf Hall of Fame 1974.

JAMES BRAID

In the history of golf and in the wonderful photographs that record the early days of the game, one of the most memorable figures will always be that of James Braid.

He was born in Elie, Fife, in 1870, the same year as Harry Vardon and a

indeed, although he himself was dissatisfied with his often suspect putting and lack of length from the tee. When, almost miraculously, he found extra length he attributed it to using a play club with a much flatter lie. With this the ball positively flew away. Forever after he remained long and accurate.

A move to Edinburgh in 1891 enabled him to play regularly and he won the

James Braid: winner of five British Opens in ten years.

few months before John Henry Taylor. A vintage period, for the 'Triumvirate' had all arrived within little more than 12 months of each other.

At that time, the professional golfer was little more than a superior caddie, so of necessity, golf took second place to Braid's work as a joiner. He would play whenever he could, and by the time he was 16 he was a very fine golfer

Edinburgh Thistle Club's Gold Medal on numerous occasions.

In 1893, he moved to London to take a job as a clubmaker at the Army & Navy Stores, and played his first professional match at Limpsfield, where his cousin Douglas Rolland was the pro. Playing as a pair they emerged triumphant, James holing a long putt on the 18th to win in the afternoon.

The Open was next, in 1894, and James was steady enough to finish equal tenth.

At the end of 1895 the tall, angular young man with the impressive walrus moustache began to amass greater fame, playing a match against J. H. Taylor – then Open champion for the second time – and squaring it on the 36th hole. It was the making of him, and the following spring he took his first full professional post at Romford, where he remained until moving on to become the first pro at Walton Heath.

Braid next contested the Open in 1896, at Muirfield, and finished a respectable sixth to Vardon, winning £5 into the bargain. The next year he lost the championship by a putt to the brilliant amateur Harold Hilton. Three more years were to pass before his first Open victory, at Muirfield in 1901, and this time his touch with a new aluminium Mills putter was described as pure delight.

Emerging from his lean period to take the Open, he especially delighted Scottish supporters, for this was the first Scottish victory since Willie Auchterlonie in 1893. Winning by four strokes from Vardon and Taylor, Braid wrote his name into the history books, and the Triumvirate was now complete. From then on he, Taylor and Vardon travelled the country demonstrating their skills.

He had to wait until 1905 for his second Open title, this time at St Andrews, and he followed it by winning again in 1906 at Muirfield, at Prestwick in 1908, and made it five in ten years with his last win at St Andrews in 1910. Popular, calm, unassuming, and liked as much by his opponents as by his supporters, he holds a special place in the history of golf as a giant of the game.

Braid was consulted on the design and layout of many golf courses; more than a hundred, it is claimed, bear the marks of his intelligence, while his most lasting legacy is the King's course at Gleneagles.

From his 70th birthday onwards he accomplished a round of golf on his beloved Walton Heath in a score equal to his age. On all occasions he carried his own clubs. This great man's personality dominated the game, and he will be held in affection for ever.

James Braid, born Fife, 1870. Died 1950. British Open Champion 1901, 1905, 1906, 1908, 1910. PGA Matchplay Champion 1903, 1905, 1907, 1911. Elected World Golf Hall of Fame 1976.

JOHN HENRY TAYLOR

Alongside Braid and Vardon making up the game's famed Triumvirate, J.H. won the Open in 1894, 1895, 1900, 1909, and 1913, was second five times, and third once.

He accompanied Vardon to America in 1900 and was second to the great man in the US Open that year. He also won the French Open twice, the German Open and captured the PGA Championship in 1904 and 1908.

He learned his golf at Westward Ho!, which he regarded as the finest course ever. The blustery conditions prevalent there served to teach him accuracy and to cultivate the ball control for which he became famous. From working as a caddie he entered the professional world at Burnham in Somerset, and while there he was matched against the famed St Andrews' professional Andrew Kirkaldy, beating him soundly.

Andrew was in awe of this new tiger, and when Taylor appeared at Prestwick for the 1893 Open he was regarded as the man to beat. Straightness was his forte, and in shooting the then-record round of 75, it seemed likely that he had the championship firmly in his grasp, though torrential rain was to be his downfall. Thoroughly soaked in the second round, he began to miss more than his share of putts and a score of 89 put him out of contention, with Willie Auchterlonie scoring his only Open victory.

Saddened by his loss but profiting by it, J.H. was to win the first of his five Open titles the following year at Sandwich, recording a winning score of 326. By today's standards that must seem high, yet those who know the course only as is it today, and playing it with titanium, graphite, and unbelievably long balls, must take it on merit as being creditable in the extreme. He defended his title successfully at St Andrews, although a first round of 86 almost put him out of the running. A storm in the final round destroyed the chances of the leader, Herd, who had the worst of it, and it all but submerged Taylor as well, but he had less of it to suffer

J. H. Taylor: a master of links golf.

His final Open title was to come in 1913 at Hoylake, where again he demonstrated that his controlled, compact swing was more than a match for the other competitors. Hitting the ball as though the wind didn't exist, he made it look simple, his secret being never to under-club or press.

In many ways the ideal advertisement for golf, J.H. established himself as the spokesman for his fellow professionals at a time when they were not always seen to be getting a fair deal, and helped establish the PGA. He was a fine speaker, a self-taught, well-read

and with waterlogged greens he was able to pitch with the boldness that was his great attribute. He won by four strokes.

In 1896 he tied with Vardon at Muirfield before being beaten in the play-off, while a year later it was the turn of the great amateur, Harold Hilton. Vardon was to win again in 1898 and 1899 but in 1900 Taylor was supreme, winning at St Andrews with a magnificent display of arrow-like accuracy.

The next few years were monopolized to a great extent by the third member of the aptly named triumvirate, James Braid, and it was not until 1909 at Deal that J.H. was to reassert his dominance on the Championship.

man, of whom it was said that in golf the guideposts were his only obstacles! Trite perhaps, but it sums up the man to a tee.

During his long career he also manufactured golf clubs while devoting considerable time to golf course architecture, as a partner in Taylor and Hawtree, a company that exists to this day.

He died in 1963, shortly before his 92nd birthday.

John Henry Taylor, born Northiam, Devon, 1871. Died 1963. British Open Champion 1894, 1895, 1900, 1909, 1913. PGA Matchplay Champion 1904, 1908. French Open Champion 1908, 1909. Elected World Golf Hall of Fame 1963.

EDWARD RAY

The trademark plus fours, felt hat and briar pipe.

TED RAY

One of Britain's top players in the early part of the twentieth century, though he lived in the shadow of Vardon, Braid and Taylor, Ted Ray had a golf career that spanned four decades.

If he was not quite able to match the Triumvirate's peerless abilities, he certainly gained inspiration from them, while being their match with the putter. He won the Open in 1912, was second twice and in the top ten 15 times over 25 years.

Big, cheerful and calm, he was a long driver with a slow, easy swing and identifiable on the course by his big moustache and full felt hat. Always in plus fours, Ted was seldom without his briar pipe; indeed he gained a useful secondary income by featuring in tobacco advertisements, at a time when smoking was quite the done thing.

Like the great Vardon, Ted was born in Jersey, and with his fellow Channel Islander he helped spark huge American interest in golf when they toured the States together, giving golfing exhibitions in 1913 and 1920. Ray won the 1920 US Open at Inverness at age 43, but is best known, by Americans certainly, for the 1913 US Open, when the high point for them was when he and Vardon were beaten by the then unknown prodigy, Francis Ouimet.

Ted played in two GB versus USA Matches and captained Britain in the first Ryder Cup. His last recorded victory, in an exceptionally long career, was in 1935 in the Hertfordshire Open when he was 57. He was pro at Oxhey Golf Club, in Hertfordshire, from 1912 until his retirement in 1941.

Ted Ray, born Jersey, Channel Islands, 1877. Died London 1943. British Open Champion 1912. US Open Champion 1920. GB versus USA 1921, 1926. Ryder Cup 1927 (captain).

WILLIE ANDERSON

When Willie Anderson gave up his job as a North Berwick greenkeeper to seek his fortune in the United States at the turn of the century, people doubted his sanity. They knew there were only a handful of courses in America at that time and doubted that any youngster with golf on his mind was ever likely to make it in that far-flung quarter. How wrong they were.

Willie was the first great player to emerge from the US, though it is impossible to gauge his degree of greatness because there were so few courses, while the accoutrements of the game were hand-wrought and often somewhat crude. Nevertheless, he fared very well, while helping also to raise the profile of the game.

This dour, flat-swinging Scot set

Willie Anderson.

a record in 1905 that has been equalled only twice in almost a hundred years – and never bettered. That was the year he won the US Open for the fourth time – the last three in a row, a feat not yet matched.

Sturdily built and short on conversation, he first won the US Open in 1901 when he defeated Alex Smith, of the famous Smith brothers, in a play-off, scoring 85 to Smith's 86. He missed out the next year but in 1903, 1904, and 1905 he triumphed, with scores of 307, 303, and 314 respectively. He was 25 years old in 1905. Five years later he was dead.

Though alcohol is often blamed as the cause of his early demise, and he was certainly an enthusiastic drinker according to at least one contemporary, he is officially listed as having died of arteriosclerosis.

The only two players since Anderson to have won the US Open four times are Bobby Jones and Ben Hogan.

Anderson's first victory was accomplished with the gutta-percha ball, his last three with the 'bounding Billy', the Haskell rubber-core that transformed the game. His score in 1901 was 331, well over over 80 shots per round, yet in 1904 he set a record for the US Open by shooting a 73, and the next year scored a 72.

Willie B. Anderson, born North Berwick, Scotland, 1880. Died America, 1910. US Open Champion 1901, 1903, 1904, 1905. A charter member of the PGA Hall of Fame, established in 1940, he was voted into the World Hall of Fame in 1975.

GEORGE DUNCAN

He was the gambler – the man who never feared to take a risk and who so often brought off the impossible.

Everyone who knew of George Duncan knew him as the golfer of perfect action. His was an immaculate style with a perfect stance assumed almost at the run, for he was the quickest player ever, though never careless.

Golfers who bemoaned slow, methodical players would say: 'Look at George Duncan. He never wasted a second yet he won the Open.' Others thought if he had only slowed down he might well have won several more.

Having driven off, he would snatch a club from his bag in readiness for his next shot – he knew exactly which club he would need – and upon arrival he would approach from behind. Down would go his right foot, his left then tiptoed into the correct position. He never waggled or shuffled and, once the stance was set, he would execute the perfect swing and away would soar the ball, usually to drop gently into the desired spot. Vardon thought him the greatest shot-maker of the generation in which he played.

World War I interrupted Duncan's career and it was not until 1920 that he won his Open title. But what a victory. He started 13 strokes behind the

George Duncan: quick, fearless and often brilliant.

leader at the end of 36 holes. In those days the Open meant 36 holes a day – four rounds over two days – and in everyone's opinion Duncan was considered done for, especially in view of his 'weakness'.

If there was a weakness in Duncan's character it was that he was unphilosophical. His impatience with the bad shot or indifferent lie cost him dearly. Often it was said that he was not interested enough to win the great championships.

Came the final, however, and Duncan for once mastered completely his lack of self-restraint and set about demonstrating his brilliance, as only he knew how. Thirty-six holes later he was champion, his score of 143 a record that was to remain unbeaten for 15 years. He said later that it was only being so far behind that had spurred him on to really try to win.

The year he took the Open he swept the board for trophies, and throughout his career he scored many successes in tournaments and international matches, but he was never again to win an Open. It was source of amazement to his contemporaries, who thought him capable of repeating the feat many times over. He came close and was runner-up in 1922 at St George's after very nearly tying with Walter 'The Haig' Hagen.

But it was always said that it was Duncan – playing with his inimitable brilliance and abandon – mercilessly crushing Hagen that gave the British team the stimulus to win the Ryder Cup in 1929 and end a string of US victories.

Duncan was known as the 'good player's doctor'; his unique qualities led many famous players to call on him for consultations – even the great Bobby Jones sought him out for a 'cure'.

George Duncan, born Scotland 1883. Died 1964. Belgian Open Champion 1912. PGA Matchplay Champion 1913. French Open Champion 1913, 1927. British Open Champion 1920. Ryder Cup player 1927, 1929 (captain), and 1931.

WALTER HAGEN

He said he didn't want to be a millionaire; he just wanted to live like one – and he did. Gene Sarazen wrote of Hagen: 'All professionals who have a chance to go after big money today should say a silent prayer to Walter each time they stretch a cheque between their fingers. It was Walter who made professional golf what it is.'

The first giant of American golf, prominent both on the links and in elevating the status of his professional brethren, Walter's first ambition was to become a baseball player. He wound up winning 11 national championships – four British Opens, two US Opens, and five PGA crowns. And before he was through, he had so seized our imagination that golf professionals – hitherto treated as second-rate citizens and barred from most clubhouses – were given the respect that they were due.

He made a million dollars in a period when that was all but unthinkable – and he blew the lot. He was utterly confident and

Walter Hagen: 'Never hurry, never worry, and be sure to smell the flowers on the way.'

spectacular in his shot-making. Above all, he was a consummate showman.

In Hagen's first US Open, at Brookline in 1913, he finished only a shot behind Ouimet, Vardon and Ray. The next year he won, and in 1919 he won his second. The riotous twenties followed, in which he won four US Opens, in 1922, 1924, 1928, 1929, and five US PGAs, in 1921, 1924, 1925, 1926, 1927. At one point he won 22 consecutive matches, until Leo Diegel finally stopped him.

Hagen never could say how many tournaments he had played in; some were 'locals' set up almost as a stage for his performances, but is estimated that he played in over 200 official tournaments in his career and that he won more than 60. He also played around 1,500 exhibitions.

He inflicted the worst defeat ever suffered by Jones, winning 12 and 11 in 72 holes. He suffered his own worst defeat in one of these matches, when Archie Compston beat him 18 and 17, for a then huge purse of £500. That was in 1926 and Hagen followed the defeat by winning the Open.

He starred in five Ryder Cup teams, 1927, 1929, 1931, 1933, 1935, and was non-playing captain in 1937. He lost only one match, to the brilliant George Duncan.

Hagen's swing reflected his style in life: relaxed beyond belief and so laid-back. He took a rather wide stance and swayed backwards perceptibly. He would hit several bad shots in the course of a round, but said that he expected to and they didn't bother him. He was a master of recoveries from seemingly impossible situations, and a great putter, especially from middle distances.

In 21 US Opens he finished in the top ten 15 times, and as high as third in 1935, when he was well into his forties. His long career as a contender spanned the greatest of all periods, from Vardon to Nelson. Above all, Hagen was a great competitor, as well as a great showman.

'Never hurry, never worry, and be sure to smell the flowers along the way,' typified The Haig's attitude to golf and to life.

Walter Charles Hagen, born Rochester, New York, 1892. Died Traverse City, Michigan, 1969. US Open Champion 1914, 1919. USPGA Champion 1921, 1924, 1925, 1926, 1927. British Open Champion 1922, 1924, 1928, 1929. Ryder Cup 1927–1935, non-playing captain 1937.

TOMMY ARMOUR

Like many a Scot before him, Tommy Armour decided in 1924 to emigrate to the United States, to become a professional golfer.

Three years earlier in 1921 he had represented Britain in amateur play at the highest level, in an official match that was the forerunner to the Walker Cup. Though he didn't know it at the time, he was to become the only man to play for Britain and for America, for after arriving in the United States and turning pro, he played with an American team against the British, in an international match before the Ryder Cup was established.

One of the great figures of international golf, Armour had many distinctions, though one distinct minus was his slow play. When criticized, he would retort: 'Who says the game should be played fast? The tempo of the game has slowed down as efficiency has increased.' He scored a remarkable victory in the US Open in 1927, holing a four-yard putt to tie with Harry Cooper for the title and defeating him in the play-off. He won the USPGA Championship in 1930, beating Gene Sarazen by one hole, and in 1931 he scored his greatest success, victory in the Open Championship at Carnoustie. It was a memorable championship. At the start of the final round, it looked as if the talented Argentinian Jurado would triumph, but Jurado faltered and Armour, with a near-faultless 71, took the Championship by a single stroke. The Scots were especially delighted, for an émigré Scot winning the title was almost as good as if he had just sailed across the bay from St Andrews.

Tommy became a striking figure, chisel-featured and with prematurely grey hair, which gave him his nickname Silver Scot. He was also a fluent public speaker and raconteur and the author of perhaps the most successful instruction book ever – *How To Play Your Best Golf All The Time*. His advice to any golfer trying to qualify still makes good sense: 'Take no sixes, no double

Tommy Armour (left) receivng the British Open trophy at Carnoustie in 1931.

bogeys, and remember there are lots of ways to make four.'

On the links Armour was famous for his long-irons, rifling his shots to the target with almost monotonous regularity, while also being a glorious wooden-club player with prodigious length. He was deliberate in his game and his great secret was perfect timing. He would waggle many times before starting his swing, then practising what he always preached, he would hit the very hell out of it with his right hand.

Thomas (Tommy) D. Armour, born Edinburgh, Scotland, 1895. Died Larchmont, New York, 1968. British Open Champion 1931. US Open Champion 1927. USPGA Champion 1930.

BOBBY JONES

Incomparable in his era, Bobby Jones has had myriad volumes written about his achievements, but they can be summed up in a single sentence: He was the greatest golfer the world has ever known.

There are those who would argue, with great reason, that Jack Nicklaus rivals Jones for the title, but Jones' record of 13 major championships over a span of eight years is unmatched. And he was the only man to complete the Grand Slam of the US and British Open Championships and the US and British Amateur Championships in the same year, 1930. And that while he was still an amateur.

Having completed the Grand Slam, Bobby Jones walked away from competitive golf at the age of 28. And then he created the Masters.

Jones, like others before him, had experienced a period of disappointment before he reached the top. His golfing career started about 1916, when, at the age of 14, he won the Georgia State Amateur championship. The following year he won the Southern Amateur. From then until 1922 he entered 11 major events and never won a single one.

But by 1923 he had broken through. In July he defeated Bobby Cruickshank in a play-off for the US Open and from then on there was no stopping him. The national championships in both Britain and America became 'Jones odds-on to win' and with good reason.

He won the US Open again in 1926, 1929 and 1930; the US Amateur in 1924, 1925, 1927, 1928 and 1930; the Open in 1926, 1927 and 1930; and the British Amateur in 1930.

Jones was tutored by Stewart Maiden, a Scottish professional who had emigrated to Atlanta, Georgia, from whom he adopted one of the smoothest swings in the game. Today, film of Bobby's action, remastered from old newsreels, show that he possessed a full, fluid, graceful swing, was long off the tee, and was an excellent putter. His was a picture swing, although a little loose by today's standards.

How could anyone so talented suddenly turn his back on the game? Jones says it wasn't difficult. His family came first, then his career as a lawyer, then his golf, which, he said, was nothing more than a game.

In the early years of his retirement, Bobby and a partner bought an old fruit farm and, working with the greatest of all golf course architects, Alister Mackenzie, created a course where he and a few old friends could play golf in the winter away from the fans who had followed him in their thousands during his career and whose presence had unnerved him. The end result was the Augusta National.

Sadly, when a spinal ailment confined him to a wheelchair in his later years, his partner ruthlessly cut Jones out of the running of the club. His skill and his manner had already made him a national hero, and his courage in adversity became an inspiration to golfers everywhere.

Bobby Jones once remarked that 'a man's priceless treasures are his friendships, and a man who has many friendships has a rich life indeed'. No person could have claimed more friends than he.

Robert Tyre (Bobby) Jones, born Atlanta, Georgia 1902. Died Atlanta 1971. US Open Champion 1923, 1926, 1929, 1930. US Amateur Champion 1924, 1925, 1927, 1928, 1930. British Open Champion 1926, 1927, 1930. British Amateur Champion 1930. Bobby played in six Walker Cup Matches, in 1922, 1923, 1924, 1926, 1926 and 1930. He won six individual single matches and four double matches, and lost only once. Elected to USPGA Hall of Fame 1940; World Golf Hall of Fame 1974.

Bobby Jones: the only man to achieve the Grand Slam of golf.

GENE SARAZEN

One of golf's all-time greats, with one of the longest careers, Gene was a former caddie from a poor family. He once said that no golfer could achieve greatness unless he had experienced hunger. As one who had known hunger and poverty, he was absolutely driven to do his best and in due course he gained his reward.

Certainly, Gene was not the golfer of copybook perfection, for he was on the short side and somewhat thick-set. His hands were chubby and his fingers too short for him to use the orthodox grip. So he adopted an interlocking grip, good enough for those with smaller hands, indeed good enough for Jack Nicklaus!

Small hands, maybe, but Gene stood like a rock, while his upper body was clearly built for power. And he was possessed of a resilient intellect to harness the whole package.

In 1922, when only 20, Gene sprang to fame by winning the US Open and followed by winning the USPGA Championship, both of which, in those days, were decided by matchplay. With these successes under his belt, he travelled to Scotland for the 1923 Open at Troon, but failed to qualify by a single stroke. It was a disappointment, but the fighter in him determined he would return, and return he did. Five years later he was runner-up to Walter Hagen at Royal St George's. In 1931 he tied for first, then finished third behind Armour and Jurado in the play-off. In 1932 his dream came true. He dominated the championship, his fitness and ball finesse a match for everybody, and he won by five strokes from Macdonald Smith, with a new aggregate record of 283, which was not beaten for 17 years.

During this period, Gene saw the potential for a new club, and was the first player to develop the sand wedge, which he is credited with having invented. Later, in 1932, he won the US Open for the second time, playing his last 28 holes in a remarkable 100 strokes. He played on the Ryder Cup team six times from 1927 to 1937.

In 1935 Gene struck one of golf's most amazing shots, still talked of in awe to this day, his famous double eagle on the 15th hole at Augusta National in the 1935 Masters. He needed three birdies to tie the leader, Craig Wood, and in the last round he stroked his ball over the water-protected 15th

Gene Sarazen: cutting a dash in tie, plus fours and correspondent shoes.

green with a four wood. It bounced twice and disappeared in the hole for a 'golden eagle'. It was a miracle. He tied with Wood, and won by five strokes in a two-round play-off.

Gene, who has always worn plusfours on the course, is one of only four golfers in history to have won both the British Open and that of the United States, the Masters, and the PGA Championship. A fast player, Sarazen, with George Fazio, played the final round of the 1947 Masters in just under two hours. What is more, he scored a 70.

Though officially retired from active tournament play, Gene returned at age 71 for one last sentimental journey to Troon for the 1973 British Open. Fifty years earlier he had made a disastrous start in his Open debut, but on this occasion he went round in 70, one under par, and included a hole-in-one on Troon's 126-yard eighth hole, the marvel captured on TV and flashed around the world for all to celebrate. Gene still plays, and is one of three honorary starters at the Masters. Though now over 90, he still thumps the ball straight and true.

Eugene Saraceni (Gene Sarazen), born Harrison, NY, 1902. US Open Champion 1922, 1932. USPGA Champion 1922, 1923, 1933. British Open Champion 1932. Masters Champion 1935. Winner of 38 Tour events 1922–1941. Ryder Cup player 1927–37.

HENRY COTTON

Heredity may have played a hand in shaping the career of Henry Cotton. His father was an excellent player, and the youngster spent hour after hour at home pounding balls into a net rigged in the family garage. At the age of 16 he turned professional.

As the junior at Fulwell he spent his days sandpapering clubheads and shafts, and though he thought this a dreary task, it did much to strengthen his forearms and hands. Later he became assistant at Rye and in 1926, when he was 19, he began his first full pro job at Langley Park, Kent.

Winning the Kent Professional title five years in succession gave impetus to his golfing ambitions. He enjoyed some successes, including coming runner-up in the *News of the World* Match Play Championship in 1928, an event he was later to win three times. His burning ambition, however, was to win the Open Championship.

With this in mind he decided to plunder his savings on a trip to America, to study American style and method – 'to find out what makes them tick'.

It was a wonderful but austere regime for the youngster, for he was grouped with other young men who had to win to make enough money to eat. It was while in the States that Henry perfected his style of playing from 'inside to out', drawing the ball in from the right. Meanwhile he still kept trying for the object of his ambition: the Open. In 1933, at St Andrews, he led at one stage and finished only three shots behind the winner, Densmore Shute.

His dream came true at Royal St George's, in 1934. Speaking of it later, he said: 'I could see my end of the rainbow when I did 67 and 65 to lead by seven shots at the halfway stage; but my greatest triumph was in overcoming violent stomach cramps in the final round, to win by five shots. It is also satisfying to reflect that my 65 is still the lowest score of the Open, and to have achieved a 67 and a qualifying round of 66, all in one week on that great course, was one of the highlights of my career.'

Henry won again at Carnoustie in 1937, during a torrential storm when the tournament was close to being abandoned on that final day. His final 71 was heralded as the finest of his career – just one short of the course record. Needing a four for the record 70 (the last hole is tough indeed, with two burns to cross), he ignored any thought of safety and hit his second with conviction

A portrait of Henry Cotton by J.A.A Berrie.

into the hole-high bunker. The sand was hard and wet, and he came out safely. With two putts, he was down in five, winning by two strokes.

The war years robbed Cotton of more honours, and it was not until 1948 that he won his last Open, at Muirfield, by five shots on this toughest of courses.

Before beginning his second round, he had been introduced to King George, and later declared that the meeting had inspired his score of 66, which crowned success.

The author of several books, Henry was also involved in course architecture, his designs including several 'beginner' courses, and his jewel, Penina in Portugal. He was knighted in 1987, though sadly he did not survive to collect the honour.

Henry Cotton, born Holmes Chapel, England, 1907. Died 1987. PGA Matchplay Champion 1932, 1940, 1946. British Open Champion 1937, 1946, 1948. Ryder Cup player 1929, 1937, 1946. Captain 1937, non-playing captain 1953. Vardon Trophy 1938. Elected to World Golf Hall of Fame 1980.

BEN HOGAN

Ben Hogan's golfing career started when he was an 11-year-old Texas caddie, and his initial efforts as a professional, begun while still in his teens, were thwarted by financial difficulties.

The effects of the depression prevailed when Hogan and his wife, Valerie, set out on the tournament trail. The going was rugged, to say the least, for though Hogan was gradually finding his game through constant practice and experience, his returns measured a total zero.

The couple were about to turn back for Texas, their funds practically gone, when Hogan managed to put four good rounds together and ended well towards the top in a Californian event. This revived his spirits and bankrolled his continuing quest for glory. In 1940, Ben won his first semi-major event, the North and South Open, and he ended the year as the leading money winner. In 1941 and 1942 he again led in earnings. After returning from World War II service, he immediately picked up where he had left off, winning everything in sight in 1946, 1947 and 1948, and by this time he had developed machine-like accuracy, cultivated by hitting literally thousands of practice shots, and had became known as the Iron Man.

It was in 1946 that he finally won his first major golf title, the USPGA championship at Portland, Oregon, while in 1948 he won no fewer than 11 tournaments, including his first US Open, his second USPGA championship and his second Western Open.

In 1949, however, disaster struck. Hogan won two of the first four tournaments that year, before a car accident almost took his life and broke almost every major bone in his body. Though little hope was held that he would ever play golf again, he came back to win nine major titles after the accident. What is more, there were many who thought, had he been in better physical condition, he would have won several more. They point to the fact that many times he appeared physically exhausted when limping over the finishing holes during those later tournaments, and it was guts alone, his supreme will to succeed, that kept him grinding away.

But grind away he did, and in 1950 he was back on the tee at Los Angeles and tied Sam Snead for top honours, only to lose after a play-off. However, the biggest play-off of the year was the US Open at Ardmore, Pennsylvania, where Ben defeated Lloyd Mangrum and George Fazio after a three-way tie to win his second US Open title.

In 1951, Hogan continued his remarkable comeback when he won his first Masters title, his third US Open and his second World Championship. In 1953 the courageous little professional won the three leading championships

of the world. He entered five tournaments, ranging from the Colonial National at Fort Worth to the Open at Carnoustie, and captured them all. His first win was the Masters, where he scored a record 274, topping the old record by five strokes. Then came the Pan-American Open with a winning score of 286. He followed with a victorious 282 at the Colonial National. Then the US Open at the rugged Oakmont layout, where the little man was victorious for his fourth Open title. His score broke the course record and he was six strokes in front of the second man, Sam Snead. Up to this point, Hogan had won every major championship except the Open, in which he had never participated. Though a world-class player, he was openly criticized for not entering this unique event before 1953.

Now he threw down the gauntlet. The golfing world was sceptical of his prowess on the ancient windswept links, which required a different brand of golf, with a smaller ball than that which Ben

Ben Hogan: forever in pursuit of perfection.

normally used. His score – 284 – won by four strokes and was another record for Carnoustie. Ben Hogan had won every major golf championship in the world.

William Benjamin (Ben) Hogan, born Dublin, Texas, 1912. British Open Champion 1953. US Open Champion 1948, 1950, 1951, 1953. USPGA Champion 1946, 1948. Masters Champion 1951, 1953. A total of 57 wins between 1938 and 1959. Ryder Cup player 1947, 1949, 1951, non-playing captain 1967. Sportsman of the Decade 1946–1956. Bobby Jones award 1976.

BYRON NELSON

In 1944, Byron Nelson entered 23 tournaments and won eight of them. In 1945 he followed with a domination that no professional has ever matched, entering 31 tournaments and winning 18, 11 of them in a row.

Furthermore, in 17 consecutive rounds his score was never higher than 70. His scoring average for the 30 tournaments he played was 68.33, though sadly no Vardon Trophy was awarded during that year of the war.

If figures like these seem almost too much to take on board, consider also that during his professional career Nelson never, ever, finished over par in any four-round tournament. Both are records that still stand. It also makes him the most consistent golfer of all time.

The war, and the fact that some top players were not in contention that year, has been used to belittle Nelson's achievement in 1945, but his scores nevertheless make him stand on his own record. On the other hand, if they hadn't suspended the US Open during 1942–5, or the Masters for three years, or the Open hadn't been put 'on hold' for the duration, his record would surely have been greater still. (Nelson was exempt from military service during World War II because he was a haemophiliac.)

Nelson turned pro in 1932 and was the top golfer of the late 1930s and 1940s, winning 49 PGA tournaments. He won the US Open in 1939, and was runner-up in 1946, losing in a play-off. He won the USPGA Championship in 1940 and 1945 and the Masters in 1937 and 1942. He was the top US money winner in 1944 and 1945; and won the Vardon Trophy for a low scoring average in 1939. Byron was elected to the PGA Hall of Fame in 1953, and to the World Golf Hall of Fame in 1974. He was a member of the US Ryder Cup team in 1936 and 1947. Some golfer, some record! His play was so consistent and powerful throughout his career that he was sometimes called Mister Mechanical.

Byron Nelson: 11 tournament wins in a row in 1945.

Byron is still in demand today, as a TV commentator and as one of the world's leading authorities on the golf swing. They say he can watch someone's swing for 30 seconds – and then put it right. He's a long-time friend of Tom Watson, who is Byron's personal protégé. Tom's own record of five Open titles stands as much as a testimonial to Byron as to Tom's own considerable skill, and he freely acknowledges it as such.

John Byron Nelson Jnr, born Fort Worth, Texas, 1912. Masters Champion 1937, 1942. US Open 1939. USPGA 1940 and 1945. Winner of 52 Tour events. Money winner in 113 consecutive tournaments.

SAM SNEAD

One of only a handful of players who are considered to possess the perfect swing, Sam probably has had the longest-lived successful career in golf. An amazingly lithe man, even in the autumn of his life, Snead, born in 1912, likes nothing better than to prove his agility by kicking his foot up to the ceiling.

Sam has a record of seven majors, and in all truth that sets him alongside the gods, but he never won the US Open. He tried so often, was placed second four times, and came perilously close in almost every one he entered, but he never took the victor's crown. Even as late in his career as 1974, when he was 62, he was placed third in the US Open behind Lee Trevino and Jack Nicklaus.

He won 81 USPGA tournaments since first hitting the Tour in 1937, far more than anyone else. He is believed to have hit over three million golf balls in the thousands of rounds played, and has been credited with over 150 tournament wins. His many victories include the Masters in 1949, 1952 and 1954, the PGA Championship in 1942, 1949 and 1951; and the Open in 1946.

Always a big money winner, he led the league tables in 1938, 1949 and 1950, while winning the Vardon Trophy in 1938, 1949, 1950 and 1955. His scoring average of 69.23 in 1950 was a record for many years.

A legend of longevity, for many years he was the oldest player to win a PGA event, the 1965 Greater Greensboro Open, while in his fifties. He also holds the record for the most wins in a single event, eight in the Greater Greensboro Open over three decades.

As if this were not enough, Sam holds a remarkable record of play in the Ryder Cup, teeing off in seven Ryder Cup events, while being the team's non-playing captain in 1969. He was on the US World Cup team in 1956, 1960 and 1961, all victorious years for America, and won the individual title in 1961.

'Slammin' Sammy', famed for his trademark straw hat, still plays golf almost daily and is happy to take on all comers, always provided the stakes are high enough and stacked in his favour. Frankly, a man would be a fool to play Sam for money, and it is rumoured he has a fortune stacked away in tin boxes, supposedly never having held great trust in bankers.

'Slamming' Sam Snead.

The major flaw in his game over the years has been his putting, and the croquet style he adopted is now outlawed. He still competes periodically on the Seniors Tour, of which he was a founder, and has won the World Seniors title five times.

Sam's career earnings run well in excess of a million dollars, although most of his play was in days when cheques were miserly by today's standards. Though he may have failed to chalk up a US Open title, he has won the US Senior Championship six times. He's now in his eighties, and to see him today one might easily believe he will go on swinging sweetly for ever.

Samuel Jackson Snead, born Hot Springs, Virginia, 1912. British Open Champion 1946. Masters Champion 1949, 1952, 1954. USPGA Champion 1942, 1949 and 1951. Winner of 81 US Tour events from 1936–65.

MAX FAULKNER

Max Faulkner.

The colourful Faulkner, adored by a veritable army of fans during his heyday, was a man who could never resist the temptation to fool around – the blueprint for Trevino's later antics, perhaps – and he could as easily have been a comedian as a professional golfer.

But as well as being always an amusing storyteller with an engaging manner and winning ways, Max was also a fine ball striker with a powerful physique who won the British Masters, the Matchplay Championship, and numerous other fine Open tournaments.

His greatest distinction, however, was to win the Open Championship at Royal Portrush in 1951, at a time when British golf was in the doldrums. After Max it was another 18 years before a Briton lifted the Claret Jug, the jinx finally being broken in 1970 when Tony Jacklin triumphed at Royal Lytham.

At times during the final round Max's game went off the rails, and he played with less confidence than he had shown the night before when he had been signing autographs 'Open Champion 1951'.

Working once alongside the greenkeeper at a course in West Sussex which he built and developed, Max spied a golfer hacking the turf to shreds. Uncharacteristically wearing ragged trousers hitched with twine, along with a battered trilby, Max sauntered over and took the offending golfer's club, settled into his stance and proceeded to give the fellow a ten-minute lesson. 'You've got a bloody cheek,' the golfer said. 'Just who the hell do you think you are?' To which Max replied: 'Guvnor, I'm just the mole-catcher, but I can play this game a bit.' There were red faces all round in the clubhouse when the truth was later revealed

Max Faulkner, born Bexhill, Sussex, 1916. Ryder Cup 1947, 1949, 1951, 1953, 1957. British Open Champion 1951. Spanish Open Champion 1952–53, 1957. British Professional Matchplay Champion 1953. British Seniors Champion 1968, 1970.

BOBBY LOCKE

Though best known for his painstaking putting style, South African Bobby Locke was no slouch off the tee. At a time when length was perhaps not the be-all and end-all it is today, nevertheless Bobby found his natural fade costing him some 30 yards, so he set about perfecting the right-to-left shape – the draw – that is the standard fare of Tour professionals today.

Nobody knows for sure if he coined the phrase, but his motto was 'drive for show but putt for dough', and time and again he proved the adage.

Bobby was not an exceptionally strong man, but what he lacked in power he made up for in craft, and having been nicknamed Bobby (his real name was Arthur) after the great Bobby Jones, he tried to emulate the great man himself.

Indeed two heroes featured in his thinking: Bobby Jones for his smoothness of rhythm and Walter Hagen for his skills at close range. These were to remain key features of his game throughout a long and successful career.

Contemporaries opined that Locke's driving lacked the lazy elegance of Jones, though in mirroring Hagen he was, if anything, the better player. Above all, he was a phenomenal putter.

His was a fussy routine: he was the archetypal 'pacer' of his time. Once ready – sometimes taking minutes – he would swing through the ball, applying topspin by keeping his hands moving on the same plane. It worked like a charm, and though it was hard to copy, it influenced amateurs and professionals for years to come.

An Air Force veteran of World War II, Bobby established himself as one of the greatest of the overseas golfers by winning the Open four times, in 1949, 1950, 1952 and 1957.

Although he had won everything possible to win in South Africa, first as an amateur and then as a pro, he first attracted international attention when he defeated Sam Snead in 12 of 16 matches they played in South Africa. Snead urged Locke to give America a 'crack', and in 1947 he travelled to the US and proceeded to win seven tournaments. His best showing in the US Open was a tie for third, three shots behind Worsham and Snead in 1947. He was also third in 1951, though well behind Hogan. He was fourth in 1948 and tied for fourth in 1949.

In all Locke won 15 events in the US, but as the Open Champion he opted in 1949 to remain in Britain, which caused a furore in the United States, where it was claimed he already had commitments to play in several tournaments. This displeased his sponsors, while the authorities claimed he had broken contracts. He was barred from the US Tour, where it was said his fellow pros, perhaps envious of his financial success, had hastened the action.

Bobby remained faithful to his loopy, inside-out swing, with a draw on most shots. Indeed it was claimed he even hooked his putts, and that they nearly always dropped.

Bobby Locke showing off the Open trophy after winning at Troon in 1950.

Arthur D'Arcy (Bobby) Locke, born Transvaal, S. Africa, 1917. Died 1987. British Open Champion 1949, 1950, 1952, 1957. French Open Champion 1952, 1953. German Open Champion 1954. World Cup 1953–1956. Vardon Trophy winner 1946, 1950, 1954.

ROBERTO DE VICENZO

Argentinian golfer Roberto De Vicenzo was one of the greatest globe-trotting players ever, winning more than two hundred tournaments around the world, including the national Open championships of 12 countries.

De Vicenzo, the son of a poor family, grew up near a golf course in Buenos Aires, and learned the rudiments of the game as a 'pond boy' or caddie's assistant – the title summing up the worst parts of the job.

He won the Argentine Open and PGA in 1944 and first played in the United States three years later. Although he never won the US Open, he made his presence felt there by winning various events on the USPGA Tour, spanning 17 years from 1951 to 1968. The final triumph – the Houston Championship – came a few weeks after his blackest moment. At the 1968 Masters he signed an incorrect scorecard, awarding himself a 66 instead of the 65 he had scored. By the rigours of the laws of the game, the erroneous scorecard had to be accepted, leaving him in second place instead of in a play-off with Bob Goalby. After the event he was philosophical, remarking in broken English: 'What a stupid I am.'

Though his carelessness had robbed him of a major title, he had succeeded one year earlier, having won the 1967 Open, finishing two shots ahead of Jack Nicklaus. The Open was a title he doggedly pursued after finishing third at his first attempt in 1948. He added a second place in 1950 and came third in 1949, 1956, 1960, 1964 and 1969.

De Vicenzo, a frank, wholehearted person whose geniality made him

Roberto de Vicenzo: from 'pond boy' to British Open champion.

universally popular, enjoyed a long career as a productive player. He was an outstanding striker of the ball, but was often let down by his indifferent putting.

Roberto De Vicenzo, born Buenos Aires, Argentina, 1923. British Open Champion 1967. USPGA Seniors Champion 1974. Winner of more than 40 National Tournaments worldwide. Bobby Jones Award 1970.

ARNOLD PALMER

Arnold Palmer revolutionized golf in the late fifties and sixties, and at his best was the most exciting player in living memory. With a characteristic hitch of his pants, and a bold, dashing style, he became the focus of such a huge following that his fans were dubbed 'Arnie's Army'.

Born the son of a Latrobe, Pennsylvania, greenkeeper and professional in 1929, Arnie was coached by his father. He won his first important title, the US Amateur, in 1954, turning pro a year later and winning his first title, the Canadian Open, within months.

There is little doubt that professional golfers are, or should be, deeply indebted to Arnold Palmer for it was he who first showed the world the sheer excitement of the game, capturing attention as never before and drawing in crowds, sponsors and money.

It was not only golfers who sat up and took serious notice, for as Palmer emerged in the 1950s as a dynamic new force in the game, an aggressive player, especially with his trusty blade putter, he managed to convey the sheer exhilaration of striking a golf ball to an entirely new sector of the public.

Britain has particular reason to venerate Palmer: his commitment to the Open Championship, which had been foundering as a world-class event, re-established it as a truly international competition. He first entered in 1960,

at St Andrews, losing out to Kel Nagle, but he followed up by winning the title the next two years in succession.

A rising generation of American stars followed Palmer to Britain to take on the Open and his presence in the tournament re-established it as the summit of golfing ambition to get to raise the old Claret Jug.

Though his place in the record books is secure, with one victory in the

Arnie Palmer: arguably the most popular player ever.

US Open and two in the British Open Championships, it is in the Masters that he became a super-hero, for he seemingly was able to conjure great shots just when they were needed. Leading the Masters in 1960, he came to the final round needing a birdie at one of the last two holes to clinch the title. He birdied them both.

In the US Open at Cherry Hills, trailing by seven shots, he was stung into action by a chance remark from a journalist, who said he had 'no chance'. He shot 65 to win.

From turning pro, Palmer formed a partnership with the young Mark McCormack, now the world's pre-eminent sports agent, and transformed the money side of golf. Palmer was the first player to exceed $100,000 in a single season (1962), and the first to surpass the million-dollar mark, this time in 1968. The trophy presented annually for the leading money winner in America is named after him.

As one who can count seven major titles among his 61 Tour victories, Arnie has rightly earned his exemptions. Palmer, and any other ex-champion, can now compete in the Open until the age of 65, while as a former Masters winner, he is entitled to play at Augusta for life. The PGA of America honoured him with a lifetime exemption to its championship in 1984, despite the fact he has never won the event. A charter member of the US Senior Tour, Arnie still enjoys the call to battle and continues to delight several generations of his legion of fans.

Arnold Palmer, born Latrobe, Pennsylvania, 1929. US Amateur Champion 1954. Masters Champion 1958, 1960, 1962, 1964. US Open 1960. British Open Champion 1961, 1962. World Matchplay Champion 1964, 1967. USPGA Seniors Champion 1980, 1984. US Seniors Champion 1981. Ryder Cup player 1961–67, 1971–73 (captain 1963, non-playing captain 1975). Bobby Jones Award 1971. Elected World Golf Hall of Fame 1974.

PETER THOMSON

Winner of the Open Championship five times, and a player who commands great respect throughout the international golfing world, Thomson has always been badly underestimated by the Americans.

He played in the US on several occasions, won the Texas Open of 1956 and was fourth in the US Open and in the 1956 and 1957 Masters, yet finally

Peter Thomson: a master of the bump and run shot, ideal for links golf.

he began to make his visits few and far between, not returning until he became a senior.

The finest golfer to emerge from Australia, Greg Norman included, Thomson proved he was world-class when in 1965 he won his fifth Open title and beat a field that boasted Nicklaus, Palmer and Lema, all previous champions. If ever there was a necessity to quash the suggestion that his wins had come against weak opposition, this victory certainly settled it beyond doubt.

Thomson, apart from being blessed with the gift of calmness, boasts a game that is ideally suited to seaside courses and to places that require improvisation. On typical American courses, which are lush and well watered and demand great accuracy with the pitching wedge, Thomson seemed less at home. Thus Americans found it difficult to comprehend how he could win the British Open five times and yet fail so frequently in their country.

Thomson could hook the ball and get great distance on hard, windswept links, while the same shot left him far short on lush terrain. Nevertheless, his great record outside the United States, made on a wide variety of courses under all conditions, is evidence of his right to be classed among the great players. In the Open Championship, he holds the almost unbelievable record of finishing either first or second for seven straight years from 1952 to 1958.

On leaving the regular Tour and becoming a senior golfer, Thomson began designing golf courses. He has also taken to contesting his skills in America again, and in 1985, his best year, he won no fewer than 10 times on the US Senior Tour.

Peter Thomson, born Melbourne, Australia, 1929. British Open Champion 1954, 1955, 1956, 1958, 1965. Australian Open Champion 1951, 1967, 1972. PGA Seniors Champion 1988. World Cup 1953–57, 1959–62, 1965, 1969.

GENE LITTLER

For the sheer joy of watching perfection at work, 'Gene the Machine', as the golf writers christened him, has no parallel. Many believe that his effortless, silky-smooth action produced the finest swing of all time. He looked as though he could go on hitting exactly the shot he wanted to from now until eternity. Gene Sarazen thought so too, commenting: 'This kid has a perfect swing like Sam Snead – only it's better.'

His record shows this isn't far from the truth, even with golf being the unpredictable game that it is. Littler won 29 Tour tournaments since he began in 1954, a year after he won the US Amateur Championship.

Winning the San Diego Open as an amateur, and thus collecting no cheque, Gene promptly turned pro and was soon 28th on the money list – a figure below which he dropped only once until 1972, a remarkable performance.

Gene Littler: the greatest swing ever?

In 1961 he won the US Open, becoming only the eighth man to take both its Amateur and Open titles.

His record of consistency was outstanding. Among his many triumphs were a remarkable three-in-a-row in the Tournament of Champions, in 1955, 1956, 1957, the cash-rich Thunderbird in 1962, and the Canadian Open in 1965.

In 1972 Littler underwent an operation for cancer of the lymph glands, and it seemed his career might be over; that the Machine had finally run down. But a few months later he was back on the Tour, playing in only 11 events but collecting cheques on six occasions.

A member of the Ryder Cup team seven times, from 1961–75, Gene received the Golf Writers' Award for courageous recovery after adversity andthe Ben Hogan Award for distinguished sportsmanship. His total earnings have been great enough to allow him a demanding hobby – collecting vintage Rolls-Royces.

Eugene (Gene) Littler, born San Diego, California, 1930. US Amateur Champion 1953. US Open Champion 1961. Winner of 29 events on the Tour 1954–71. Ryder Cup player 1961–71.

BILLY CASPER

A great putter, a superb shot-maker, and a giant among his peers, Billy Casper's record of 51 tournament victories is a colossal achievement. Only five other players can boast the same: Snead, Nelson, Nicklaus, Hogan and Palmer. Yet Billy Casper is underrated in the history books – because he didn't blast the ball off the tee like Nicklaus, nor fly his irons quite like Gene Littler. If he lacked just one thing, it's that elusive quality known as charisma.

Casper turned pro in 1954, and went on the Tour in 1955. He won his first tournament the following year, then rose to the top like a rocket, winning

Billy Casper.

at least one title every year for the next 15 years. Only Nicklaus and Palmer (with 17 consecutive years) have bettered this total. He won the US Open in 1959 and 1966, the Masters in 1970, the Canadian in 1967. Fifty-one Tour tournaments all told, the second-highest in the modern, or post-Hogan, era.

Billy will perhaps be best remembered for his 1966 victory over Palmer, considered a classic, though often remembered more for Arnie's collapse than Billy's grinding down of his most fearsome opponent.

Although the two players were tied after 36 holes, Palmer romped ahead in the third and stretched his lead during the ultimate round, holding a seemingly unbeatable seven-shot advantage with nine to play. Somewhere Casper's God was urging him on, and he made birdie after birdie to score 32 on the back nine. Palmer's 39 gave each man a 278 score, and they were back to the course the following day for an 18-hole play-off. Palmer again was firing on every cylinder, forging ahead with a two-stroke lead after nine holes, though Casper was far from done. His long putts began dropping – for birdies – and his score of 69 beat Arnie by four. Arnie had won eight majors in his time, but he was never to win another.

Casper won the coveted Vardon Trophy five times and was voted PGA Player of the Year in 1966, 1968 and 1970. He played on every Ryder Cup team from 1961–75, eight times in all.

Billy is a swift player with one marked feature in his swing: he drags his right foot on every full shot. His marvellous putting is done with a wristy tap. Plagued by allergies and weight problems, he has tried such exotic foods as elephant and buffalo meat and of late seems to have defeated the problems, certainly the former. When Billy left the regular Tour for senior ranks he'd won 51 tournaments and almost two million dollars. This man has blessed the game without any unnecessary fireworks – and is much loved for his winning ways.

William Earl Casper Jnr, born San Diego, California, 1931. US Open Champion 1959 and 1966. Masters Champion 1970.

TONY LEMA

Some players gather mere fans, others capture hearts. Tony Lema, the Californian who won the Open Championship at St Andrews in 1964, also won a place in the hearts of everyone who saw him play. His performance on the course at once launched him into the annals of golfing legend.

St Andrews golf-watchers are noted for their canniness, convinced they can spot a giant-killer two fairways distant. Equally, they're convinced that it takes years to master the Old Course, certainly several rounds to learn even its rudiments – it is known for its bite.

So what did they make of this player, a man who had never played links golf before and who had arrived just 48 hours before the first man drove off in the Championship? There were grave mutterings.

But there was a touch of canniness in Tony Lema too, for he had hired 'Tip' Anderson, perhaps the town's most astute caddie. On his first links sortie he hit the ball where Tip told him he should, and it worked, though just nine holes was the sum of his links knowledge before he teed off in quest of the title. For all his skills, the task seemed impossible, yet the

knowledgeable hordes of St Andrews golfers who had watched his practice put him in with a chance.

He began with a 73, the first complete round he'd ever played on the course, and took the lead with a 68 in the second round. By now people realized he had both the technique and the temperament to win. Meanwhile, Jack Nicklaus, his most serious threat, had rounds of 76 and 74. Lema's

Tony Lema hugging the Claret Jug after taming the Old Course in 1964.

championship was not set to be a walkover though, for in the morning round of the final day Nicklaus suddenly found his touch and began to drop putts from every angle. Tony started poorly, losing eight strokes to Nicklaus in those first nine holes, though he was able to conjure a magic spell of golf that included five successive 3s, finishing 3, 4, 4, 3, for a 68, recovering to lose just two strokes to Nicklaus overall. In the final round Lema cruised to a five-stroke victory with a 70; he had won the Championship at the first time of asking, and by a substantial margin, from a great field.

As was Tony's custom, champagne was brought into the Press Tent and he joined journalists in celebrating a victory as good as St Andrews had ever seen. He went on to finish the year in great style, taking the Crosby, the Thunderbird, the Buick and the Cleveland Opens that year.

In July 1966 he and his wife died in a plane crash. Champagne Tony Lema, gifted with perfect swing and perfect manners, was lost to golf at the age of 32.

His list of successes was not long, but who knows but that he would have equalled or even outstripped every rival had not his life ended so abruptly? It will not be by his golf alone that his name will be remembered, for his refreshing behaviour, his cheery outlook on life, his unfailing courtesy, all marked him as someone apart – a true champion.

Anthony David Lema, born Oakland, California, 1934. Died in a plane crash July 1966. British Open Champion 1964. Ryder Cup player 1963 and 1965.

GARY PLAYER

They call him Mister Endurable, and his longevity as a golfer of world class cannot be better illustrated than by the fact that he won his first Open Championship at the age of 23, while at 48 he was still good enough to be

Gary Player, unmistakable in his customary black outfit.

second behind Lee Trevino in the 1984 American PGA championship.

One of only four men to have won the four majors of golf, Player graduated to become one of the Big Three, along with Palmer and Nicklaus. Player was also the king of matchplay. Having been seven down to Tony Lema in the 1965 World Matchplay Championship – an event he was to win five times – he succeeded in clawing back the deficit to win at the 37th, following this by beating Peter Thomson in the final.

Training, dogged determination, muscle-building and mind-over-matter exercises; all it seems are credited as contributing factors to his continuing success, while commentators so often miss out the most important one of all: Gary has a fantastic golf game.

Look at his record: winner of over 100 tournaments worldwide, the Open three times, the Masters three times, the US Open once and the USPGA twice, plus a whole host of Senior Tour victories. The span of 15 years between his first Open title and his third covered three decades

(1959,1968,1974) while being the longest since those times of John Henry Taylor, who put two decades between his first and last victories, and Harry Vardon, who spanned 18 years.

In his early years he was unmistakable in outfits that were always entirely black, giving him the aura of some Western gunslinger and adding to the invincibility of his image.

Always a home lover with a strong sense of family values and a passion for his homeland, he has preferred to travel to and from South Africa, where he farms a large ranch. Indeed it is said he has flown more miles than any other player in search of success. Player's sincere approach and unfailing politeness have endeared him to many, and he gained more fans when he gave away his total winnings of $25,000 from the 1965 US Open – part to promote junior golf and the rest towards medical research.

Though a constant 'tinkerer' with his swing these days, he is enjoying a whole new career on the US Seniors Tour, where he is still winning huge sums – his official earnings in 1996 topping the half-million-dollar mark.

Gary Player, born South Africa, 1935. British Open champion 1959, 1968, 1974. Masters Champion 1961, 1974, 1978. US Open champion 1962 and 1972. South African Open champion 14 times.

LEE TREVINO

It is hard to image that anybody loves the game more than Lee Trevino, the Clown Prince of Golf. He gives the impression he would play every day just for the fun of it, while positively revelling in building upon the fun image that surrounds him. In truth, in contrast to his flamboyant public image, he is a very private man. He is also a superb golfer.

Lee was born into a desperately poor Mexican-American family and grew up in Dallas in an atmosphere dominated by concern about where the next dollar was coming from. He openly admits to having been a hustler, and understands the meaning of pressure, for on many occasions in his early days he gambled for big stakes, purely on his golfing ability, all without so much as a copper coin in his pocket. He used to take money off wealthy players by betting he could beat them while using only a large soft-drinks bottle wrapped in tape. He could.

Always in a class of his own as a shot-maker, from being the best player on the Tour for several decades, Lee, or SuperMex, as he is known, is now making a massive impact on the US Seniors' Tour, where his official tournament winnings in 1996 alone easily topped half a million. In cash terms, he is in that select bracket of golfing supermen – one of the top five money winners of all time.

His wisecracking between shots became his indelible trademark. His humour – he is the creator of thousands of brilliant one-liners – drove some of his opponents mad, but it made the public adore him all the more.

Although he had played golf while in the army, he emerged from almost nowhere to win the 1968 US Open, in a scrambling, unorthodox way, the shot-maker defeating the classicist Bert Yancey, who finished second.

Ready for another wisecrack: Lee Trevino, the Clown Prince of Golf.

In 1971 Lee pulled off the most amazing triple, winning the US Open, Canadian Open and the British Open, all in just four weeks. The only player one might compare him with is Seve Ballesteros. Just as exciting and as much a swashbuckler, Lee is gifted with an unbelievable variety of strokes. His flat swing, so instantly recognizable and so often scoffed at, is really beautifully styled, for it allows him to keep the club face square through the ball marginally longer than normal, which increases his control. This in turn permits him to play the delicate, magician-like touch shots which so delight his supporters. Who, for example, will ever forget his holing-out, seemingly from nowhere, at Muirfield's 17th, on that final day of the 1972 Open? Jacklin should have won, but was crushed by Trevino's outrageous conjuring tricks.

Some players match their game to their personality. Lee Trevino might be the best example of that, for though outwardly a joker, he is also a combative person, and when he is on his game there is no one more aggressive on the course. His record in winning major titles is simply enhanced by being one of golf's all-time good-guy heroes.

Lee Trevino, born Dallas, Texas, 1939. British Open Champion 1971, 1972. US Open Champion 1968, 1971. USPGA Champion 1974, 1986. Five times Vardon Trophy winner and six times a Ryder Cup competitor. Elected to the World Golf Hall of Fame in 1981.

JACK NICKLAUS

Awesome. Jack Nicklaus is the greatest living player in the game of golf. Before he was 28, Nicklaus had won two US Opens, three Masters, a USPGA, the British Open, and two US Amateur titles.

Nicklaus knew that only the majors counted when it came to making history, so he set his mind out to win every one – and ended up winning more of them than any other golfer in history.

Golden Bear Jack Nicklaus: the greatest player ever.

By the time his career as a regular Tour player was drawing to a close, he had won six Masters titles, five USPGA Championships, four US Opens and three British Open Championships.

Nicklaus was good enough to win the US Amateur at the age of 19, and finish second in the US Open at 20, bringing inevitable comparisons with the great amatuer Bobby Jones. But then if you make a name for yourself in golf, people always make comparisons, and within a short period, Nicklaus was being compared with Ben Hogan. But in the World Amateur at Merion, in 1960, Jack scored 269 for four rounds over one of golf's most testing layouts – and when Hogan had won there in 1950, he'd only managed 287.

Further comparisons were considered futile when Nicklaus lowered the Iron Man's record for both the Masters and US Open. After winning his second US Amateur, in 1961, he turned pro, and the following year he defeated Palmer in a play-off to win the US Open at Oakmont. After that people stopped comparing him with other golfers – he was simply the best.

But the man who is now seen as the most respected statesman of world golf, whose advice saved the Ryder Cup competition from collapse, whose course designs figure among the finest, and whose character earns nothing but respect, took some time to endear himself to golfing fans.

When he first hit the headlines he was perceived as unglamorous, with crew-cut hair and a bulging waistline; he was seen as just an overweight athlete who could thrash the ball a mile. By his mid-twenties Nicklaus had decided to change his image and within months presented an altogether different figure, with a modern hairstyle and a hugely slimmed-down waistline.

He became the idol of the masses, as adored as anyone has ever been. Though he never relied on subtlety, being one of the game's first power merchants, in his new slim guise he retained all his strength, while polishing his short game to perfection. It all combined to make him perhaps the most feared man in the game.

Motivation and concentration have been the key to his success. He says he is aware that he will never play the perfect round of golf – but that will never stop him trying to. He is driven by an absolute hatred of failure: not of losing, but of failing to live up to the standards he sets himself; so when he does fail, even in the execution of a single shot, he is overwhelmed by the need to improve. He said once: 'I am easily embarrassed by myself. No single emotion is more responsible for whatever I have achieved.'

Nicklaus has been the leading money winner on the US Tour a record eight times, while never being lower than fourth until he cut back on activities in the late 1970s. A lean spell ended at St Andrews in 1978, where he took his third Open title, though he followed this with an indifferent 1979, and one might have forgiven him for thinking of retirement. Instead he continued to practise, and in 1980 it paid off, with a win in the US Open at Baltusrol.

Was there anything left to prove? Well, maybe not, but in 1986 he scored his most memorable victory, summoning up hidden depths to produce a seven-under-par final round at Augusta to win the Masters by one stroke from Greg Norman and Tom Kite. It was a devastating reply to those who had been foolish enough to think of him as 'yesterday's man'.

Jack's record of 20 major victories is astonishing in itself, as the great Bobby Jones had previously set the record at only 13 and that had been considered beyond the reach of other mortals until Nicklaus proved otherwise.

Only three other golfers have succeeded in winning all the majors at least once – Gene Sarazen, Ben Hogan and Gary Player – but once only. Nicklaus has done it three times. At last count, he had won around 100 tournament victories worldwide.

Seeking new mountains to climb, Jack began his formal golf course design career as a consultant, co-designing courses with architects Pete Dye and Desmond Muirhead. He shared in the design of several of America's finest, including Harbour Town, and the legendary Muirfield Village. It was this variety of experience that gave him real expertise in course design. He formed his own company in 1973, establishing a worldwide reputation, both for interpretation and execution of his designs.

As a brilliant course architect, he is part of an elite group, just as being at the very pinnacle as a golfer places him in another. His golf has excited millions; now his magnificent courses bring pleasure to golfers of all levels. Excellence is the very hallmark of the man they call the Golden Bear.

Jack William Nicklaus, born Columbus, Ohio, 1940. British Open Champion 1966, 1970, 1978. US Open Champion 1962, 1967, 1972, 1980. USPGA Champion 1963, 1971, 1973, 1975, 1980. Masters Champion 1963, 1965, 1966, 1972, 1986. Ryder Cup player eight times. Bobby Jones Award 1975. Elected World Golf Hall of Fame 1974.

RAYMOND FLOYD

Raymond Floyd has at times mixed mediocre years with moments of sheer brilliance. He won his first title, the 1963 St Petersburg Open, when he was just 20 – and yet when he joined the Tour that year he had failed to make the cut in ten previous appearances. Then for a couple of years Floyd disappeared from view, content perhaps for a time to enjoy the party life, while also managing an all-girl rock

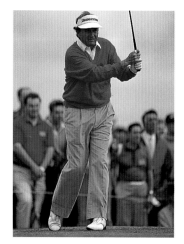

Raymond Floyd.

band known as the Ladybirds. He emerged only briefly with just one win, the St Paul Open.

It was not until 1969, when he won the Jacksonville, the American Classic, and finally the PGA Championship, that his name was made – only for him to disappear again just as quickly for another six years before he won again.

He finally hit his second peak by winning the 1976 Masters, leading all the way and winning by a record eight strokes with a score of 271. In that year he was second in the US Open and fourth in the British Open. Since 1974 he has only once failed to top $100,000 on the US Tour, though by his own high standards the wheels did wobble somewhat in the late 1970s, when he failed to qualify in the 1979 US Open, was 36th in the British Open, 17th at Augusta, and way, way down in the USPGA Championship.

Yet in 1981 he won $317,000 in just eight days, taking the Doral Open and the Tournament Players' Championship titles. In 1982, at the age of 40, he won the USPGA at Southern Hills and his opening round of 63, even by his own ultra-critical standards, was held by him to be his best ever. Next he won the US Open at Shinnecock Hills, becoming the oldest winner of the title and capturing it by again pulling low numbers from his bag, shooting 66 in the final round.

Floyd has won 18 regular tour events and played in six Ryder Cups. He has also won in Brazil, South Africa, Costa Rica, Canada and Japan. Of late, he has made a new and highly lucrative career on the US Seniors Tour, in 1996 winning well in excess of $1 million.

Raymond Floyd, born North Carolina, USA, 1942. USPGA Champion 1969 and 1982. US Masters Champion 1976. US Players Championship 1981. US Open Champion 1986. Ryder Cup player 1969, 1975–77, 1981–85, 1991–93 (non-playing captain 1989). Vardon Trophy 1983. Elected to World Golf Hall of Fame 1989.

TONY JACKLIN

Tony Jacklin became a national hero at Lytham in 1969 when he was the first Briton to win the Open in 18 years. For the nation it had been a long time coming, and for Jacklin the victory came as he reached the peak of his prowess, and he won the US Open the next year by seven strokes, the biggest margin since Jim Barnes's victory in 1921. In winning, Tony became the first Briton to hold both American and British titles at the same time.

Tony Jacklin and his late wife Vivienne display the British Open trophy to the Lytham crowds.

Jacklin had turned pro in 1962, and in 1963 was named Rookie of the Year by Henry Cotton. Soon after, Jacklin's boss, Bill Shankland, prompted him to try his luck in America. Previously inclined to swing the club like lightning, he soon learned the importance of tempo and to swing smoothly, and he began to put together a fine, controlled, all-round game.

Seemingly saving his best for the grand occasion, Tony certainly played his finest at Royal Lytham in 1969, beginning his first round with a birdie and finishing with a 68. Bob Charles, however, was in the lead with a 66. Next day a 69 kept Charles ahead and with two rounds to go he led the field at 135. Jacklin with 70 was third at 138. Charles seemed to lose his touch in the third round, and he disappointed with a miserable 75, while Jacklin had a smooth 70, giving him a two-shot lead. The two men were paired in the last round, and Tony soon established a lead with birdies on the third and fourth, and by the turn he was five ahead.

Looking now very much the winner, Tony began to show nerves for the first time but he saved himself with glorious bunker shots around the green, each time holing out with a single putt. On the last tee, two shots ahead of Charles, he cracked a 'corker'. The crowd was in raptures. He struck a glorious second, and with two routine putts, a British golfer had won again. Bob Charles finished second, with a strong final round of 72, with Thomson and de Vicenzo tied for third.

Tony was to have another memorable Open at St Andrews in 1970, reaching the turn in his first round in a record 29. He began the return 3, 3, 4 and 4, and at eight under looked set to break the Old Course record. Sadly, a vicious storm broke, the greens became flooded, and play was suspended. The next morning, poor Tony began with a six. Twelve hours earlier he had looked good for a 61 or 62. Now this dream vaporized as quickly as the inspiration drained from him and he scored a disappointing 67. In the event he finished fifth.

Then, in 1972 at Muirfield, came Jacklin's Nemesis in the form of Lee Trevino. Tony had looked a certainty to take his second Open. He came to the 17th tied with Trevino who, having played too strongly, was considered out of it – his ball off the green in four strokes while Jacklin was safely on in three.

There has never been anyone quite like Trevino, and he proved it that day, holing his chip for a five. Shaken, Tony took three putts, and Trevino went on to steal a title he had mentally conceded. As an individual player Tony Jacklin never seemed to recover from this blow, though he enjoyed a brilliant inspirational period as Ryder Cup captain, leading the European team to two great victories. Now a senior, Tony is enjoying a new career on the US Seniors Tour, where his winnings in 1996 exceeded $300,000.

Tony Jacklin, born Scunthorpe, England, 1944. Dunlop Masters Champion 1967, 1973. British Open Champion 1969. US Open Champion 1970. British PGA Champion 1972, 1982. Winner of 13 PGA European Tour events. Ryder Cup player 1967–79 (non-playing captain 1983–89).

JOHNNY MILLER

Probably the most important player to emerge in the 1970s, Miller had won the American (USGA) Junior Championship in 1964, and, while still a teenager, finished eighth in the 1966 US Open. In 1969 he turned pro, and from then on almost always finished in the money.

Throughout the 1970s he won 15 PGA events, including the 1971 Southern Open, the 1972 Heritage Classic and the 1973 US Open, in which he completed his final round with a record 63. He also won the World Cup championship for America.

Always a 'streak' player, Johnny had an incredible 1974 season, winning a record $353,021 and eight events, the most by any player in a single year since Arnold Palmer 14 years earlier. He was the first in PGA Tour history to win the first three events of the season, and rounded up splendidly by winning the Tournament of Champions, the World Open, the Westchester Classic, the Heritage Classic, and the Kaiser International – earning the

Johnny Miller: dominated world golf in the early 1970s.

honour of election as PGA Player of the Year. He finished the year by winning Japan's Dunlop Open.

In 1975 he started out by winning the Phoenix Open by 14 strokes, the largest margin since Ben Hogan won the 1945 Portland Open by 17. Then he won the Tucson, the Bob Hope and the Kaiser, while also playing on the US Ryder Cup team. He had total earnings through 1975 of $947,152, finishing second in the year's earnings behind Jack Nicklaus.

Winner of the 1973 US Open, he won the British Open at Birkdale in 1976, forging so far ahead of his nearest rival that he could afford to spend the final few holes encouraging the emerging youngster Seve Ballesteros, telling him not to forget about second place.

Strangely, 1976 was to be Miller's last great year. By 1977 the magic had evaporated and he had dropped to 48th on the money list, while in 1978 he had sunk to 111th. Some say he soon became bored.

Johnny Miller is one of those who have been familiar with the wilderness in recent years, having made vast sums very quickly and, perhaps, having taken a great talent too much for granted. But he is in great demand as a TV commentator and analyst, where his pithy comments and acute observations have made him highly regarded.

Johnny Miller, born California, 1947. US Open Champion 1973. British Open Champion 1976. Winner of 24 US Tour events. Ryder Cup player 1975, 1981. Player of the Year 1974.

TOM KITE

A historian searching the record books of just a few years ago would find it hard to find the name of the 1997 American Ryder Cup team captain featured anywhere.

There are hundreds of pages extolling the achievements of the great players on the Tour, and they mention Ballesteros, Norman, Nicklaus and so on, which is only understandable – but how could anyone leave Tom Kite's name off the list?

As much as he impresses as a player – he is an awesome golfer and a credit to his profession – he impresses still more as a gentleman. This is the ultimate Mister Nice Guy.

Tom Kite hits so consistently well that one wonders if he ever has a bad ball-striking round by any normal player's standards. He's incredibly straight, but he also has all the shots and his putter is often possessed of magic. He's calm and disciplined, especially under pressure, and so consistent, easily the most on the US Tour, which is the ultimate compliment for a pro since that's what all top players strive to achieve.

Tom's only problem is winning. Granted he has won regular Tour events – although he was the first to amass $5 million in Tour earnings (putting him $500,000 ahead of Nicklaus by 1989), and although he has now doubled that total to almost $10 million, to be the second highest money-winner of all time – he has won only 15 events to Jack's 70-plus total.

Not without perseverance, Tom finally shrugged off the ignominious title of 'Best Player Never To Win a Major' when he scored his deserved triumph at Pebble Beach in the 1992 US Open. There were many who tried to topple him – Colin Montgomerie and then Jeff Sluman both seemed at one point to have the title sewn up – yet in the kind of gale-force winds that only a hunting dog could love, Tom's resolve carried him to his finest victory, bringing a run of near misses finally an end.

He was named captain of the American team in 1997, visiting Spain in defence of the Ryder Cup.

Tom Kite, born Texas, 1949. European Open Champion 1980. US Players' Champion 1989. US Tour Champion 1989. US Open Champion 1992. Walker Cup 1971. Ryder Cup 1979–1989. Bobby Jones award 1979. Vardon Trophy 1981–1982. USPGA Player of the Year 1989.

Tom Kite: quiet and self-effacing, but the most consistently succesful golfer in the last 15 years.

TOM WATSON

There is no doubt that Tom Watson, like Tom Kite, will go down in history as one of the game's great champions and gentlemen. He symbolizes everything that is fine in the game, captivating galleries with his play and demeanour.

Modest, courteous and strong in adversity, he is nevertheless one of the most aggressive of players, as well as one of the greatest champions of the

Tom Watson: still looking to match Harry Vardon's six British Open titles.

modern era. He is blessed with a wonderful, philosophical approach to the game and to life, believing that 'the beauty of golf stems from the fact that success, as well as failure, comes from within'.

He turned pro in 1971, and scored the first of his remarkable run of victories in the Open Championship at Carnoustie in 1975. As well as winning five British Open titles, he has twice won the US Masters and once the US Open. Although he lacks the PGA to complete a career Grand Slam, his place in history is secure. He holds three of the lowest winning totals at the Open, 268 at Turnberry in 1977, 271 at Muirfield in 1981 and 275 at Birkdale in 1983. Only four players have won more pro majors – Nicklaus, Hagen, Hogan and Player.

Although his form has kept him from the winner's rostrum of late, people still remember when Tom went head-to-head with Jack Nicklaus in the famous 'Duel in the Sun' in the 1977 Open at Turnberry and won, following on to became the dominant player in the game for a considerable period.

Possessed of a glorious, copybook swing, and for a decade one of the best and most aggressive putters on the Tour, Tom shows his weakness now with the short ones, which elude him just when he seems to have rekindled the old fire. He desperately wants to win a sixth Open to equal Harry Vardon's record, and who is to say he won't make it? We haven't seen the last of Tom Watson. We may not have even seen the best of him.

Tom Watson, born Kansas City, Missouri, 1949. British Open Champion 1975, 1977, 1980, 1982, 1983. US Masters Champion 1977, 1981. US Open Champion 1982. Ryder Cup player 1977, 1981, 1983, 1989 (captain in 1993). USPGA Player of the Year 1977, 1978, 1979, 1980, 1982, 1984. Arnold Palmer Award 1987. Vardon Trophy 1977, 1978, 1979. Bobby Jones award 1987. Elected to World Golf Hall of Fame 1988. Old Tom Morris Award 1991.

BEN CRENSHAW

Known as 'Gentle Ben' because he is softly spoken and polite, Crenshaw has a reputation as a fine golfer, which is reinforced by his being a putter without parallel. This is the man most current golfers would choose to make a crucial putt for them.

His career started with a bang in 1973, when as a rookie he qualified at Tour school by a massive 12-stroke margin, won the Texas Open, his first pro event, and finished second a week later in the World Open.

Ben continued to fare well, finishing second on the 1976 money list and fifth in 1979 and 1980. In finishing second in the 1976 and 1983 Masters, the 1978 and 1979 British Opens, and the 1979 US Open, he began to acquire a reputation as the 'nearly man', a player who could excel in regular Tour events but who seemed incapable of winning a major. He finally sank the myth and got his name on a major title in 1984, winning the Masters by two strokes over Tom Watson. From this euphoria he moved into something of a slump, later diagnosed as having been caused by an overactive thyroid gland. Recovered, he came close to winning the Masters again in 1989, but failed with an uncharacteristic missed putt on the final hole, which meant he would not play off with Nick Faldo and Scott Hoch.

In 1995, fate dealt him his finest hand. In an emotion-packed final round at Augusta National, Ben enjoyed flashes of his old brilliance, while occasionally suffering the odd setback that kept the championship tense to the very end. Coming to the final hole with a two-stroke advantage over Davis Love III, Ben chose to hit his four wood and thus avoid the tricky fairway bunker on the left. His drive was accuracy personified, allowing a clear shot to the green, but his approach was short, his chip a trifle long, while his first putt was uncharacteristically off line. The huge gallery crowd

Ben Crenshaw: twice winner of the Masters' Green Jacket.

held its breath as he lined up for the final putt – under two feet – that would guarantee his victory, then burst into tumultuous applause: Ben was the Masters Champion again. After that final putt, his emotions took over: relief, disbelief and joy. Weeping without restraint, while being hugged by his long-time caddie Carl Jackson, Ben declared: 'I don't know how I made it.' There was never a more popular victory.

Ben Crenshaw, born Austin, Texas, 1952. Irish Open Champion 1976. Mexican Open Champion 1982. US Masters Champion 1984 and 1995. Winner of 21 Tour events 1973–1996. Ryder Cup player 1981, 1983, 1987. Bobby Jones award 1991.

GREG NORMAN

Greg Norman: if only he was lucky.

What does Greg Norman want more than anything? The 'super-golfer', who is the world's top-rated player, can buy virtually anything he wants with the prize money he has won – except the green jacket that is the mantle of a Masters winner.

He wants one so badly, it makes him ache. It would crown his career, especially after the grandest collapse ever witnessed in major golfing history, which saw his lead of six strokes in the 1996 Masters swallowed by his own bad play and the ruthless consistency of Nick Faldo. But the man who seems to keep on winning is left to dream when he gets to Augusta.

He is in his forties now, but Greg Norman still thinks he can slip that cherished scrap of worsted over his shoulders; he has believed it for years. Others wonder if his phenomenal talent is too often deserted by the other essential in a world-class golfer's bag – luck.

Norman has finished second over 50 times in his 21-year career, including three runner-up finishes in the Masters.

He had a phenomenal year in 1986. He topped the US prize-money list and won the Open Championship at Sandwich by a commanding five strokes, helped by a closing round of 64, one outside the course record. His aggregate score of 267 was a record, beating Tom Watson's 1977 figure by one stroke.

He also led going into the final rounds of both the Masters and US Open, but they slipped through his grasp. After winning the Open, Greg found himself again in contention, in the final round of the USPGA, though this time Lady Luck took a hand, when Bob Tway holed a seemingly impossible bunker shot. The Old Lady was up to her tricks again a few months later at the 1987 Masters. In a play-off, she laid her blessing on Larry Mize, who conjured a Tway-like miracle by holing a chip from way off the green, to defeat Greg by a single stroke. Fated, it seems, but what is a mere mortal to do?

Greg's second Open triumph, at Royal St George's in 1993, by a two-stroke margin from Nick Faldo, was impressive, though it is remembered as much for his ovation as his golf. Gene Sarazen, 91 years old and as sprightly as ever, presented Greg with the old Claret Jug. It was a poignant moment, as Sarazen had won his Open in 1932 just a mile away, at Princes. In a speech that left many moist eyes, Sarazen the veteran observed that Greg played a game that he could scarcely comprehend. 'Oh boy,' he said, 'isn't this guy something else? He's just awesome.'

Greg was voted 1995 USPGA Player of the Year; in 1996, the same. In one of his best seasons, if one discounts the Masters débâcle, he headed the money list, despite playing in only 16 tournaments, and remains the top-ranking player in the world by miles. His wins in the 1996 Australian Open, near wins in the Masters and the US Open, and possession of the Tour's lowest scoring average all add up to the Great White Shark being everybody's bet to remain at the top for a very long time. More major titles will undoubtedly fall to him. Since the invention of the Sony World Rankings, Norman has topped the list for over 200 weeks, while no one else has topped the 100 mark.

Gregory Norman, born Queensland, Australia, 1955. Open Champion 1986, 1993. Australian Open Champion 1980, 1985,

1987, 1996. World Matchplay Champion 1980, 1983, 1986. US Players' Champion 1994. Winner of 73 tournaments worldwide. Harry Vardon Trophy 1982. Vardon Trophy 1989, 1990. Arnold Palmer Award 1986, 1990.

BERNHARD LANGER

A man of remarkable tenacity and determination, Bernhard Langer was a near-invincible star on the European circuit. He won the US Masters in 1985, and followed this in 1993 with a second, glorious victory. In between, he dissected course after course with his precise iron play, winning a string of championships in Europe, Asia and America.

This cool, meticulous, stroke-maker first emerged as Seve Ballesteros' greatest European rival, and in recent years has eclipsed the Spaniard, starting near favourite at just about any tournament.

He's an exceptionally gifted iron-player, and if his game has an Achilles heel, it is his putting. Where once he had success with an old Acushnet 'bull's-eye' – a favourite with generations of pro golfers – for a long time he used an incongruous two-handed method, one hand gripping the other arm in a stiff fashion.

He joined the American PGA Tour in 1985 and, along with Greg Norman, Nick Faldo and others, demonstrated to the American professionals that a 'buck' would never again be quite as easy to win on home ground.

Born in West Germany, in 1957, Bernhard always had ambition to play golf at the highest level and he turned professional in his mid-teens. By the end of 1986, he had won two dozen or more international tournaments, including four German Opens, two Irish Opens and one each, French, Spanish and Dutch. The grand total now stands at nearer 40.

With his second Masters title, and his greatest triumph, in 1993, Langer

joined that select group of 12 men who have won it more than once, while becoming the fifth international player to triumph in the last six years. Langer came home in that final round, with a four-stroke advantage over Chip Beck, giving a Hogan-like exhibition of his iron mastery throughout. Though he

Bernhard Langer: constantly trying new methods on the putting green.

somehow made it look easy, his fellow competitors knew differently. 'He is a tactician beyond description,' says Dan Forsman.

Bernhard Langer, born Anhausen, Germany, 1957. German Open Champion 1981, 1982, 1985, 1986, 1993. US Masters Champion 1985, 1993. European Open Champion 1985. Australian Masters Champion 1985. British PGA Champion 1987, 1993. Ryder Cup player 1981–95. Vardon Trophy 1981, 1984.

NICK FALDO

It is difficult to know quite where to begin with Nick Faldo. Recognized as one of the world's most complete golfers, he boasts a record that is already hugely impressive, and like that of Nicklaus, Hogan, even Bobby Jones perhaps, his talent and dedication is such that one must believe his best is yet to come.

He enjoyed a brilliant career as an amateur, and much had been expected of Nick, not least by himself, as a pro. Through the mid-1980s, however, it seemed that his promise might fall short of being truly fulfilled. For a time he became known as 'El Foldo', after consistently frittering away seemingly invincible leads.

In 1984 he turned for help to the golf guru David Leadbetter, but was scared off by the prognosis: 'Take two years off and rebuild your swing.' Six months later he was back at Leadbetter's doorstep. He said he wanted to be the best – to understand his swing, rather than just fix it – and from then on they worked together.

His victory in the 1987 Open Championship at Muirfield was a turning point, for, although he'd believed his swing was too loose to hold up under pressure, the results with the newly fashioned Leadbetter swing – made up of minute but significant changes – were plain for all to see. His final 18 holes were played absolutely in strict par, hole by hole, despite awful weather conditions.

Two years later he won his first Masters, a second Masters in 1990, and another Open the same year, and again in 1992. In 1993 he finished second in the Open and third in the USPGA Championship. Then, for a while, he slid back.

Ice-cold, utterly dedicated to being the best, Faldo has lost media support because his concentration allows him little room for on-course banter. But to the public he is always potentially the most deadly player in the world, and is very much admired by them for it.

Nick had often openly criticized British golf course conditions, at least the conditions in which greens are presented for major tournaments, so he travelled to America. Specifically, he wanted to work on his putting and found the consistency of America's manicured bent-grass greens very much to his liking.

Then came the Masters of 1996. Greg Norman began the final day looking

Nick Faldo: no one tries harder.

bulletproof, only to suffer his biggest let-down, agonizing as Faldo tore into his six-stroke lead. While Greg collapsed, Faldo triumphed. As they played together in this final round, it was a case of Faldo chipping away at Greg's lead by methodically producing his best golf ever, for a final round of five under, twelve under for the tournament, and a five-stroke advantage over the Great White Shark.

Unbelievable? Perhaps, but appropriate too: Faldo had taken up golf at the age of 14 only because he had been inspired by watching on television as Jack Nicklaus triumphed at Augusta in 1972.

Faldo held the Sony Ranking as number one in 1993–94 for a record 81 weeks. At Augusta he was crowned king, again. Long may he reign.

Nick Faldo, born Welwyn Garden City, England, 1957. British Youth Open Amateur Champion 1975. English Amateur Champion 1975. British Open Champion 1987, 1990, 1992. Masters Champion 1989, 1990, 1996. World Matchplay Champion 1989, 1992. European Open Champion 1992. World Championship 1992. Ryder Cup player 1985–88, 1991, 1993, 1995. Dunhill Cup 1985–88, 1991, 1993. Vardon Trophy winner 1983, 1992. USPGA Player of the Year 1990.

Seve Ballesteros: the master of the miracle recovery shot.

SEVE BALLESTEROS

Spectacular, inspirational, everything that sporting heroes are made of, Seve Ballesteros hit shots that defied belief, let alone description.

He's simply a genius with a club in his hand, especially around the greens, and there's no doubt that he will go down in history as one of the truly great champions. His record of majors is not perhaps in the league of Nicklaus, and his finest days are now behind him, but Seve remains arguably the most charismatic player in the world. He's daring, exciting to watch, and he wears his heart on his sleeve.

Seve, one of four golfing brothers, was born in Pedrena, Spain. His first stabs at the game came as a child with ill-fashioned, makeshift clubs, with which he learned to be resourceful – to fabricate and create shots seemingly from thin air. Legend has it that he would hit stones and pick-ups with a cut-down three iron until the thing disintegrated, then find another and repeat the exercise.

Even as a professional Seve would practise his golf not from the fairways, but from the rough, from between trees and in sand – just so that he could cope with anything that came his way. It proved wise, not just because of his ability to manufacture brilliant recovery shots, but because his huge but erratic driving so often put him into some awful spots.

Though he is now a seasoned campaigner blessed with consummate track craft, he still conjures new and exciting shots, almost to order, and many believe he's one of the most gifted iron players of all time.

Though still a mere stripling of nineteen, Seve had been a pro for over three years, when he set his sights on the 1976 Open Championship. For three rounds he matched the best and held off Johnny Miller, who was in the middle of his hottest streak. Miller won, but Seve tied for second place with Jack Nicklaus. For two years thereafter, Seve was unstoppable, leading the European money list and winning in every corner of the globe, taking titles in Australia, Holland, Ireland, Kenya and Switzerland, among others.

Seve took the first of his two British Open titles in 1979 at Lytham, edging Ben Crenshaw and Nicklaus by three strokes, the first Continental to win since the Frenchman Arnaud Massy in 1907, and a year later he made history by winning his first Masters title at Augusta National, the first European ever and only the second non-American (Gary Player had triumphed in 1961).

One of the longest hitters on the Tour, he found Augusta National again to his liking in 1983 as his length, coupled with uncanny accuracy, gave him his second green jacket, while earning him the adoration of every Southern belle in the State of Georgia.

Ballesteros whipped the cream yet again at St Andrews in 1984, his second Open title coming after he held off Tom Watson and Bernhard Langer by two strokes. Four major titles in six years put him among the immortals. There was to be one more. After seeming to lose touch, Seve fired back in 1988 and triumphed in typical dashing style, winning his third Open in appallingly wet conditions at Royal Lytham. Some say it was his finest ever.

In discussions about the best player in the world, certainly Ballesteros is up there with Bobby Jones, Hogan, Palmer, Nicklaus, and a handful of others in history. Though probably not quite the greatest ever, he is certainly the most charismatic. When golfing magicians are at work you should watch them if you ever get the chance. They have genius, and they are few and far between.

Severiano Ballesteros, born Pedrina, Spain, 1957. British Open Champion 1979, 1984, 1988. US Masters 1980, 1983. Five times World Matchplay Champion, 51 European Tour victories. Vardon Trophy 1976–78, 1986, 1988, 1991.

TIGER WOODS

It would normally be considered ridiculous that a player could win just one Major, be on his first year as a professional, and yet immediately be classed among the all-time-greats of golf's centuries-old history. But for the game played by Tiger Woods, the word normal simply does not apply.

It was not so much the winning, as the manner of it. That such a young man could beat the very best golfers in the world by 12 strokes; that he could break the record of 271 set by Jack Nickaus twenty-two years earlier and equalled only by Raymond Floyd 11 years after that. (And it is worth mentioning that the record was beaten by only one shot because the 21-year-old experienced a nightmare opening nine holes costing 40 shots.)

The simple truth that emerged over four glorious days at Augusta was that if he is on his game, Tiger Woods cannot be beaten. Tom Watson did not exaggerate when he said that this kind of player comes round only once every thousand years.

Not that his astonishing performance in turning one of the toughest courses in the world into a pitch-and-putt came out of the blue. He started imitating his father's golf swing at the age of six months; appeared on TV with golf fanatic Bob Hope at the age of three, and by four he shot 48 for nine holes!

He was the youngest ever Junior champion, youngest ever Amateur champion, and won the very first event he played on the pro circuit, pipping Tom Lehman on the first extra hole with a near hole-in-one. Tiger has always been special.

His extraordinary power comes from his immensely fast turn of the shoulders as he strikes the ball. He does not need the massive backswing used by other players to achieve distance. Averaging 337 yards off the tee, his game is so long that par fives no longer seem to exist. Yet the world was able to see at the Masters how good his short game is too: his putting was faultless. Jack Nicklaus thinks his own incredible records are now certain to tumble. 'Tiger is playing a game with which we are not familiar. If he is playing well, any golf course in defenceless.'

Tiger Woods: simply a phenomenon.

in a positive way, then I believe that's what was intended for me.'

That he should achieve his victory on a course that until 20 years ago allowed no black players, and until Tiger won the green jacket had only two black members, adds further joy to his triumph. He is open about the dangers of racism in the game; he is an icon, and inspiration, and a money-earner without compare – his first contract with Nike was for 40 million dollars.

The word great is widely over-used, especially in sports writing, but for Tiger Woods the word becomes wholly inadequate. He is nothing short of a phenomenon, and with good fortune he will bring the world many more years of his magic.

Tiger Woods, born Cypress, California, 1975. US Junior champion (youngest ever) 1991, 1992, 1993. US Amateur

But then add to that his character – smiling, easy-going, patient, charming. Able to talk to youngsters in the crowd and to relate to his own skills with charm: 'I think I now understand why the big guy in the sky has given me some of these talents. The main reason is to help people. If I can influence their lives

champion 1994 (youngest ever), 1995. Walker Cup team 1995. Mercedes Championship, Asian Classic and US Masters, 1997. Selected for Ryder Cup, 1997.

David White

A WAITING GAME

'EVERY TIME I PLAY IN A PRO-AM THE GUYS THINK THAT THEY

CAN OUT-DRIVE ME BECAUSE I AM JUST A WOMAN.'

Marie-Laure de Lorenzi

Introduction
by Laura Davies

The history of women's golf has been one of constant struggle. Women were neither liked for taking up the game, nor welcome in the clubhouse. Few people either expected, or wanted, them to do well.

The determination of women players over the centuries has brought us to the excellent position we are in today. But we still need to go forward, bringing more youngsters into the game and helping develop their natural talents.

And while I am very much opposed to 'men-only' golf clubs, I don't see them as being too serious a threat, because I don't think they will be around for very much longer.

The real battle women face today is less against discrimination and lack of recognition, (although at one stage last year I had won two major titles and very little was printed in the golf magazines, which only focused on the men!) but more a struggle to find the sponsors with the money and interest to take the women's game seriously onward, into the Millennium.

We need to find support that will not only reward the winners, the fortunate golfers playing at the top of their game, but equally to make sure that those girls lower down in the field can get money to cover their costs and expenses so that they can keep taking part, and keep learning and contributing all the while.

Some time ago I won the Standard Register Ping Tournament in Phoenix, Arizona, for the fourth year in succession. It put my name alongside those of Gene Sarazen and Walter Hagen, as one of the few people to win an individual tournament four years in a row.

I am deeply proud to have done it, and to be the only woman in that triumvirate. It's hard to believe that this should all come true when my initiation to golf was so routine. I only started to play because my brother, who is three years older than me, used to. I had a go just so that I could join in with him; playing with him and against him, wielding a single five iron, until eventually I got into a club.

One of the hardest challenges for girls these days is just getting the chance to play. It is not easy, especially for youngsters, male or female, to get into a club and it should be made far simpler. If people want youngsters to have a chance, if they want to build great players for the future, the clubs have

'As a professional women's tour player, if you are good, it is a great way to live; a relatively easy life and great fun. We travel the world and earn a great living. We play for fortunes.'

got to give them every chance, and that means letting them join and letting them play.

The last few clubs who persist in refusing to allow juniors to win prizes are facing a backlash from the English Ladies' Golf Association, which is banning such clubs from taking part in ELGA special events – and quite rightly too. We have to encourage more girl golfers; they are in short supply.

Going on to becoming a professional is not just a matter of natural progression; if you are good enough, then golf takes over, and becomes your goal. I left school at 16 in order to play golf. I was absolutely determined. I wasn't frightened about what was involved. I absolutely knew that that is all I wanted to do. I wanted it to be my life.

And as a professional women's tour player, if you are good, it is a great way to live; a relatively easy life and great fun. We travel the world and earn a great living. We play for fortunes.

At times, if you are not playing so well, it is hard work, but in truth it really is a fantastic life. It was no fun missing cuts again and again, but even at the worst moments of it all there wasn't anything else in the world that I would rather do.

You must always set goals. That is what drives you on, what you are doing it for. There is no point playing if you do not have that determination.

Playing in a competition like the Solheim Cup really drives you on. There is a real edge when you are playing with friends trying to beat other friends. When you are out on the course the competition is so intense. I still feel sick with nerves at the excitement of winning a point for my country or even blowing it.

As to the future, I really believe that the women players of Europe are going to dominate by the year 2000; the young girls we have coming up in the game are developing far better than the Americans. In a few years the competition will really turn and we will be the ones teeing off first.

I have never played in tweed skirts, and I have no intention of doing so. I am lucky enough to be able to pick and choose from golfing fashions made for me by the designers at Maruman; clothes which carry my name across the world.

But I am deeply thankful to the women who did play that way all those years ago; out on the fairways in restrictive clothes and facing even more restrictive attitudes. They had to put up with criticism and obstruction in order to do something they enjoyed. The ones who played at the top of their game – like Joyce Wetherhead, and Babe Zaharias – are remembered. Many, less able or less fortunate, have been forgotten; but they enjoyed their golf and by continually playing they did so much to set the path for today's lady golfers.

Golf is great fun. We should all be grateful to the strong women who helped make it that way – and we should try to do the same for the lady golfers of the future…

The biggest single short-sighted, self-centred and sinister influence on the women's game? Men. They have set women's golf back by a century, driven on by the emotions encapsulated in the old drinking toast, 'To the ladies. God bless 'em and keep off the golf course.'

Before World War I, golf courses were dubbed 'the Garden of Eden – without the influence of Eve'.

When the Ladies Golf Union tried hosting the first British Women's Open in 1962 they had to cancel the contest because they couldn't find a sponsor. But at last, after the determined efforts of a succession of brilliant sportswomen, the walls are tumbling down.

How many male golfers do you know who could live with the game of Laura Davies? Marie-Laure de Lorenzi smiles at the thought of it all when she talks about playing with men.

'Every time I play in a Pro-Am the guys think that they can out-drive me because I am just a woman. Most of them don't even come close, but they are so desperate that they keep trying and trying and the ball goes all over the place. They hate the thought of being beaten by a woman.'

And of course, now that women professionals are taking part in Pro-Ams

Mary Queen of Scots returns to the links.

on the world circuit they are facing another new obstacle: men who can't keep their hands to themselves. The situation is so bad the Women's European Tour is including a how-to-deal-with-men course at its training school. Seriously.

There are now formal guidelines that, come 10 p.m. at the after match dinner, the women will leave, says tour chairman Terry Coates. Mixed messages apparently started to arise when successful putts were celebrated with a kiss. Now girls are encouraged to keep the flagstick firmly between themselves and the advancing kisser, and are warned that while the friendly male has the potential to be a sponsor (most important) or a husband (not quite so good), he is more likely to be a hooligan.

Women have been playing golf for hundreds of years, but it is only since around the World War II, notably by the advances made in America, that they have begun to get the recognition they deserved.

Mary Queen of Scots was undoubtedly the most famous early golfer on record – and she was roundly criticized in 1567 for being out on the links with another woman player instead of mourning her husband, who had been murdered a few days before!

The third Ladies' golf championship at Royal Portrush in 1895. The winner, wearing a tam-o-shanter, was Lady Margaret Scott. Miss E. Lithgoe (second from right) won the silver medal and Miss H.G. Willcock (first left) and Mrs Ryder Richardson (first right) shared the bronze medal.

At St Andrews a women's golf club had been formed by 1867, and by 1893 the Ladies' Golfing Union launched the first annual championship – won, over 27 holes, by Lady Margaret Scott.

But the first significant change came after the death of Queen Victoria when shifts in attitudes allowed women to challenge the conventions that precluded physical exercise. Not that it was easy. Medical science was of the general opinion that women had a limited supply of energy, which should be dedicated to home-making and child-bearing, and that it was too easily wasted with exercise. That mature women were prone to fainting spells was put down to their inherent physical weakness – overlooking the fashion dictates that forced them into corsets designed to create 19-inch waists.

Sport was seen as essential to train a boy in the rigours of the life that lay ahead – moulding him as a disciplined and sturdy member of the ruling sex: politician, educator, professional, economist. Women, who by society's rules would be expected to be none of the above, were left to sit at home drinking tea and doing embroidery.

But as the years went by golf – mild, leisurely golf – gradually came to be seen as being such a gentle form of exercise that it might, occasionally, be tried by the female of the species.

Unfortunately, the case of women's development was hindered not only by the male. Equally tradition-bound women went to war over the increase in physical exercise.

As one fervent commentator, Mrs Alec Tweedie, wrote in 1902, golf and other sports were the curse of femininity.

'Over-exercise among girls is surely a bad thing. A finely-developed woman is a joy – a tall, over-grown, leggy, scraggy-armed female is an eyesore. Women are certainly inclined to take too much physical exercise today. After all, a woman's first duty is her home, and it is just as much her duty to make things run smoothly for her father and mother as it is, later, for her husband and children.

'Every girl's work lies before her – the daintiness of the home depends on her. If she can cover the furniture – and this is quite an easy matter – she is showing her usefulness. If she can cook she can teach and save in the kitchen; if she can make her own dresses and trim her own hats she deserves praise, and can make a ten-pound note go as far as five times that amount in less capable hands.

'After all is it not much finer to make a home and its inmates comfortable than to win a cup for golf?'

Fortunately, she wrote, 'golf is a comparatively new introduction, and one in which none of the hard-working folk of America have time to take part to any extent, although people are beginning to play round New York, where clubs are therefore springing up with mushroom-like rapidity.

'There is no doubt about it, however, that on the whole Americans take much less exercise than Britishers. Now the overgrown girl is not so often met with in the States as she is in England; indeed, the American woman, however young, is usually well developed, with an excellent carriage and presence; she has a good figure and great repose of movement.

'Two rounds of golf on a man's links means a great deal of exercise besides a ten-mile walk, which in itself is a good deal for a woman. She has to play just as hard and swing her club with as much strength as the man against whom she is pitted, and it is these girls who do so much who stoop, get narrow chests and rounded backs.

'A masculine woman is as bad as a feminine man – both are anomalies, both are objectionable.'

In some respects, women golfers on both sides of the Atlantic did little to help their cause. In England, the Suffragettes carried out a bomb attack on Lloyd George's new country house overlooking Walton Heath golf course, where the politician was a regular player. Had it been his *town* house, scarcely an eyelid would have been batted. But on the heath!

The Suffragettes also began digging up the greens at some of the finest courses. According to the police at the time, two young women arrested after one attack were found to have bags containing flammable materials saturated with oil, a handsaw and an electric lamp.

Later in the day they were taken before magistrates at Richmond and charged with maliciously setting fire to a building. One of them hurled a heavy book at the head of the presiding magistrate. Not surprisingly, bail was refused.

We must go back a few years to report one early *faux pas* in the United States, where the very innocence of the women of Mrs Henry Hopkins' Morris County Golf Club in north-eastern New Jersey caused embarrassing problems. When Mrs Hopkins founded the club in 1893, the rules decreed that it should be a women-only organization. However, there would be honorary membership for members of the clergy, and 200 associate memberships – for men.

Two years later, when they elected a man as president, he changed the rules – and that was the end of the women's influence.

But there were spectacular achievements, too, in the early part of the twentieth century, including a golfing battle of the sexes in 1910, which saw 19-year-old Miss Cecilia Leitch play a 72-home match with no less a golfing figure than H.H. Hilton, twice winner of the Open.

By the 14th hole in the first round, Hilton was four up, and the crowd began to murmur 'This is farcical.' Leitch, destined to be one of the greats of all times, showed 'indomitable pluck', according to observers, and by the end of the round had reduced the lead to one. At the beginning of the afternoon round, Hilton was again three up, but Leitch wiped off the deficit,

'Indomitable pluck.'
Miss Leitch tearing
into another drive
during her
momentous win
over Harold Hilton.

went two up and finished the day one down after 36 holes.

Huge crowds followed the match, which was wayward at times. Spectators crushing on to the course were hit at least six times, and on the way to the first hole Leitch's tee shot hit a pram carrying two infants. However, they were untroubled by the incident.

The second day brought one of the most exciting matches ever. Everything was against the dauntless Miss Leitch during the morning round. There was an awkward wind and the rain came down in torrents, soaking her to the skin. Hilton was on the top of his form, and went in two up.

After the third hole of the final round, sodden Cecilia ('Cecil', as she was

Hilton (left) pictured with John Ball. His game went to pieces in the final 18 holes.

known) was five down. The turning point of the match was at the fourth hole. Hilton putted carelessly and lost the hole. He didn't recover form after that, and from that point won only a single hole. Leitch won the match outright on the 17th green, two up with one to play.

Not all would-be champions waited until they were 19, however, as this report from the Daily Mail of 1919 shows:

GOLF'S BABY-GIRL, 'LOST' IN THE ROUGH

'White socks peeping above bronze shoes, a little jumper frock of white, fair hair hanging in plaits from under a panama – that was Miss Nancy Griffiths, aged 12,

who stepped on the first tee at Stoke Poges, Bucks, yesterday in the girls' golf championship. Straightaway, without a waggle of the club, she hit a drive with a swing of confidence that drew experts into her 'gallery'.

'She and her sister, Miss Barbara Griffiths, a year older, had begun the day unhappily. The car in which they were travelling with their father from their home at Sunningdale collided with another at Windsor, and both were severely shaken. Securing a taxicab, they reached the course in time, although Miss Barbara's right hand had to be bound before she could play.

'Miss Nancy opposed Miss Mollie Nicholson, of Bradford, some eight years her senior. Her figure splendidly erect, head thrown back, 'the baby' set about her task with complete composure. Success did not elate her nor adversity dishearten.

'Losing the first, she won the second and third. Going to the fifth both were bunkered. Miss Nicholson was in a desperate position. Miss Nancy stood watching her opponent's heroic endeavours. Then she looked up archly at the referee when Miss Nicholson had played five in the bunker. 'I hope you're counting all these,' she said quietly.

'Miss Nancy was two up. From every tee she was driving about 180 yards, dead straight in most cases. Once she went into the long grass to play a shot, and disappeared from view. When a search party might have been organised, her panama was seen moving among the rank vegetation. Presently, having studied her bearings, out she came.

'She was still one up at the turn, but the stroke that beat her was a putt of ten yards, which Miss Nicholson holed to square at the tenth. After that little Miss Griffiths went off her putting. She looked nettled for the only time when, at the fourteenth, she was twice short. She was beaten on the sixteenth. Still, it was a great effort of a maid who uses her six clubs and grips – overlapping – like a Vardon. Her sister was beaten by Miss Sarah Thompson, of Newmarket, by 6 and 5. Miss Barbara, swinging exactly like Miss Nancy, would not agree that her cut hand had contributed to defeat. "It didn't hurt a bit while I was playing."

'Qualifying for the tournament, she did a 71 on the women's course at Sunningdale – four below par – aged 13.'

Such achievements did little to change the views of those who thought they knew where a woman's place should really be – even if they *did* allow golf to play a small part. Even then, it was only to make them better wives.

A 1920 treatise on the essentials of wifehood laid down the following guidelines:

'She must be good to look upon. If she is not pretty she can be dainty, fresh, and well groomed.

'She must be a good and prudent house-keeper, and be able to cook, even if she can afford servants.

'She must have tasteful ideas about house decoration, making her home a place of rest and comfort.

'She must be a companion to her husband. Sympathy is not enough. She must be able to discuss work, literature, and politics, intelligently with him and his friends.

'She must be a devoted mother realizing to the full the responsibility, resting with her, of giving to her country moral, healthy, and helpful citizens.

'And, with all these duties, she must never be for a moment without love.

'To perform all these things to their uttermost is no easy task, but all wives and wives-to-be who are desirous of reducing matrimony to a fine art should consider the following practical details.

'Self-education. Insist upon having a morning paper of your own and devote half an hour each afternoon to an intelligent perusal of it; an hour a day should also be given over to good reading.

'Personal appearance. Never consider it unnecessary to dress daintily for the evening. Your husband is just as appreciative of pretty dresses, neatly dressed hair, and a charming appearance as he was before you married him.

'Companionship. When your husband returns after the day's work, household duties must be laid aside and all your attention given to him. Interest yourself in his interests. If he plays golf, learn to play also, and thus make yourself indispensable to his pleasure as well as to his work.

'All this may seem to demand rather too much of a woman's life and of self-denial, but in practice it will be found to bring more happiness and content than any other method; and she will have the satisfaction of realizing that every day so spent is furthering the great ambition to make a true art of wifehood.'

In some quarters, women themselves were beginning to be worried about the effects the 'masculine' pursuit of golf were having on them. In the United States, in 1926, according to a Dr Frederick Graves, 'The American woman is seriously concerned because she has been told that her ankles are thickening, and she is reported to be very busy soaking, massaging, and strapping her ankles in rubber bandages every night.' The cause? Golf, and the Charleston.

Surprisingly, while social critics condemned the women's game, advertisers adored it. Not in terms of putting money into it – more a case of making money out of it. Pictures of women playing golf appeared everywhere, on calendars, on porcelain, on posters, cards, book covers, postcards, clothing catalogues, music sheets and chocolate boxes.

The image of women in golfing costume was elegant, racy, beautiful and independent. They were seen to have a fresh attitude of mind, and a physicality that was enticing and sensual.

Of course those women who managed to make it out on to a golf course found the game less than a thrilling – or sensual – experience, hampered, as they were, by the physical restrictions of the clothes they were forced to wear. Try swinging a club behind your head when you are wearing two petticoats, a pair of corsets, knickerbockers, a plaid jacket and a wet tweed skirt clinging to your ankles.

Men came to reason that, because they made and enforced the rules, then women would be no threat – as long as they played only when it suited men, and as long as they were banned from bars, committees, and in many cases, membership.

And largely, they were encouraged to play only with other women. What men hadn't bargained for was womankind's easy appreciation that golf, being less a game of brute strength but rather a mixture of guile, gamesmanship, strategy and style, might have been created for women.

Opposition to their playing golf became focused off the course rather than on and again it was largely centred on the perceived physical changes that such activity was inducing in the modern woman.

One critic raged: 'During the last twenty years and more we have never ceased to plume ourselves on the supposed fact that, with the improvement of modern conditions, and the increasing attention to physical exercise, our

ABOVE AND RIGHT: A new target for advertisers. Pictures of women playing golf appeared everywhere.
PREVIOUS PAGE: 'To the ladies. God bless 'em and keep off the golf course.'

Not all women who played golf were '...flat-chested, colourless, and lacking in reasonable proportions.'

women have greatly added to their health and beauty.

'The result is that our women have deteriorated physically. She shoots up tall, flat-chested, colourless, and lacking in reasonable proportions. Dried and atrophied by rough wear and unseeming habits, that delicate form shrinks and withers from the norm of health and beauty. No longer have our girls pleasant contours and healthy lines.

'The chief charm in woman, as well as the end Nature had in view for her, is her femininity. When that goes she loses her birthright. Whether this is an argument which will avail with women I cannot say. But perhaps they may be affected by the undoubted fact that they are deteriorating in beauty and in physical attractiveness.'

While some progress was being made and more women took up golf, some of the leading figures in the women's game were taking one step forward and three steps back.

In the United States, rapidly becoming the pace-setter in world golf, the LPGA was founded under the leadership of the brilliant player Betty Hicks. Despite high ideals, it collapsed within five years, the victim of underfunding and a string of inter-factional battles that produced irreparable divisions.

Hicks herself penned a savage obituary. 'The first organization of women's professional golf was conceived in wrath, born into poverty and perished in a family squabble ... a bawling scrawny child of early day feminists, a beggar of a child pleading for tournaments.'

And the collapse of the LPGA meant that the begging and pleading for tournaments would continue, for its collapse furthered the belief of potential sponsors that women's golf was a dud: unattractive, uncompetitive and unable to organize itself in anything like the manner needed to merit major investment.

Lady golfers in the 1880s. In windy conditions their long skirts would often billow up and obscure
their sight of the ball when playing a shot. Some used a device called 'Miss Higgins' – a large
elasticated belt that could be moved down from the waist to the knees to stop the skirt flapping.

What the women's game really needed was a catalyst to make the money men and the crowds begin to pay attention. The miracle arrived in the incredible form of Babe Zaharias, one of the greatest athletes of all time.

Babe was already a national heroine in the USA when, in 1934, she turned exclusively to golf. A former professional basketball and baseball player, she excelled in athletics, and in the 1932 Olympics, set in her own 'back yard'

ABOVE: Pioneers of the women's game: Glenna Collett (left) and Joyce Wethered.
RIGHT: A Dominican Republic stamp commerates Babe Zaharias's three gold medals in the 1932 Olympic games.
OPPOSITE: Although golf was considered the curse of femininity, lady golfers were often depicted as glamourous and elegant.

REPUBLICA DOMINICANA

CORREO AEREO 17¢

1932 - MILDRED DIDRICKSON

of Los Angeles, she won gold in the javelin, 80-metre hurdles and high jump. Having the high jump medal snatched away, when she was disqualified for using a technique considered unladylike, only enhanced her reputation.

When she took up golf after the games, she won her very first event by 13 clear strokes. Then she won the Texan Amateur title – again only to be disqualified on the grounds that earning a living as a basketball player made her a 'professional' when it came to golf. It took five years to get her amateur status back, and when she did, she won 17 tournaments in a row, and became the first American to win the British Amateur title in 1946.

In 1951, in a superb stroke of PR, she led a team of American women players against a men's team of British amateurs playing off scratch. Playing level par with the men and with Babe ignoring the women's tees, they won every game of singles. She was the crowd-puller who gave the game the impetus it needed.

The injection of money into the game has been such that the leading US money-earner at the height of Babe's career was earning one-twenty-eighth of what her male equivalent made. But by the mid-1990s, the leading female money-earner was making slightly over half what the leading man made.

Today the women's game is a major crowd puller, and a massive source of advertising, fashion and sponsorship revenue, thanks to the efforts of pioneers such as Cecilia Leitch, Glenna Collett, Joyce Wethered, Catherine Lacoste, and the first champion of them all Lady Margaret Scott. And to the brilliance of modern legends such as Laura Davies, Nancy Lopez and Annika Sorenstam.

It is a professional game calling for massive dedication and the level of skills displayed on the tour circuit bring records and incidents that would awe those pioneers, who faced prejudice and ignorance on their journey.

Helen Ducker

LEADING LADIES

'I'LL TAKE A TWO-SHOT PENALTY, BUT I'LL BE DAMNED IT I'M

GOING TO PLAY THE BALL WHERE IT LIES.'

Elaine Johnson *(After her tee shot bounced off a tree and nestled in her bra.)*

LADY MARGARET SCOTT

I t was Lord Wellwood in 1890 who started it all, after authoritatively stating that 70 or 80 yards was the limit of a feminine drive, 'not because we doubt a lady's power to make a longer drive, but because that cannot well be done without raising the club above the shoulder. Now we do not presume to dictate, but we must observe that the posture and gestures requisite for a full swing are not particularly graceful when the player is clad in female dress.'

The noble lord's opinion was still wreathed in after-dinner cigar smoke when he and the rest of the masculine world were utterly confounded by the appearance of Lady Margaret Scott, who proceeded to win the first three British Ladies' Championships, in 1893, 1894 and 1895, fairly launching the ball into orbit at every attempt.

She not only drove considerably farther than 80 yards by raising the club above the shoulder, but contrived to look remarkably smooth, elegant and ladylike while doing so. Her style of play was described as 'dashing, fearless, fascinating', and her great advantage was in her powerful second shots, particularly when faced with horrible lies.

She was, undoubtedly, in a different league to her contemporaries, though she did not achieve her unquestioned supremacy over her rivals by discarding any of the approved feminine accoutrements of the time. Like them, she wore thick ankle-length skirts, abundant and flowing, which had to be anchored by lead weights and webbing, and existed on a foundation of several petticoats. Following her hat-trick, Lady Margaret retired from golf and never played competitively again.

Looking at illustrations of her swing today, it is easy to see why she had such mastery of her game. Lady Margaret's style depicts text-book excellence of an entirely different, later era – she was ahead of her time by a country mile. It shows.

Lady Margaret Scott, born 1875. Died 1938. British Ladies Open Amateur Champion 1893, 1894, 1895.

Lady Margaret Scott as depicted by P.A. Staynes in 1910.

'CECIL' LEITCH

Cecil Leitch was the first female power player, the first woman to give the ball an almighty thump. Born Charlotte Cecilia Pitcairn Leitch, she was known simply as Cecil. She had the good fortune to be born of a Fife doctor who practised at Silloth, and who founded a golf course there, close to the present 18-hole championship links.

Taught by her father, she and her sisters regularly played together with cut-down clubs and soon became very proficient at battling against the heather and stiff westerly breezes. It was good fortune that took 'Cecil' and her sister Edith to St Andrews for the British Ladies' Open in 1908. They had been 'discovered' by a a female friend who persuaded the family to let them go, saying that the experience would do the girls good.

The girls' debut was to be the beginning of a new era in women's golf. Edith had made it to the third round. Her sister reached the finals of the championship — her first serious competition — and proceeded to stamp power and authority over all comers until her only wood broke in the semi-final and she lost to the eventual winner. It was a miserable way for the 17-year-old to bow out, but the golfing world saw, even at this early stage, that the girl had masses of talent and that it would be only a matter of time.

It was not until 1914 that Leitch gained her acceptance as Britain's finest, winning both the British Championship and the English title. World War I intervened, but in 1920 'Cecil' was off again, chasing titles and demonstrating her remarkable powers. At the height of her career she held more than twenty course records, winning the British Championship again in 1921 and then in 1926. She won the Canadian Open in 1921, the English in 1914 and 1919, the French in 1912, 1914, 1920, 1921 and 1924 and was an English

Cecil Leitch put everything into her drives.

International for twelve years, winning 29 of her total of 33 matches.

It was her matches with Joyce Wethered that focused attention on women's golf, elevating coverage from the sports pages to the national news. Their classic battles did much to add to the rising popularity of golf for women, and they raised the accepted standards of play to a degree previously thought unbelievable.

'Cecil' and Joyce first met in the final of the English in 1920, when Joyce scored a surprise victory. One year later the roles were reversed, 'Cecil' gaining revenge with victory in both British and French Opens. They met again in the finals of the British in 1922 and again in 1925, though on both occasions Joyce Wethered prevailed.

'Cecil' Leitch wrote books about golf and was prominent in the affairs of the LGU.

'Cecil' Leitch, born Silloth, 1891. Died 1977. French Ladies' Champion 1912, 1914, 1920-21, 1924. British Ladies' Champion 1914, 1920–21, 1926. English Ladies' Champion 1914, 1919. Canadian Ladies' Champion 1921.

JOYCE WETHERED (LADY HEATHCOAT-AMORY)

Often compared with Bobby Jones, with whom she toured the United States in 1935, Joyce was summed up by Bobby himself: 'I have never played golf with anyone, man or woman, amateur or professional, who made me feel so utterly outclassed ... she is the finest golfer I have ever seen.'

As a 19-year-old unknown, Joyce entered the 1920 English Ladies' Championship at Sheringham and to everyone's amazement, none more than her own, she beat 'Cecil' Leitch, then the dominant figure in the game. It was a turning point, marking the beginning of an epic series of matches between these two great players, though Cecil got her revenge in 1921 with

two victories over her rival. From that point they played in the tightest of battles and together provided galleries of adoring fans (nobody was ever neutral) with displays of absolute wizardry, but Leitch never bettered her.

Joyce's record is without parallel. She won the English Championship five times in succession, involving 33 matches without defeat, while the British Ladies' Championship was a similar story. Here she won four titles and lost only two matches, one to Cecil Leitch in 1921 and to Mrs Allan Macbeth in the semi-final of 1923. In all she won 38 matches out of a possible 43 – incredible.

Not just a great ball striker, Joyce was captivated by the artistry of the game, the perfection of a faultless style. Most photographs show her almost on tip-toes

Joyce Wethered's swing was perfect. 'The finest golfer I have ever seen,' said Bobby Jones.

at impact, though there was never a hint of anything other than perfect balance and poise, and her full pivot gave her unconstrained movement while producing clubhead speed and crispness – and therefore distance – at impact. She was as graceful as any ballerina.

Having achieved supremacy she went into retirement, but after four years she was persuaded to return, in 1929, for just one more attempt at the

British Ladies' Championship crown. She scored a memorable victory over the American Glenna Collett in a titanic 36-hole battle, after being five down after nine. Entertaining a rapturous St Andrews crowd as only she could, Joyce finally overcame her rival with a 3-1 triumph. While she declared her victory 'the most satisfying win of my career', it was to be her final Championship appearance (though she played and won her singles match in the first Curtis Cup in 1932). Like Bobby Jones, Joyce retired from major competition at the age of 28, there being no more worlds to conquer.

Thereafter she appeared only in the Worplesdon Mixed Foursomes, which she won eight times with seven different partners. Bernard Darwin saw the fun in this, describing the astonishment of her partners, who were 'successively amazed by her accuracy and appalled by the number of times she had to play from positions into which she would never have got herself'.

Today Joyce lives in retirement in Devon, where a cherished collection of her trophies and memorabilia is housed within the Heathcoat-Amory estate.

Joyce Wethered (Lady Heathcoat-Amory), born Surrey 1901. English Ladies' Champion 1920-1924. British Ladies' Champion 1922, 1924–5, 1929, runner-up 1921, semi-finalist 1923.

GLENNA COLLETT

It would be hard to argue against the claim that this was the greatest American woman amateur ever. Glenna Collett's first enthusiasm was for baseball. Press-ganged into golf by her anxious mother, who thought the boys' game altogether too rough, she nevertheless did not take the game up until her teens. Within a few years she had developed exceptional talents and in the 1920s and 1930s she so dominated the amateur scene that her record has only been approached in more recent times by the great JoAnne Carner.

Glenna Collett was the ultimate matchplay golfer and mainstay of the American Curtis Cup team for over two decades.

One of golf's all-time heroines and a dominating figure in the roaring twenties, she became one of the best match players of her time. Indeed, in 1924 she lost only one match out of sixty played, in the US Ladies' semi-finals — and even that was a fluke. She and her opponent, a champion tennis player called Mary Browne, were all square going to the 18th. With Glenna safely on the green, Mary muffed her shot and it sailed into the trees, only to rebound on to the green and into the hole!

Glenna soared to great heights, winning the US Women's Amateur in 1922, 1925, 1928, 1929, 1930 and 1935 – a record for USGA competitions – while being runner-up in 1931 and 1932 and medallist on four occasions. In total she won 49 amateur championships in 18 years, while scoring victories in 19 consecutive matches from 1928–31, another USGA record.

She won the French Women's Amateur in 1925 and the Canadian in 1923 and 1924. She was a member of the US Curtis Cup team in 1932, 1936, 1938 and 1948; captain in 1934, 1936, 1948 and 1950. Perhaps her greatest match was in the 1929 British Women's Amateur. Alas, she met Joyce Wethered in the final and though Joyce had 'retired', she had been coaxed to return by the prospect of a week of golf at St Andrews. Glenna played the first nine in 34, was five up at one time, but couldn't withstand Miss Wethered's miracle finish and lost, three and one. In 1925 she had met Joyce for the first time and lost when the great stylist shot four pars and six birdies over ten consecutive holes.

Undoubtedly the greatest golfer among American women of her period, she might even have been heralded the greatest champion of all had she captured the British title just once, but that was to resist all attacks until the Babe came along after World War II. Glenna's record was unsurpassed at least until after the war, when the girls began devoting all their time to the game as paid professionals.

Glenna Collett (later Vare), born New Haven, Connecticut, 1903. Died 1989. US Women's Champion 1922, 1925, 1928, 1929, 1930 and 1935.

GLORIA MINOPRIO

I f ever a woman golfer deserves her corner in the game's history, it is Gloria Minoprio. She did not win much, indeed the record books are largely inclined to ignore her, yet her contribution to the golf game is priceless.

Gloria hit the headlines – and by capturing the attention of newspaper editors she became front-page copy throughout 1933 – largely because, socially, she was light years ahead of her time. Tall, dark and decidedly

Gloria Minoprio, with her glamour and eccentricity, took golf on to the front pages.

glamorous, she was the first woman to wear slacks on a British course.

It caused uproar, of course. The Ladies' Golf Union was up in arms. In the first round of the English Women's Championships her vanquished opponent moaned that 'It was hard on me to have to play against an opponent who wears such unusual clothes. It was like playing someone in fancy dress.'

While the popular press went to town, and the letters columns were packed with the rights and wrongs of the issue, the LGU went on record by stuffily decrying her contribution to the 'dignity and deportment of the game'. Their formal statement 'deplored any departure from the traditional costume of the game'.

But Gloria didn't much care; the rules did not specifically forbid her supposed eccentricity, so on a colourless October day at the start of the 1933 English Championship, she breezed up to the steps of Westward Ho! clubhouse in a chauffeur-driven yellow Rolls-Royce, wearing a turtleneck sweater, a beret and trousers, all in a fetching shade of navy blue. To add to this perceived outrage, Gloria, a former conjurer's assistant, wore mask-like white make-up.

It would provide a splendid twist if we could record her magnificent and inspired path to victory, but sadly she failed even to qualify, moving Henry Longhurst to title his *Sunday Times* feature 'Sic Transit Gloria Monday'. Five times in succession she failed in the first round, but on the sixth occasion she qualified for round two, thus Henry's headline became 'Sic Transit Gloria Tuesday'.

She was also a pretty unusual golfer: she only used one club – a flat iron – with which she drove, chipped and putted. She said: 'I use one club because I know that club, and have completely mastered it. More clubs would only make the game more difficult.' Yet by the time she had played 40 rounds of golf she had a handicap of four.

A brilliant card-sharp, a sheep farmer, a magician, she was for three years, the most exciting figure at every championship. Gloria was unabashed by public criticism, much of it from women, saying simply that trousers were easier to play in than skirts. 'I have strong ideas about doing anything I like provided it does not give pain to anyone. I don't mind if it merely offends old-fashioned convictions.' Within three years women playing golf in a skirts were exceptions rather than the rule.

Gloria Minoprio, born Littlestone, Kent, 1910. She married into Polish aristocracy at the outbreak of World War II and moved to Canada, where she died in the late 1950s.

MILDRED (BABE) DIDRICKSON ZAHARIAS

One of the best athletes of her time, and possibly the greatest all-rounder of all time, Mildred Zaharias acquired her nickname through her skill at baseball during Babe Ruth's reign, and earned a living by playing both baseball and basketball.

She was an extraordinary sportswoman, and first captured worldwide attention in the 1932 Olympics, when she set three records in hurdles, javelin and high jump – the only three events in which she was allowed to qualify!

She began playing golf in the 1930s and was an immediate success, taking a medal in her first event. She won the USGA Women's Amateur title in 1946 at her first try and followed this by capturing the British Women's Amateur title in 1947 – the first American to win it – after which she turned pro.

Described once as 'an earthquake personality who could hit the ball past almost as many men as she claimed she could', she convinced all who saw her that she was the best since Joyce Wethered. It is an unfair comparison, though, as the two women were poles apart in physique, temperament,

Golf wasn't Babe Zaharias' only game. She played both basketball and baseball professionally and won three gold medals at the 1932 Olympic Games.

outlook and technique. For the record, they met just twice – in 1935 – and Miss Wethered won both times.

Utterly extrovert, the Babe loved publicity and could entertain an audience as well as any pro. Able to outdrive and outplay most men, and prepared to flout convention by wearing outrageous clothes, she brought a mass following to the women's game at a time of crisis and was a founding member of the LPGA.

She would hit upwards of 1,000 practice balls a day, joking almost non-stop while ridiculing the current fashions. 'Do I wear girdles and bras and the rest of that junk? What d'ya think I am? A sissy?'

There were some who resented her, others who could find no common ground, even though they conceded she gave massive impetus to the women's professional circuit. One contemporary, Betsy Rawls, recalled in later years that 'Babe added a lot of colour to the tour when it was needed, but she did not add any dignity to the game.'

But what courage! Having won a couple of dozen tournaments in less than a handful of years she was diagnosed with cancer and a major operation was performed in April 1953. Experts said she would never play again, but she confounded them all by teeing up in the All-American some 14 weeks later, shooting 82, 85, 78, 84. The following week she was third in the World Tournament, and she finished the year sixth on the money list. She was just warming up, and in 1954 she won five events, including an incredible 12-stroke victory in the US Open.

Pain finally overcame her in 1954 and for the next 18 months she suffered agonies, while spending much time in hospital. She finally succumbed to the disease in September 1955.

Mildred (Babe) Didrickson Zaharias, born Texas, 1914. Died 1955. British Women's Amateur Champion 1947. US Women's Open Champion 1948, 1950, 1954. Winner of more than 50 events worldwide.

'Friendly and honest, devoid of shyness and of conceit,' Pam Barton was popular everywhere she played.

PAM BARTON

When Pam Barton was 12 years old her father gave her a golf lesson in their back garden on the outskirts of London. At her first 16 attempts she missed the ball every time. At the age of 17 she narrowly lost in the final of the English Women's Championship; and again the following year.

By 19, she had performed the astonishing double of winning the English Championship and the American Championships. Three years later, she won them both again. It was unheard of.

A remarkable natural talent, Pam Barton has a double place in the history of the game – for the golfer she was, and for the golfer she might have been.

Naturally attractive, she was a sturdy redhead with a big swing and an infectious smile. Her fine rhythmic style was amplified by her ability to hit the ball truly hard. She was admired for her golfing abilities, and admired again for her character, which was 'friendly and honest, devoid of shyness and of conceit'.

She became one of the most popular sporting figures of her generation, and in America they dubbed her England's Wonder Golfer. She played for Great Britain against America in the Curtis Cup and for England against Scotland, Ireland, Wales and France on numerous occasions.

Pam's favourite partner was her sister Mervyn, and together the two girls were almost unbeatable, with Mervyn's putting probably better than Pam's.

She was a vociferous backer of the rights of the spectator, claiming that most courses offered substandard facilities for the competitors, but nothing whatsoever for the members of the public who were charged for the privilege of walking the fairways.

Then, at the height of her fame – she became a guest partner for celebrities and visiting royalty – and perhaps not even near the height of her skill, the Pam Barton story came to a sudden end.

She served as an ambulance driver during the Blitz, and in 1941 joined the Women's Auxiliary Air Force as a radio operator, rising to have 600 WAAFs under her command. In November 1943 the plane she was in crash-landed on return to base, and she died at the age of 26.

Pam Barton, born Barnes, London, 1917, died 1943. English Ladies' Champion 1936, 1939. American Ladies' Champion 1936, 1939. Elected to the US WPGA Hall of Fame 1966.

CATHERINE LACOSTE

Catherine was the daughter of Simone de la Chaume who first won acclaim at the age of 14 by taking the 1924 British Girls' title, defeating Enid Wilson and Dorothy Pearson. Though petite, she had remarkable determination, and for a while was easily the finest French woman golfer, beating a whole string of seasoned campaigners.

She took the French Closed title at 15 and at 17 contested the British Championship as the best player in Europe. The odds were against her beating the best American players in 1927, but the 1924 Girls' result was exactly repeated, with Simone beating Enid Wilson in the semi-final and Dorothy in the final, making her the first foreign player to take the British title. Her private life was no less successful, for at the pinnacle of her career she married the great French tennis champion René Lacoste.

Genes will out, they say, and Simone's golden touch proved hereditary, with their daughter Catherine becoming a giant-killer in the amateur arena, even beating hardened professionals at their own game.

Born of such sporting pedigree, Catherine had the capacity, clearly inherited from her mother, to propel the ball enormous distances, while from René she took the innate dedication to succeed.

Catherine enjoyed a sparkling career from the very beginning, but even

Catherine Lacoste was the first to break the American monoply of the US Women's Open in 1967. She was also the youngest ever winner.

with a growing reputation and an enviable European tally of victories, she looked out of her depth in the 1967 US Women's Open against all the top American professionals. Nevertheless she began steadily, made precious few mistakes, and led comfortably going into the final. It was Louise Suggs who gave her a jolt, for having been far adrift she shot eight birdies in 15 holes. It was a challenge like no other, but Catherine kept her nerve and birdied the 17th to move finally beyond Louise's reach. An amateur had achieved the impossible!

Two years later, Catherine proved her superstar status by winning three Continental titles before tackling the British and US Amateur titles. Arriving at Royal Portrush a week before the British Championship, she practised

diligently with her mother, and progressed through each round without mishap. The final was a different matter. Playing against Ann Irvin, Catherine hit a wild drive at the 10th that was destined OB until it struck a spectator and bounced back into play. Ann Irvin lost by a single stroke, declaring 'You cannot compete with luck of that magnitude'.

One month later Catherine travelled to Texas in her quest for the 'grand slam' of amateur golf, and in baking temperatures she defeated Shelley Hamlin in a nail-biting final.

With the discipline that only great champions can afford to exercise, she declared that that was enough. A year later she married, decided against a professional career, and settled in Spain to raise a family.

Catherine Prado (née Lacoste), born Paris, 1945. US Women's Champion 1967. Ladies' British Open Amateur 1969. French Ladies' Champion 1967, 1969, 1970, 1972. French Ladies' Close Champion 1968-69. US Ladies' Amateur Champion 1969. Spanish Ladies' Amateur Champion 1969, 1972, 1976. First amateur, first non-American and youngest player at the time to win the US Women's Open.

LAURA DAVIES

Unquestionably the best-known woman golfer in Britain, possibly in the world, long-hitting Laura Davies is, quite simply, a marvel. As an amateur, she began by winning the South East and English Intermediate Championship, and later became a Curtis Cup player, though her early endeavours were limited by a shortage of money. Indeed, on one occasion club members had a whip-round in order to raise enough cash to send her to the British Women's Open.

Turning pro in 1986, Laura took a gamble when she joined the Women's

Professional Golfers (WPG) European Tour, borrowing £1,000 from her mother to get started. The gamble paid off, her mother was paid back with interest, and in 1987, having made a meaningful impact on the earnings of her European colleagues, she tried her fortunes in America.

With very little preparation, she finished in the top ten in the 1986 US Women's Open, and it became clear that earlier claims concerning her immense power had not been exaggerated.

During the next two years she concentrated on the European scene, while upon her return to the US in 1987, in just her fourth event, she tackled the US Women's Open, surprising herself by tying for first place with JoAnne Carner and Ayako Okamoto. Nobody gave her much chance against the two more famous players, but she powered her way to victory in the play-off, pocketing $55,000 into the bargain. Her victory led the US Tour to amend its constitution and she was granted automatic LPGA membership.

Laura plays a glorious game, totally attacking and daring – the female equivalent of Seve Ballesteros at his best. Her style is that of the gambler (for which she is notorious off the course). If she can reach the green she'll try her damnedest, and if she doesn't make it, then she possesses one of the finest short games in professional golf. Her sand shots and pitches are pure delicacy. She is powerful, but she is anything but clumsy. She has the authority and control to play the most beautifully executed shots around the green and her putting is reliable, sensitive, and a joy to watch.

Laura is a real crowd-pleaser, and fans love her captivating grin, wicked sense of humour and general sociability. For Laura, golf is meant to be fun.

Her record is phenomenal. In 1996 she was number one in scoring average (70·32), the longest driver (262·31 yards average), and led the world money list, with $927,302 officially, and $340,000 in the unofficial skins game. Laura

was voted Player of the Year by the Golf Writers' Association of America, the second time this honour has been bestowed upon her.

Incredibly in March 1997 Laura became the first woman in professional golf to win the same tournament four years in a row. By winning the Ping Standard Register tournament in Arizona, Davies joined Gene Sarazen and Walter Hagen in the exclusive four-in-a-row club. It also marked her 50th title in 12 years as a professional.

Laura Davies, born Coventry, England, 1963. Women's British Open Champion 1986. Women's US Open Champion 1987. LPGA Champion 1994, 1996. Order of Merit winner, WPG European Tour 1985, 1986, 1992, 1993. Curtis Cup and Solheim Cup player. Vivian Saunders Trophy 1992. GWAA Player of the Year 1994 and 1996.

David White

Laura Davies hits the ball every bit as hard as the competitors on the men's tour.

THE TOURNAMENTS

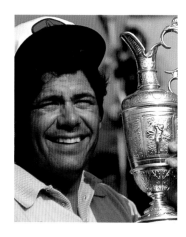

EVERY GREAT GOLFER HAS ASPIRED TO WIN THE OPEN.

MANY OF THE GREATEST HAVE GONE ON TO DOMINATE IT.

BRITISH OPEN

Built to unassuming dimensions more than 130 years ago, the British Open is the tournament that underpins world golf. None of those who watched or took part at Prestwick Golf Club in 1860 could have dreamed that the small private competition for eight Scottish professionals could grow into the tournament that has inspired so many dreams.

The Open is the biggest major of them all. It is the title everyone wants to win. Why? Because of the difficulties of links golf; because it is the oldest championship; and most of all because it has the most revered winners' board in the game.

Played over the 12 holes of the links at Prestwick, it was won by Willie Park, whose three-round score of 174 etched his name in history. The following year, the tournament became open to professionals and amateurs alike. Twelve souls battled for the red Morocco leather belt inlaid with silver, which was put up by the Earl of Eglinton; the winner was one of the greatest golfers of all time, Old Tom Morris.

For nine more years 'the Belt' was the target for all comers – until the brilliant son of Old Tom Morris, unsurprisingly dubbed Young Tom Morris, won it three times in succession to keep it outright.

For one year the tournament was held in abeyance until 1872, when Prestwick, the Royal and Ancient (St Andrews) and the Honourable Company of Golfers (Musselburgh) united to organize a revised tournament. Again the winner was Tom Morris Jnr; this time his was the first name to be engraved on 'the Cup' – the stunning silver claret jug that is desired the world over.

Prestwick, the Honourable Company of Golfers and the Royal and Ancient in turn held the annual contest until 1892 when the Honourable Company of Golfers moved down the East Lothian coast from Musselburgh to

Willie Park Snr wears 'the Belt' after winning the first ever British Open in 1860.

Muirfield. It was at Muirfield that the tournament was extended to its present format of 72 holes. Two years later it was played in England for the first time – at Royal St George's – with a record entry of 94 contestants. The Open had arrived.

Traditionally played on links courses, the Open offers an extraordinary challenge. Links courses compel a variety of different shots: the bump-and-run into the green; the controlled hit of the ball into, across or with the wind; and the clean strike off sloping lies. They call for imaginative play and produce great champions – one look at the list of Open winners proves that.

Only 14 courses have been used for the Open. By far the most famous is St Andrews, the home of golf. The course has been played on for over 400 years. It has never been formally designed, but has gently evolved over the years. Many of its hundred bunkers were originally created either as wind shelters for sheep, or by people digging for shells.

Bobby Jones was unimpressed by his first visit in 1921. In the third round of the Open, after triple-bogeying the par-3 11th while already many shots over par, he tore up his scorecard in exasperation. However, he grew to love the course. As he said: 'The more I studied the Old Course, the more I loved it, and the more I loved it, the more I studied it. So that I came to feel that it was for me the most favourable meeting ground possible for an important contest. I felt that my knowledge of the course enabled me to play it with patience and restraint until she might exact her toll from my adversary, who might treat her with less respect and understanding.' The townsfolk of St Andrews loved him in return and called the 10th hole of the Old Course after him.

Every great golfer has aspired to win the open. Many of the greatest have gone on to dominate it, from Vardon, Braid, Taylor and Jones, to Hagen, Locke, Thompson, Palmer, Player, Nicklaus, Trevino, Watson, Ballesteros and Faldo.

Few have managed to monopolize it quite like the father and son combination of Old Tom Morris and Young Tom Morris, the oldest and youngest winners.

Old Tom, the father of the game, won the Belt four times and was also runner-up four times – on two of those occasions he was beaten by his son. Old Tom is not merely respected, he is revered, and in his home town of St Andrews the last hole is named after him.

But it is his son who is considered the first golfing immortal, winning his

Bobby Jones (right) chats to clubmaker Ben Sayers
at St Andrews in 1921.

first Open at the remarkable age of 17, and going on to win next three in succession. There can be little doubt that his mastery of the game would have been unrivalled for years to come had tragedy not intervened. Golf meant nothing to the brilliant young player when it came to his love for his bride. When she died prematurely in 1875, he was overwhelmed. A few months later, Tom Morris Jnr died of a broken heart at the age of 24.

His death robbed the game of an immense talent. In winning his third Open he completed the 578-yard par-5 first hole at Prestwick in three shots – and that with hickory-shafted clubs and the old gutta-percha ball.

He was the first man to achieve a hole-in-one in Open history, when he sank his tee shot at Prestwick's 145-yard eighth in 1868.

But the untimely removal of the great young player did nothing to weaken Scottish dominance of the tournament. Both Jamie Anderson and Bob Ferguson won the trophy three years in succession (although, unlike their predecessor with the Belt, they were not allowed to keep the Cup.)

Then, from the 1890s through to World War I, three English professionals, J.H. Taylor, Harry Vardon and James Braid, became almost impossible to beat, winning 16 Opens between them.

Braid, the first man to win five Opens, was said to hit the ball with 'divine fury' but possessed an extremely equable temperament; Vardon won the tournament a record six times and was responsible for popularizing the now modern overlapping grip – the Vardon V – that was invented by John

VARDON. BRAID. FERNIE. TAYLOR.

FAR LEFT: The Great Triumvirate of Vardon, Braid and Taylor.
LEFT: The Vardon V.
ABOVE: An oil painting of Young Tom Morris' last game.

Laidlay; and Taylor, also a five-times winner, was renowned for his matchless ability to combat agonizingly windy links conditions with his unerring low-trajectory driving and iron play.

The Great Triumvirate were responsible for the first golfing boom. Large numbers of new courses were built, often under their supervision, to cater for the demand prompted by their popularity.

As a columnist wrote in the London *Daily Mail* in 1913: 'One of the new movements of the immediate future for the physical and mental good of the people at large will take the form of municipal golf, that is, golf courses provided by the municipalities in convenient places on which the public may play free of charge or by payment of only the most nominal fee.

'It would be a safe prophecy that in ten years from now every township in our country with a population of fifty thousand or more will have its public links; if I had to express a private belief in the matter, I should reduce the figures of population and the period. The aldermen and councillors have been brought to see the advantages and even the necessity of coming into this movement, and the people in busy places in England are beginning to demand their public golf.'

It was J.H. Taylor who did much to help raise the profile of the golf professional as the doyen of golfing correspondents, turning 'a feckless

Bobby Jones receives a hero's welcome in New York after winning the 1926 Open.

company into a self-respecting and respected body of men'.

In the 1920s, the Open became truly international with the successful invasion of great American players such as Walter Hagen, Bobby Jones and Gene Sarazen. Hagen, known to all as 'The Haig', did as much as anyone to glamorize the Open. His stylish play, flamboyant dress sense and general air of composure that was almost contemptuous (and which, incidently, hid nerves of steel) made the man and the game itself front-page news. The public adored him, and vast armies flocked to watch him play.

He was generous too. After his 1928 win he gave the whole of his £100 first prize to his caddie. Hagen was an irrepressible showman with a fine sense of occasion. Witness the 1926 Open at Lytham where he needed an eagle two at the last to tie with Bobby Jones. He flamboyantly ordered the flagstick to be removed to make it easier to hole his 150-yard approach shot. He didn't quite make it, but he wasn't far away.

He had bravado too. In the 1929 Open at Muirfield he was seen carousing the night before the final round. Reminded that the leader, Leo Diegel, was already in bed, Hagen quipped: 'Yeah, but he ain't sleeping.' Hagen won the next day with Diegel trailing in third.

Bobby Jones might have been the most successful golfer ever if he had

Henry Cotton chipping on to the sixth green during his victorious last round at St George's in 1934.

not retired at only 28. No serious follower of the game would argue that he would not have won more than three Open titles, and in 1930 Jones achieved immortality when he won the Grand Slam – or Impregnable Quadrilateral as he called it – of the British Open, US Open, British Amateur and US Amateur, a feat never likely to be equalled.

He remained an amateur for all of his playing career – what untold riches he would have won if playing today – and possessed a smooth, flowing swing, was the purest striker of a ball and had an unwavering touch around the green. His talents were not confined to the golf course for he obtained first-class degrees in Law, English Literature and Mechanical Engineering at three separate universities.

Gene Sarazen was another hugely popular visitor, appearing first in the 1923 Open at Troon, where in stormy weather he scored 75 and 85 in the qualifying rounds. His ambition was undimmed, and he told the *Times* correspondent Bernard Darwin: 'I'll be back, even if I have to swim across.'

In 1928 at Royal St George's he was in contention until his caddie, Skip Daniels, told him to attack and try to clear the stream that runs across the par-5 14th. Sarazen failed, and Daniels, full of remorse, promised Sarazen that he would win him an Open before he died. Sure enough, at Prince's four years later, Daniels caddied Sarazen to victory. Daniels, his promise fulfilled, died three months later.

It was Henry Cotton, regarded by many as the father of the modern game in Britain, who broke the ten-year winning streak of the Americans when he emerged victorious in 1934 at Royal St George's. He played magnificent golf with a first two rounds of 67 and 65 – the famous Dunlop 65 ball was named after this second round – to forge a commanding halfway lead. Beset by illness and nerves, he struggled with a final round of 79 but still managed to hold on and win.

A player of rare intensity, Cotton won the Claret Jug twice more – in 1937 at Carnoustie, when he beat the elements and the field with a final round of 71 in a downpour, and finally in 1948 at Muirfield, where he claimed inspiration for his near-perfect second-round 66 from the appearance of George VI as an interested spectator.

The post-war years up to 1960 were dominated by two Commonwealth golfers, Peter Thomson of Australia and the South African, Bobby Locke. Thomson's experience was extraordinary – for while he went on to win the trophy five times, he never won any other Major. He had a special aptitude for links golf and was a master at the bump-and-run shot.

Henry Cotton (left) and Peter Thomson have won eight Opens between them.

Locke won four times. Although a short hitter, he manufactured a hook to add length to his drives and was famed for his crisp putting stroke.

The next to dominate were the Big Three of the modern era, Arnold Palmer, Jack Nicklaus and Gary Player. Palmer was the first golfing great of the television age, bringing a new excitement to the game, which had come to be regarded as rather staid in the post-war years. His swing with its familiar loop at the end of the follow-through was not for the purists; but it carried enormous power. And his amazing ability to conjure birdies from nothing made him a hit with golf fans, old and new.

Three-times winner (and seven-times runner-up) Jack Nicklaus, the greatest golfer of all time, followed in Palmer's wake.

The inspirational Seve Ballesteros at Lytham in 1979.

He maintained that he could never call himself a true champion until he had mastered the special bump-and-run golf of the Open. When he finally won at Muirfield in 1966 after many close attempts, the occasion was almost too much for him. Presented with the Claret Jug, he turned to the crowd and said: 'Excuse me. Do you mind if I just enjoy this moment?' That years later he named the first course he designed Muirfield Village underlines the importance he attached to that first win.

The magnificent Gary Player is the only man to match the feats of the Great Triumvirate of Braid, Taylor and Vardon by winning the Open in three different decades. No one worked harder at his game or fitness. Nor was anyone as competitive. He still regards his four wood to two feet at the long par-5 14th to set up an eagle, played in the heat of battle against Nicklaus at Carnoustie, as the greatest shot of his life.

The continuing esteem in which the British Open is held in the modern game owes a great deal to Nicklaus, Player and Palmer.

In recent memory Tom Watson and Seve Ballesteros stand out. Watson has won the Open a brilliant five times and is still chasing Vardon's seemingly unassailable record of six titles.

Ballesteros — occasionally wild, always inspirational — was the undisputed master of the miracle recovery shot. In winning his first Open at Royal Lytham in 1979, he saw little of the fairways all week but managed to conjure an effective escape each time. The best was left to the 16th on the final round. A truly massive sliced drive found its way into one of the spectator car parks. He was given a free drop from where he hit a perfect iron to 20 feet, holed the putt nonchalantly for a birdie and took an unassailable three-stroke lead. This is the man who has won a hole by hitting a drive into the middle of a lake — only for the shot to bounce off the hull of an upturned boat and ricochet back on to the fairway. American pros called him 'The Car Park Champion' but the public loved him for it.

The man to beat these days is Nick Faldo, for whom dedicated professionalism, rather than flamboyance, is the key to the game. In 1987 he reeled off 18 straight pars in the final round at Muirfield to pip Paul Azinger. Five years later at the same course, he showed true champion qualities after losing a four-shot lead by making birdies on two of the last four holes when all had seemed lost.

There have been many momentous shots in the Open, probably none more so than Bobby Jones's on the 17th at Royal Lytham in 1926. After a wayward tee-shot, Jones was faced with an unpromising lie in a bunker. Although there was nothing but scrub and bunkers between him and the green, he had to attack to maintain his challenge for the Open. He got out his mashie (four iron), hit it perfectly – he had to – and the ball sailed 175 yards on to the green and inside that of his main rival, Al Watrous. Watrous is supposed to have said: 'There goes a hundred thousand bucks' as he recognized Jones's magnificent escape. Deflated, he promptly three-putted, allowing Jones to par this and the last hole to gain the trophy. A plaque has been placed at the spot to commemorate the shot.

Arnold Palmer is the only other player to earn a plaque. When winning at Birkdale in 1961 in gale-force conditions, he hit a drive at the 15th (now 16th) into the rough and under a small bush. For most the lie would have been impossible and the ball would have been shifted merely feet. Not for Palmer. Wrapping his enormous hands round a six iron, and with massive strength, he carved the ball on to the green.

For pure theatre nothing could match the 1977 'Duel in the Sun' between Jack Nicklaus and Tom Watson. With a barrage of birdies on the third and fourth rounds, both moved out of sight of the chasing pack. The tournament was beginning to resemble matchplay as the two punched and counter-punched like prizefighters. As Watson said to Nicklaus on the 14th: 'Jack, this is what it's all about.' On the 15th Watson drew level by holing a 60ft putt and pulled ahead with a birdie on the 17th. On the 18th Watson hit his seven-iron approach to less than three feet from the hole. All seemed lost for Nicklaus as he hacked his second from gorse on to the fringe of the

The duel in the sun: Nicklaus and Watson took golf to a new level of excellence in 1977.

FAR LEFT: Doug Sanders will never forget his miss in 1970.
LEFT: Lee Trevino triumphant in 1972.

green. However, he dramatically holed his long putt for a birdie and Watson had now to hole his putt to win. He did and the most dramatic championship was his.

The Open has had its fair share of holes-in-one. None were more romantic than 71-year-old Gene Sarazen's in the 1973 Open at Troon. Returning to Britain 50 years after his first Open attempt on the same course, he hit his five-iron approach into the cup at the 126-yard Postage Stamp eighth. A delighted Sarazen said: 'I want to see that shot on the screen and want to take a copy of that film up to Heaven with me to show Hagen and Jones because they won't believe me.' It was his first hole-in-one in 40 years.

Jamie Anderson's ace at Prestwick's 17th in 1878 helped him win the tournament by a single shot. Most credit should perhaps go to R. Johnston's

hole-in-one at Muirfield's 14th in 1906. He played the whole of the tournament with just one club. It had an adjustable head.

'Champagne Tony' Lema caused a sensation when he won the Open at St Andrews in 1964, having not previously seen the course and arriving too late for a practice round. The Argentinian, Robert de Vincenzo, won in 1967 at the age of 44 on his 19th appearance.

Naturally there have been moments of great sadness and tales of what might have been. Perhaps the greatest miss was perpetrated by Doug Sanders in 1970. He had a short but downhill left-to-right putt for victory on the last hole at St Andrews. After agonizing over it for ages he stubbed it wide and finished level with Jack Nicklaus. He lost the play-off the following day. Asked recently if he often thinks about the dreaded miss, he responded: 'Not really. Some days I can go five minutes without thinking about it.'

For carelessness no one could match Hale Irwin in the third round at Birkdale in 1983. He air-shot a one-inch tap-in and lost to the eventual winner, Tom Watson, by one stroke.

Harry Bradshaw can claim to be the unluckiest golfer in the history of the Open. In an incident which could never be repeated on the perfectly maintained courses of the modern game, Bradshaw saw his second-round drive at the fifth at St George's in 1949 fly off into the light rough. On reaching his ball, he found that it was lying, of all things, in the bottom of a broken beer bottle. After consulting with a rules official, he decided to play it as it lay, smashed it free with his sand wedge and consequently took a double-bogey six. It led to a tie with Bobby Locke, who won the play-off.

In 1972 Tony Jacklin was another to suffer. On the penultimate hole at Muirfield he was tied with Lee Trevino, but was firmly in control. He was in the middle of the green in three while Trevino was in the greenside rough in four. As Trevino later recalled: 'I was very angry. I just reached over, grabbed a club, chipped and the ball went into the hole. I was careless about it. All I was trying to do was get the damn thing on the green, two-putt, play the next hole and then jump in my car and go.'

Jacklin was so stunned that he three-putted for a six from just 25ft and bogeyed the last to gift the Open to Trevino by two strokes.

Past champions gathered at St Andrews in 1905. Among them are J.H. Taylor (far left), Old Tom Morris (centre with stick), James Braid (centre with arms folded) and Harry Vardon (seated front right).

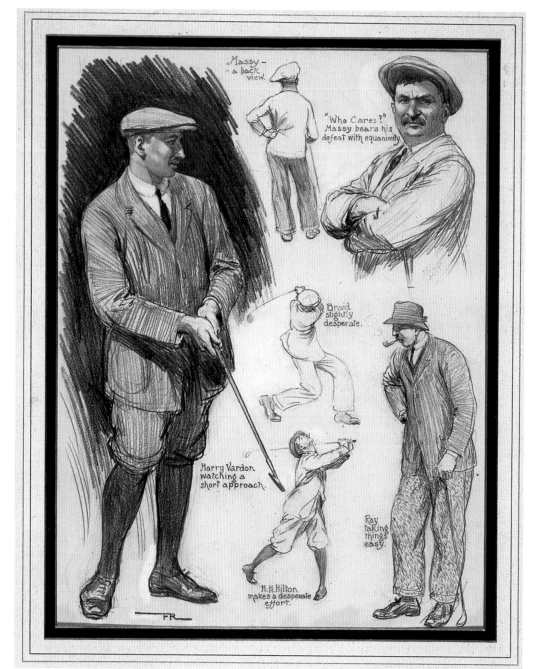

A pencil drawing by
Frank Reynolds RA,
'Harry Vardon,
Open Champion
for the fifth time at
Sandwich, 1911'.

Reynolds' sketch of the *News of the World* tournament at Sunningdale in 1903.

US OPEN

In the cold February of 1949 the brilliant golfer Ben Hogan was driving home with his wife when their car was crushed in a horrific head-on collision with a bus.

Had the devoted Hogan not flung himself sideways to protect his wife from the impact, he would have been crushed by the steering column, which ripped through the dashboard into the driver's seat.

As it was, he broke his pelvis, collarbone, ankle and ribs. Once the immediate fears for his life were allayed, even his own doctors believed he would never walk again, and told him that he was facing life in a wheelchair.

Less than 18 months later he managed to force his battered frame to the first tee at Merion to take part in the 1950 US Open.

In those days both the third and fourth rounds of the competition were

**Ben Hogan splashes out of the bunker
at Merion in 1950.**

The St Andrews club in Yonkers – the first American golf course.

played together on the gruelling final day. Hogan, still in the running after his early rounds, had no option but to endure a full 36 holes of golf for the first time since the crash that nearly killed him.

Limping and obviously in pain, he manfully covered the first 27 holes, but as he started the final nine, he was seized by cramp in his left leg. With five holes remaining he was in agony and as he passed the clubhouse on his way to the 14th tee he came close to quitting as, one shot behind, the pain became near unbearable.

Hogan forced himself on. He birdied the 224-yard par-3 17th; then he made par at the last with a perfect one-iron approach, to tie with Lloyd Mangrum and George Fazio.

The next day took his exhausted body back out on to the course to win the 18-hole play-off with a round of 69.

The display was a tribute to the heroism and the skill of an already legendary golfer. It was also a sign of the extraordinary allure of the US Open.

The formation of the Open dates back almost to the birth of golf in the United States. The first North American golf club was the St Andrews Club, founded in Yonkers in 1888 by John Reid and his friends Henry Tallmadge, John Upham and Kingman Putnam.

The game was booming. Within seven years there were 40 courses in the United States, and the first 18-hole course had been built in Wheaton, Illinois, for the Chicago Golf Club. Pioneer of that course was one Charles Blair MacDonald, the man whose inability to admit defeat was to lead to the founding of one of the world's great tournaments.

The bullying MacDonald tried to force his way to victory in the inaugural US Amateur title, forcing the annulment of two contests in which he had been beaten.

His supporters and opponents quickly divided the growing mass of the country's golfers and leading figures in the game realized that the formation of an official body was essential.

Three days before Christmas in 1894, Henry Tallmadge invited representives from five leading golf clubs to meet in New York.

The attendance list was:

Samuel Parrish and General Thomas Barber: Shinnecock Hills GC

Laurence Curtis and Samuel Sears: Brookline Country Club

Charles Blair MacDonald and J. Arthur Ryerson: Chicago GC

John Reid and Henry Tallmadge: St Andrews GC

Theodore Havemeyer and Winthrop Rutherford: Newport GC

That night, over dinner at the Calumet Club, the Amateur Golf Association of the United States, forerunner of USGA, was founded.

The objective was to 'promote the interest of the game of golf, to conduct the Amateur and Open championships of the United States and to establish a code of rules for the game of golf.'

Charles Blair MacDonald.

The following year on 4 October, the first US Open was contested by 10 professionals and one amateur over the nine-hole Newport Golf Club. Horace Rawlins won with a 36-hole aggregate of 162, beating Willie Dunn by two strokes. The premier golfing tournament in the United States had begun... but it was to be another 16 years before it was won by a native-born American.

Horace Rawlins won the inaugural US Open championship.

For the first 15 years the tournament was monopolized by Scottish émigrés. Willie Anderson won four times in this period and is still the only golfer to have won three consecutive titles (1903–5). Not far behind were the Smith brothers from Carnoustie – Alexander, William and MacDonald.

Alexander Smith was known as one of the fastest putters in the game. His motto was 'miss 'em quick'. He was also the first player to break 300 when he carded 73-74-73-75 for a four-round aggregate of 295 in 1906.

And it was in 1910 that Alexander Smith, winning the US Open for the second time, managed it in astonishing style in one of the most extraordinary contests ever – one which would have had today's media commentators thrashing around in a feeding frenzy of superlatives.

After four hard-fought rounds Alexander went into a three-way play off and won. The two men he defeated, in the kind of shoot-out that sponsors today can only dream about, included his own brother, MacDonald.

The only man to interrupt the Scottish stranglehold had been the English golfing great Harry Vardon, in 1900. He had been invited across by the A.G. Spalding ball manufacturing company to take part in a series of exhibition matches to promote their new 'guttie' ball, the Vardon Flyer. A tour that did much to popularize the game of golf was helped immeasurably when Harry happened to win the Open while he was there.

The USGA traditionally chooses some of the world's most famous old courses as venues for the Open. They trip off the awed devotee's tongue like a mantra: courses that can only be dreamed about for most players – Inverness, Medinah, Pebble Beach, Baltusrol, Oakmont, Oakland Hills, Winged Foot.

And Shinnecock Hills and the Country Club at Brookline, both founding fathers of the American game, are still used as Open courses.

The transformation in the oldest courses provides a fascinating insight into just how much the game has changed over the past century. In 1896 at Shinnecock Hills, when Jim Foulis won with rounds of 78 and 74, the course played to a length of just 4,423 yards. In 1995, when Corey Pavin won with a four-round aggregate averaging 70, it played to a length of 6,697 yards.

With the obvious exception of Pebble Beach, US Open courses are inland and vastly different from the British links courses, and wind is rarely a factor. They are situated in either parkland or woodland and are characterized by

Alexander Smith (left) beat his brother, MacDonald, in a play-off in 1910.

thin fairways and a savagely penal rough, especially around the fringes of the greens.

Seve Ballesteros believes that the US Open is 80 per cent a test of driving (which would certainly explain his marked lack of success in the tournament). But Seve is by no means the only player to protest that the rough is more vicious than anywhere else in the world; a ball straying as little as six inches off the fairway or the off green can result in the unhappy player having no shot.

Greens are prepared lightning fast, none quicker than those at Oakmont. The 1947 Open winner Lew Worsham cracked: 'These greens are so slick that nobody I know uses any kind of putter except a blade. If you use a mallet-head – well that's like getting a back-rub with a sledge-hammer.'

Imagine this: even ball markers have been known to slide away from the spot on the glassy, polished surface.

Even some of the biggest names around have argued that some of the great Open courses have been so finely tuned that they have been almost unfair, and intimate that this type of course doesn't really produce a true winner. But if that were the case why has the US Open been won so often by the greatest names in golf?

It does, however, throw up the occasional surprise winner. For instance, Andy North won the title twice yet managed to take only one other tournament in his entire career.

After the auspicious founding of the contest in 1894, America had to wait until 1911 for its first native-born winner when John McDermott, an ex-caddie from Philadelphia, won after a play-off.

For the next three out of four years the amateur triumvirate of Francis Ouimet, 'Chick' Evans and Walter J. Travis held sway. The 20-year-old Ouimet's victory in 1913 caught the public imagination most. Against all odds he managed to play the last six holes at a soggy Brookline course in two under par to level with Britons Harry Vardon and Ted Ray. In the play-off he was given little chance, but with the help of his 10-year-old caddie Eddie Lowery he won, scoring 72 to Vardon's 77 and Ray's 78. The home crowds were thrilled and a golfing boom had begun.

The period between World War I and the beginning of the 1930s is often considered as a Golden Age in American golf. Everyone from the humble bank clerk to the society girl was keen to have a go. Credit for its sudden

Walter Hagen with the Open trophy in 1914.

popularity can be given to the three golfing superstars of the age, Walter Hagen, Gene Sarazen and Bobby Jones. All brought style, grace and glamour to the game.

Hagen was the first to dominate, winning in 1914 with a record-equalling aggregate of 290. He went a long way to raising the standing of his fellow tournament professionals.

Most tournament pros were ex-caddies and regarded as an underclass by the mainly middle-class golfing community. To play golf as a gentleman, you had to be an amateur. Caddies were not allowed to mix with the great and the good in the clubhouse and the prevailing attitude was amply illustrated when the Prince of Wales invited Hagen into the clubhouse after a round. Officials told the Prince that professionals were not welcome. The Prince replied that if Hagen were not allowed in, he, the Prince, would leave immediately. The club yielded.

Even in America professionals were treated very much as an underclass and it was only in the 1920 Open at Inverness that they were allowed to avail themselves of the clubhouse facilities such as the locker room, bars, dining rooms and toilets. With typical good grace, Hagen presented a grandfather clock to the club on behalf of the grateful pros.

The inscription reads:

God measures men by what they are
Not what in wealth possess.
This vibrant message chimes afar,
The voice of Inverness.

Gene Sarazen rose to meteoric fame in 1922, when he beat off the challenges of Walter Hagen, Jock Hutchison and James Barnes to win the Open at his first attempt. 'Who on Earth is Sarazen?' people were heard to cry after his flawless last round of 68. They soon knew, as a couple of months later he won the PGA of America as well. Ten years later, with the help of his new invention, the sand wedge, he won the Open again, this time with a record-breaking last round of 66.

The brilliant Bobby Jones won the Open four times in the space of eight years. His vast dominance was illustrated in 1929 at Winged Foot. Although struggling to two sevens in the last round he managed to tie first with Al Espinosa. In the 36-hole play-off the next day he beat Espinosa by 23 strokes.

Gene Sarazen came from nowhere to win in 1922.

After World War II the man to beat was the great Ben Hogan. He won four Open titles from 1948 to 1953 and, despite his courageous performance in 1950, claimed that the greatest of them all was a year later with 'in the circumstances the greatest round I have ever played' by scoring a last-round 67 over the 'monster' Oakland Hills course to catch up five strokes on Bobby Locke and win the title. The course had been especially toughened up by the golf architect Robert Trent Jones and was seen by many as unplayable.

The only other man to equal the four Open titles of Hogan and Jones is Jack Nicklaus. He had been a pro for only three months when he beat Arnold Palmer in a play-off to win the title in 1962. In doing so he also became the first man since Jones to hold the US Amateur and Open titles at the same time. He won again in 1965 after a posting a last-round record of 65 and showed the true style

Jack Nicklaus and Arnold Palmer before their play-off in 1962.

of a champion in 1972 at Pebble Beach when his one-iron tee shot hit the pin at the treacherous long par-3 17th. He tapped in for a birdie and could enjoy the long walk to the 18th knowing that his lead was unassailable.

Tom Watson denied Jack Nicklaus a record-breaking fifth Open title in 1982 with one of the most audacious shots in Open history. With Nicklaus safe in the clubhouse, Watson was level but had yet to play two of the hardest holes in golf, the 17th and 18th at Pebble Beach. On the long par-3, he hit his tee shot just off the green into the tight, tangling rough – a bogey looked on the cards. Undaunted he chipped in for a birdie 2 and, for good measure, birdied the next hole to win by an improbable two shots. As Nicklaus said

later: 'If Tom played another thousand shots from the edge of the 17th, I don't think he would hole one.'

Since Nicklaus, no one has yet managed to make this contest his own, although Hale Irwin won the title three times and Curtis Strange won in successive years.

There have been so many magic moments that it is difficult to choose which to recount.

The little-known Ed Furgol produced something special to win the title at Baltusrol in 1954. On the last hole, a par-5, he carved his drive deep into the woods. When he got to his ball, he found no clear route back to the fairway; however, turning to his left he could see a small gap leading to the fairway on Baltusrol's other course, the Upper. After consulting officials and finding that this other course was still in bounds, he punched an eight iron on to this fairway, and using the same club struck his ball over trees to within a few feet of the flag. He holed the putt for a birdie 4 and victory.

Corey Pavin produced the shot of his career to win the 1995 Open at Shinnecock Hills. On the last hole, after hitting a very short drive, he was faced with a blind second shot, of well over 200 yards, over a hill. Hitting a perfect four wood, he raced up to the top of the hill to see where his ball had landed. It was a mere four feet from the flag and the Open was his by two shots.

In 1970 Tony Jacklin succeeded at Hazeltine by a huge margin of seven

**Corey Pavin salutes his amazing second shot at Shinnecock
Hills' 18th in 1995.**

shots to become the first Briton to win the Open in 50 years. He was also
only the fifth man to hold the US and British Opens simultaneously.

Seven years later, Hubert Green played with nerves of steel to take the
title. A woman rang the FBI to say that three men planned to kill Green
as he played the 15th. He was given the news, but insisted on playing.
Unsurprisingly, he hooked his tee shot at the 15th but recovered
to play flawless golf over the remaining closing holes and won by
one stroke.

Just as the Open has been won with brilliant golf, so has it been lost by
bad golf – often by the great players. In 1920 Harry Vardon, in the autumn
of his career and looking for a second Open title, squandered a five-stroke
lead in stormy weather over the last seven holes to lose to his compatriot
Ted Ray. Likewise in 1966, Arnie Palmer paid the price for being too
aggressive with his driving and almost unbelievably lost a seven-stroke lead

in eight holes to Billy Casper.

Sam Snead was just as generous in 1939 when, needing a par-5 at the last
to win, he carded an eight and eventually finished fifth.

Some players have been victim to outrageous ill fortune. Byron Nelson
was seemingly on his way to winning the Open until his caddie accidentally
kicked his ball into the crowd, thereby incurring a one-shot penalty. T.C.
Chen was equally unlucky. While playing the fifth hole at Oakland Hills in
1985, he hit the ball twice with his chip shot – the first time on impact and
the second time during his follow-through. It counted as two shots and he
lost to the eventual winner, Andy North, by just one shot.

Lloyd Mangrum, however, could only blame himself. On the 16th in a play-
off with Ben Hogan and George Fazio in the 1950 Open at Merion, he noticed
a bug was lying on his ball. He instinctively blew it away instead of playing
the ball as it lay, and was penalized two shots. That's golf.

**Great winners of the US Open: from left, Bobby Jones in 1923, 1926, 1929 and
1930; Ted Ray in 1920; Chick Evans in 1916; and Harry Vardon in 1900.**

US MASTERS

This is the tournament and the course that everybody who has ever played a round of golf dreams of playing. It is the epitome of elegance; perfectly groomed, utterly elitist and stunningly beautiful.

It is also the competition that has been run by one of the most self-important and patronizing groups of people ever to walk this Earth, and whose handling of their powers is less use than abuse.

They say that the easiest way for an outsider to become a member of the Augusta National golf club is to win the Masters. When Tiger Woods stormed to victory in 1997, he became only the third black member (the first had been allowed in just six years before). Until 20 years ago every member was white and every caddie was black.

Even then Masters winners aren't allowed to play at the course out of competition during the rest of the year. Tom Watson tried and they wouldn't let him. Bernhard Langer was almost stripped of membership when he complained about the stupidity of the ruling.

What is certain is that, thrilling, exacting and enviable though it is, the way the Masters is run today is far removed from the ideals of the genius who invented it – the immortal Bobby Jones.

Jones was the man who, in 1930, achieved the Grand Slam. In a single glorious, improbable year he won the British Open, the US Open and both the British and American amateur championships. Then he promptly quit competitive sport and set about building a course where he and his friends might play some winter golf. It wasn't, he said, a hard decision to make. 'My wife and children came first, then my profession [he was a lawyer]. Finally, and never in a life by itself, came golf.'

With the help of his close friend, the New York stockbroker Clifford Roberts, he discovered the ideal site – Fruitlands, a 365-acre old fruit nursery

A hand painted first day cover to commerate the opening of the Augusta National Golf Club.

in the small town of Augusta in Jones's home state of Georgia.

Roberts was a dour and autocratic figure, but regarded as the number one Wonderboy of Wall Street. The two men arranged to buy the site at a Depression price, and then enlisted the help of the golf architect Alister Mackenzie to create a golfing masterpiece. The result was the Augusta National, the best-known course in golf.

The course was completed as early as 1933 and the following year Jones invited his old golfing adversaries to compete in the Augusta National Invitation Tournament. Horton Smith won with a score of 284. The next year Craig Wood seemed to have the tournament in the bag after finishing on 282 for a lead of three shots. Gene Sarazen was the only one who could catch him. Playing the par-5 15th he hit a four wood 235 yards over the lake, on to the green and straight into the hole for an albatross 2. He finished level with Wood and won the play-off the next day by five shots.

Sarazen's amazing stroke was called 'the shot heard around the world' and instantly made the tournament famous. Soon the public and press alike were referring to the tournament as 'The Masters', and a fourth major championship had been born.

There is no doubt that Augusta and the Masters tournament are unique. 'I love this course,' says Seve Ballesteros. 'I feel I am coming home here.

That is why I'm happy. I treat it with respect, like an older person. And sometimes I take a few advantages. But there is always respect.'

Greg Norman, recalling his first invitation, said: 'I'll never forget it. This was what golf was meant to be: pure golf. This was the purest form of tournament.'

It was seeing the 1971 Masters on TV that inspired Nick Faldo to take up golf. The next day he signed up for his first lesson at his home club in Welwyn Garden City.

You play by invitation only – and as a result, it is not always the best field that takes part. In 1992, for example, Tom Kite was not invited despite being the world's leading money winner; two months later he won the US Open. No explanation was ever given for his omission. Suspiciously high numbers of leading European and Commonwealth golfers seem to be left out despite being in the world's top 50 rankings.

So why is the Masters still considered so special? First and foremost, this

Bobby Jones driving at the first hole in 1934 when the course was almost bare.

course is a one-off. The fairways are improbably wide. There is no rough. The greens are immense and undulating.

But, no, that doesn't make everything easy. For one thing, something you don't really notice as you watch on television is that the course is extremely hilly. More importantly, it is entirely strategic. This is like golf and chess rolled into one. As Bobby Jones once explained: 'This can be a very easy course or a very tough one. There isn't a hole out there that can't be birdied if you just think. But there isn't one that can't be double-bogeyed if you stop thinking.'

It is imperative that approach shots are hit to the right areas of the green, i.e. below the hole. Above the hole, even by just a few feet, can mean three or four putts. Some putts are impossible – Tom Watson, when he won the Masters in 1981, putted clear off the green at the ninth during his final round.

Although the television cameras can't truly capture the vagaries of the course, you had better get used to seeing it that way, because that is about as close to the Masters as you will ever get.

Originally, spectator tickets were issued only to friends and family of the membership, and they are passed down from generation to generation as heirlooms. General sale to the ordinary public was stopped in 1967, and a waiting list was drawn up. Even that was closed in 1978. Outsiders can buy a ticket to watch only on a practice day.

You might think that the restricted guest list would guarantee impeccable behaviour from the spectators. In fact the crowds can be partisan, ill-mannered and vociferous in their abuse.

Many a Masters has hinged on the events on the 11th, 12th and 13th holes, known collectively as Amen Corner. Why is it called Amen Corner? Television commentator Dave Marr suggests: 'If you get round it in par, you believe a little bit more in God.'

It starts with a long par-4, with a small pond eating into the left of the

Today Augusta is perhaps the most luscious course in the world.

ABOVE: The treacherous par three 12th.

BELOW: The coveted Green Jacket worn by Jack Nicklaus (left) in 1986 and Tiger Woods (right) in 1997.

green. (This hole must be a particular favourite of Nick Faldo. Twice here a play-off has been decided in his favour.)

The short 155-yard 12th has been described by Jack Nicklaus as 'the most demanding tournament hole in world golf'. (In 1980 Tom Weiskopf took 13 shots, hitting his ball into the water five times.) The slender green, sandwiched between Rae's Creek at the front and bunkers and a swale at the back, presents a daunting target, especially as the hole is prey to capricious winds. Nicklaus has taken anything between a nine iron and four iron.

The 13th is a severe right-angle dog-leg par-5 with Rae's Creek snaking in front of the green to trap an errant second shot. Byron Nelson has a particular fondness for Amen Corner. When winning in 1937 he carded a birdie two at the 12th and an eagle three at the 13th, while his closest rival, Ralph Guldhal, hit a five and six respectively. Five years later Nelson birdied

all three Amen Corner holes to help him tie with Ben Hogan.

Augusta is also extremely beautiful – a horticultural as well as a golfing masterpiece. Bobby Jones hired the grandson of the original owner of the old nursery, a Baron Berckmans of Belgium, to plant the sides of each fairway with azalea, dogwood, yellow jasmine, magnolia and more. Most are in bloom during the Masters tournament in April providing a riot of colour for the television cameras.

And like the British Open, the Masters

Gary Player captured his third Green Jacket in 1978 after a blistering final round of 64.

winners' roll is the envy of the golfing world. In its first 25 years all the great pre-war and post-war American professionals rose to victory, with Jimmy Demaret and Sam Snead standing out as the first three-time winners. From 1958 to 1966 the tournament was effectively annexed by Arnold Palmer and Jack Nicklaus. Palmer was the first to win the Green Jacket four times and, when he strode away with the title in 1964 by six shots, no one would have believed then that this would be his last major. Nicklaus did even better, winning six times.

In 1965 he smashed the record four-round aggregate with rounds of 67-71-64-69 for a total of 271 to win by nine shots.

Gary Player can claim longevity as a winner, taking his first Masters in 1961 and his third and final one 17 years later in 1978. Partnering him on that blistering last round of 64 was an awe-inspired Seve Ballesteros, who became the youngest-ever winner in 1980 when he destroyed the field, at one stage leading the final round 10 shots clear.

Ballesteros's triumph again in 1983 heralded a new era in Masters golf,

namely domination by the Europeans. From 1985, when Bernhard Langer won the first of his two Green Jackets, to the present day eight of the last 12 Masters have been won by a European. Most notable among these is Nick Faldo, who has now won three times and, like Nicklaus, is the only man to defend his title successfully.

The winners' list is magnificent, the course is magnificent, so what is it that leads many commentators to accuse the Masters of being the most insular contest in the game? Or, as the sportswriter Ian Wooldridge described it, 'an institution so smugly convinced of its place in God's First Eleven, so unutterably contemptuous of ordinary people, so unjustifiably snobbish about its brief traditions...'

Its direction altered dramatically when Bobby Jones first became ill. He developed a wasting disease that affects the spine, played his last game of golf in 1948 and died in pain in 1971. At his death a close friend commented: 'As a young man he was able to stand up to just about the best that life can offer, which is not easy, and later he stood with equal grace to just about the worst.'

As Jones's illness worsened, his early partner Clifford Roberts seized the reins and, with an eye focused foremost on money and glory, ran the Masters with a ruthlessness that appalled his friend. In 1968 he froze Jones out completely and the two men never spoke again.

Roberts strolled out on to a par-3 and shot himself in 1977, but the guidelines he had forged since seizing control linger on unpleasantly today.

Membership is restricted to rich white males; there is one black member, but probably only because officialdom threatened to boycott the tournament if the undeclared racist policy was not abandoned.

Only players liked by the committee play, and only journalists who do not offend the committee can write or commentate from Augusta. One, who described the greens as being so fast that they seemed to have been waxed like a bikini line, was told he would never come again.

Another who described the spectators as a mob was barred for seven years. Any commentator mentioning prize money is banned and CBS, who have the television rights, are forbidden by contract from saying how much they have to pay for the privilege.

There is a special locker room for past champions upstairs from the main locker room – Lee Trevino, who grew up fighting prejudice, hated this elitism and preferred to change in the car park.

But petty regulations aside, the Masters is about fabulous golf and spectacular shots and no performance has been more stunning or involved more wonderful

shots than the game played by Tiger Woods, who tore up all precedents by playing the course almost entirely with driver, putter and wedges.

Still there have been many other great moments – like Larry Mize's 1987 chip into the cup from 30 yards at the second extra play-off hole to defeat the hapless Greg Norman. A year later Sandy Lyle created his own bit of magic by hitting a seven iron out of a fairway bunker to within eight feet of the flag. Golf historian Herbert Warren Wind described it as 'the greatest bunker shot in history'. Sandy holed the birdie putt to win the Masters by a single shot.

Roberto de Vicenzo can claim to be the unluckiest player of all. In 1968 the world watched him make a birdie three on the 17th, but his marker Bob Goalby put him down for a par-4. De Vicenzo failed to notice the error, signed the card, and the wrong score had to stand. Who went on to win by a single stroke? Bob Goalby.

ABOVE: Sandy Lyle hit 'the greatest bunker shot
in history' in 1988.
RIGHT: Larry Mize leapt for joy after chipping in
from 30 yards to win in 1987.

USPGA

This is the one competition that is the absolute property of American golfers. Founded in 1916 as the annual tournament for US professionals, it has never been won by a European.

That curious fact aside, it it true to say that, despite the best intentions, the USPGA championship is now the least regarded of the four majors.

Ironically it is partly the pursuit of popularity that has seen its influence decline, although it is still undoubtedly a dream for any player to win. The competition is the only one of the majors to have undergone radical change, and it has suffered as a result.

The most dramatic alteration came in 1957. Until then the USPGA had been a head-to-head matchplay competition. But the arrival of television and its massive (even then) influence on the finances of any large sporting event brought a change in the rules. TV demanded strokeplay as more suited to its formats – easier to cover, no sudden finishes halfway through, and still full of drama.

So the professionals changed their tournament and now, with the evident popularity of the Ryder Cup and its matchplay formula, they must be ruing the day they did so.

Further, in choosing venues to hold the contest, the USPGA took on the role of pioneer. Whereas the US Open stuck to the same hard core of old courses, the USPGA from the outset looked to spread the gospel of golf to all parts of the country. Very rarely in the matchplay days was the same course used twice. But for some reason the constant selection of new venues gave the contest less rather than more allure.

The formation of the Professional Golfers' Association dates back to 17 January 1916 when 30 professionals, including Walter Hagen, met at the Taplow Club in New York. There were three points to the agenda.

'Long Jim' Barnes won the inaugural PGA title at Siwanoy.

First, to promote the game of golf to a wider audience; second, to instigate a set of regulations for fair or better treatment of tournament professionals, caddies and greenkeepers; third, the arranging of an annual national Professional Golfers' Association tournament.

Rodman Wanamaker, a department store magnate and host for the day, put up a trophy and prize money of $2,150 for the matchplay event. It took place at Siwanoy Country Club in Bronxville where James 'Long Jim' Barnes won, beating Jock Hutchison on the 36th hole.

Walter Hagen was the dominant figure in the early years. He won five PGA titles, and along with his astounding Ryder Cup record, can claim to be the best matchplay golfer of his, or any, generation. He won the title consecutively from 1924 to 1927, and by the time he finally lost in the quarter-final to Leo Diegel in 1928, he had gone 22 matches unbeaten. Not that Diegel, the eventual winner, could get his hands on the trophy, the Rodman Wanamaker Cup – Hagen had inadvertently left it in a taxi and it didn't turn up until several months later.

Gene Sarazen was Hagen's main rival. Sarazen won his first PGA in 1922 at the age of 20. He triumphed again the following year, beating Hagen in what many described as the most exciting match in PGA history and the first to go to extra holes.

The 1940s and early 1950s belonged to

Leo Diegel (left) ended Walter Hagen's run of 22 unbeaten matches.

Jack Nicklaus has won five PGA titles, three British Opens, four US Opens and six Masters.

the triumvirate of Byron Nelson, Ben Hogan and Sam Snead. Byron Nelson won twice, the second occasion in 1945 when he was in a run during which he won 11 tournaments in a row – the hottest-ever streak in golf. Hogan's PGA triumph in 1946 was his first major at the advanced age of 34; then he won another eight in the next seven years. Sam Snead became the only man after Hagen and Sarazen to win the title three times when he beat Walter Burkemo in 1951 by seven and six after beginning the final with an eagle, two birdies and three pars, going five up in the process. He even came third behind Lee Trevino and Jack Nicklaus in 1974, at the age of 63.

Since then, only Jack Nicklaus has won the PGA more than twice; he took five in all to equal Hagen's record, his last victory coming in 1980 at Oak Hill when he thrashed the rest of the field by seven shots.

The most romantic story of the PGA is one of its most recent. In 1991 Nick Price dropped out on the eve of the tournament through injury. Three reserves were offered the chance to replace him but all declined. The fourth reserve, John Daly, drove through the night from Memphis to get to the Crooked Stick course in Indiana. On arrival he borrowed Price's caddie Squeaky, and the rest, as they say, is history. Pummelling the course into submission with his huge drives, Daly put together rounds of 69-67-69-71 to win by a comfortable three shots. With his huge swing, prodigious power and quick, carefree golf – he sipped beer between shots – he became a folk hero. Not since the emergence of Arnie Palmer in the late 1950s had someone so caught the public imagination.

Another deeply popular winner was the likeable, wise-cracking Lee Trevino, who hit the comeback trail when winning at Shoal Creek in 1984. Many had thought he was finished after suffering back trouble and numerous other problems, not least being struck by lightning and suffering a heartbreaking divorce from his wife of 20 years.

And the comeback of Bobby Nichols bears retelling. In 1952, like Ben Hogan three years earlier, he was involved in an awful car accident and was told he would never walk again. Encouraged by letters of support from Hogan, he defied doctors' gloomy predictions to become a successful amateur and then professional golfer. In 1964, after opening with a first-round 64, he held off both Nicklaus and Palmer to win the tournament with a then record aggregate of 271.

The most stunning shot in PGA history belongs to Bob Tway in 1986 at Inverness. Level at the last hole with Greg Norman, he splashed out of the bunker straight into the hole for an unlikely birdie 3 and a tournament win by one stroke. Norman cannot have happy memories of Inverness. Seven years later he lost a play-off there to Paul Azinger when he three-putted from 18 feet at the second extra hole.

There have been a few mishaps too, especially in the days of matchplay. In 1926, Leo Diegel, playing the 19th of the 36-hole final, overhit his approach to the green, the ball resting under the large car belonging to Walter Hagen, who happened to be his opponent. The car was removed and the ball was found nestling in a huge rut. Diegel hacked at it three times but didn't even

move it. He lost five and three.

These things go round, though. Three years later the angels were on the side of Diegel when he played against Johnny Farrell. Twice he stymied Farrell's ball on the green in consecutive holes. Both times the unfortunate Farrell, in trying to hole out, succeeded in knocking in Diegel's ball.

(The now-redundant 'stymie' rule declared: 'If the player's ball knocks the opponent's ball into the hole the opponent shall be deemed to have holed out at his last stroke.')

ABOVE: John Daly surprised everyone by winning in 1991. LEFT: Bob Tway celebrates his marvellous bunker shot to win in 1986.

RYDER CUP

In 1926 a group of American professional golfers crossed the Atlantic to play at Sunningdale to qualify for the Open. George Duncan, a leading British player and the professional at Wentworth, challenged them to a match against a team of British pros. The challenge was accepted and, somewhat surprisingly, the British annihilated the Americans 13 points to 1.

Over drinks in the clubhouse afterwards, Duncan proposed that the match

took impressive revenge by winning 9-3. It was the first of an overwhelming string of American victories that came close to killing off what is today one of the world's premier sporting events.

'This Ryder Cup is like nothing else in golf,' says Seve Ballesteros, who has made his mark on enough of the contests. 'Here you play for your family, you play for your country and your continent. You play for your team. For once in this game you aren't playing for yourself.'

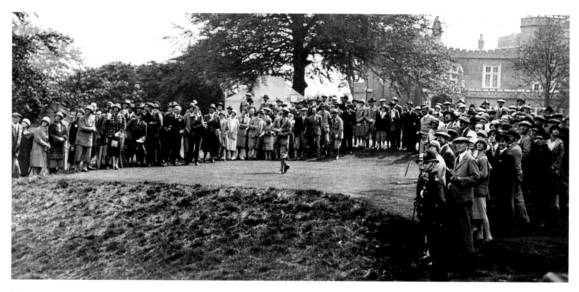

ABOVE: Captains J.H. Taylor (left) and Walter Hagen (right) shake hands before the match in 1933

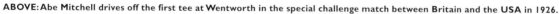

ABOVE: Abe Mitchell drives off the first tee at Wentworth in the special challenge match between Britain and the USA in 1926. as Samuel Ryder looks on.

should become a regular event, and a seed merchant, Samuel Ryder, a keen sponsor of the game, offered to provide a trophy to be contested every two years. He commissioned the silversmiths Mappin and Webb to produce the trophy, which portrayed Ryder's own personal professional coach Abe Mitchell – known as the 'finest player never to win the Open'.

The first official Ryder Cup match took place the following year on 3 and 4 June at the Worcester Country Club in Massachusetts and the Americans

But in the 1970s, it came close to extinction. As Michael McDonnell wrote in the Daily Mail after the 1975 match: 'The Ryder Cup passed away yesterday. Not just for another two years but almost certainly for ever. There is no further point to this charade.

'The last rites of this contest which had endured on American goodwill for most of its 48 years were performed before lunch with a total and humiliating defeat of Britain and Ireland.'

Following the first four matches, when the home side was successful on each occasion, the Americans dominated the Cup, winning every match bar two between 1935 and 1983. There were some especially humbling defeats for Great Britain. In 1947 they were routed 11-1 by a very strong American side containing Ben Hogan, Byron Nelson, Lloyd Mangrum and Jimmy Demaret; and in 1967 and 1975 both matches had already been lost before the afternoon singles had started. By the time Tom Weiskopf declined his invitation for the 1977 Ryder Cup to go elk hunting, something clearly had to be done or the tournament would be lost for ever.

It was Jack Nicklaus who, in 1977, suggested to Lord Derby, the president of the British PGA, that the Britain and Ireland side should be turned into a European team. 'Please don't think me presumptuous,' he said, 'but I want to be honest about this. The matches are just not competitive enough. Even the British and Irish players must be frustrated by the futility of the results.'

Derby, the most influential figure in British golf, took heed and the PGA, which had since 1967 been refusing American hints that it include Commonwealth players in the team, saw sense at last and included Ballesteros and Antonio Garrido for the 1979 match at Greenbrier.

In their first two matches the new European team showed little improvement. But in 1983, on American soil, they ran the home team very close and lost by only a single point, bringing a new competitive element that transformed the Cup. Since 1987 no more than two points have ever separated the sides, and each contest has been unbearably close.

Perhaps the finest of all Ryder Cups was played at the magnificent but treacherous Kiawah Island course in 1991. After three days of bruising matchplay golf – it was dubbed 'The War on the Shore' – the match was to be decided on the last hole of the last singles between Bernhard Langer and Hale Irwin. If Langer were to win the hole Europe would retain the Ryder

Cup. He had to putt from six feet for it and agonizingly missed. The cup went back to America.

Walter Hagen, the captain of the American team for the first six matches, was the guiding light behind the Ryder Cup in the early years. He did much to foster good golfing relations between America and Britain. Although his long game was sometimes fragile, he had a deadly touch around the greens and was the consummate match player. 'Who's gonna be second?' he would often declare on the first tee. It was very rarely him, for he lost only one of his Ryder Cup matches when trounced 10 and 8 by George Duncan in the singles in 1929.

Many of the American players have, not surprisingly, great Ryder Cup records. Billy Casper still holds the record for winning the most points – 23 – while Arnie Palmer can claim the most wins with 22. America can also boast that they fielded the strongest ever side in 1981 when they included Ryder Cup stalwarts Tom Kite, Jack Nicklaus, Tom Watson, Lee Trevino, Johnny Miller, Ray Floyd, Hale Irwin and Larry Nelson. Their play was typified by Kite in the singles when, even though his opponent Sandy Lyle scored

Arnold Palmer is the most successful Ryder Cup player.

The world's best pairing? Jack Nicklaus and Tom Watson teamed up at Walton Heath in 1981.

eight birdies, he scored ten to beat him three and two. Europe didn't have a snowball's chance in Hell.

Tony Jacklin did more than anyone to revive Europe's fortunes when he took office as captain in 1983. He made sure that his players were looked after – they travelled on Concorde and were given team 'uniforms' – so that they could concentrate solely on their game. He fostered a new sense of self-belief. Although failing narrowly in 1983, Europe won triumphantly at the Belfry in 1985 and then two years later upset the Americans again at Muirfield Village, inflicting their first home defeat.

Jacklin's chief lieutenant has been the inspirational Seve Ballesteros, who seems to thrive on beating the Americans. His partnership with Jose-Maria Olazabal has been nothing short of stunning. Of the 15 foursome and fourball

matches they have played together, they have lost just two. Ballesteros does have a talismanic effect on his fellow European players. Who else could have hit a three wood out of the bunker 245 yards to the middle of the green on the last hole to halve the match against Fuzzy Zoeller in 1983?

Nick Faldo has played more Ryder Cup matches than anyone. Since his debut in 1977, when he beat the Open champion Tom Watson in the singles, he has played in every match. His most stirring act came in 1995 at Oak Hill. It was imperative for him to beat Curtis Strange in the singles if Europe were to succeed. On the 18th, and the match level, all seemed lost as Faldo drove into the rough and had to chip out on to the fairway while Strange had hit the perfect drive. However, Strange mishit his second shot into the rough before the green and Faldo responded with a perfect 100-yard wedge to within four feet of the flag. Strange crumpled, hitting a poor chip and two-putting for a bogey. Faldo rolled in his putt to win the hole – and a massive bear hug from a tearful Ballesteros.

One of the greatest highlights of an often one-sided contest was the tied match in 1969 at Royal Birkdale. As was to happen at Kiawah Island in 1991, the match came down to the last singles, which was between the two premier golfers of the day, Jack Nicklaus and Tony Jacklin. The score was 15 points each and the result hinged on their battle. At the 17th Jacklin holed an enormous putt to win the hole and draw level. The tension was almost

Jose-Maria Olazabal and Seve Ballesteros were almost invincible as a Ryder Cup pairing.

unbearable. As they walked up the 18th fairway, Nicklaus asked Jacklin if he was nervous. Jacklin replied: 'I'm petrified.' Nicklaus responded: 'Well, if it's any consolation, I feel the same way.'

Both hit good second shots to the heart of the green. Jacklin putted first to two feet. Nicklaus followed, charging his first putt past the cup and bravely holing his second from four feet. He then picked up Jacklin's marker – the putt was by no means dead – and gave it to him saying: 'I know you won't miss that putt, Tony, so I'm not going to give you the opportunity.' The match was halved and the Cup was tied. It was the supreme sporting gesture.

The 1933 match also went to the last putt. Briton Syd Easterbrook and American Denny Shute were level going up the last. Shute three-putted, allowing Easterbrook to hole a brave four-footer for the hole, the match and the Ryder Cup. This exciting conclusion, watched by the Prince of Wales, caught the imagination of the public and brought mass popularity to the Ryder Cup for the first time.

The most important match, it could be argued, was in 1985 at the Belfry when Europe won, for the first time in 28 years. America was faced with real competition at last. For the whole three days the European home team, enjoying huge popular support, were cheered to the echo as they first matched the Americans in the foursomes and fourballs and finally dismantled them in the singles 7-4. The enduring image was of Sam Torrance arms aloft after holing an 18-foot putt on the last green to beat Andy North and win the Cup.

Over the years there have been stunning moments of individual brilliance. Ben Hogan in 1951 was meeting unexpected resistance from Charley Ward in their singles match, and at the par-5 10th at Pinehurst he looked likely to lose a hole when he drove wildly into the trees. He chipped

back on to the fairway, selected his two wood and smashed the ball on to the heart of the green 280 yards distant. He holed the putt to take the hole.

Arnold Palmer underlined what a supreme matchplayer he was in 1965. On the long par-5 18th he closed his singles match with Peter Butler with a driver and three wood to three feet from the flag for an eagle. It was the

The European team of 1985 that broke the American stranglehold.

coup de grâce for Great Britain.

Lanny Wadkins has one of the best Ryder Cup records. In 1983 he showed why when gaining a birdie at the last hole to halve with Jose-Maria Canizares and win the match for America. He achieved it by hitting a pitch shot to 16 inches from the hole – team captain Jack Nicklaus was so delighted he was seen kissing the pitch mark.

Sometimes it is the less celebrated players who are the heroes. In 1987

Agony: Bernhard Langer misses the putt that cost the Ryder Cup in 1991.

it was Eamonn Darcy who, by holing a sliding downhill five-foot putt, closed the door on Ben Crenshaw and inflicted America's first-ever home defeat. In 1989 it was Christy O'Connor Jnr who played the shot of his life when he hit a full-blooded two iron across the water at the Belfry's 18th to within a yard of the flag. He holed the putt to beat Fred Couples and gain a vital point to secure a tie for Europe. In 1995 Philip Walton made it an Irish treble when he hit the putt that won the Ryder Cup.

And there has been plenty of despair. In 1985 Craig Stadler missed an 18-inch putt on the last hole. If he had sunk it, he and his partner Curtis Strange would have beaten Sandy Lyle and Bernhard Langer and America would have gone into the last foursomes still in the lead. Many saw this as a turning point in the match, giving hope to the Europeans

Ecstasy: Tom Watson in 1993.

and demoralizing the Americans. In 1991 Mark Calcavecchia was dormie 4 against Colin Montgomerie. He then proceeded to score a 7, 6, 6 and 5 to lose all four holes and allow Montgomerie an unexpected half. Calcavecchia was inconsolable and was hardly unable to face his American teammates. Then Bernhard Langer missed the final putt, meaning defeat for the Europeans. Calcavecchia smiled again; Langer didn't. In the entire game of golf, no emotion comes close to losing the Ryder Cup.

SOLHEIM CUP

The fledgling international women's team challenge, the Solheim Cup, owes its existence to the success of the Ryder Cup, and earned its name in similar fashion.

Leading figures on the women's circuit argued that if men could produce one of the great sporting spectacles, surely the world's greatest women golfers could do the same. While there was enthusiasm for the concept, the experience of the fallow years of the Ryder Cup, when America dominated the matches, was enough to bring doubts.

When the Women Professional Golfers' European Tour (WPGET) proposed the idea of a match to the Ladies' Professional Golf Association of America (LPGA) in 1988, the overture was quietly rejected. The Americans believed (with some justification) that their players were far too strong for the European golfers. However, the emergence of world-beaters such as Laura Davies and Liselotte Neumann put a different aspect on the challenge and it was accepted in 1990 in a match at Lake Nona in Florida.

The victorious US team at the inaugural Solheim Cup in 1990.

Karsten Solheim and his wife with European captain Mickey Walker (centre).

Karsten Solheim, the owner of Karsten Manufacturing Corporation, makers of the world-renowned Ping clubs, provided the financial backing to kick-start the competition, and, as the Samuel Ryder of his day, the cup was named after him.

Of the four Solheim Cup matches to date, America have won three to Europe's one. In the inaugural match, the European team were overwhelmed, defeated comprehensively in the foursomes, fourballs and singles to lose the match 11-4.

It is fair to say that the majority of the Europeans were genuinely starstruck when faced with such golfing legends as Nancy Lopez, Pat Bradley, Betsy King and Beth Daniel. The Americans had to play only an average game to obliterate the awestruck Europeans.

Two years later, Europe were brilliantly motivated by Mickey Walker, team captain in all four Solheim Cups, who was determined to do better. She demanded total commitment from her players and instilled a new confidence.

But the icing on the motivational cake came in an aside from the controversial American Beth Daniel, who remarked: 'You could put any of us [the American players] in the European team and make it better.'

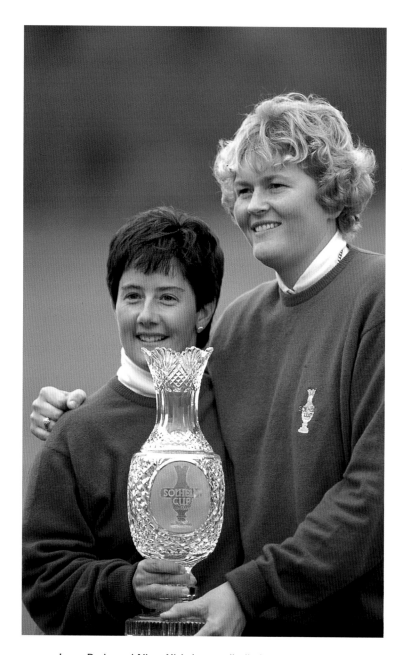

Laura Davies and Alison Nicholas proudly display the Solheim Cup after victory at Dalmahoy.

The Europeans were livid and the United States side got the shock of their lives as they were swept aside by the comfortable margin of 11-6. Dottie Pepper summed up her team's feelings. 'We weren't supposed to lose. We had what you might well have called the dream team over there. But we just got hammered.'

The 1994 match couldn't come soon enough for the American team. Although honours were even after the foursomes and fourballs, America convincingly won the singles 8 points to 2 to win the match 13-7.

The 1996 Solheim Cup at St Pierre was remarkably similar. Again the Europeans were more than a match for the Americans in the fourballs and foursomes – now extended to two series – but were dismantled in the singles, losing them 10 points to 2.

The American dominance in the singles does suggest a lack of depth in the European team, especially now that the team numbers have been increased from 10 to 12. Do Europe rely too heavily on their superstars Laura Davies and Liselotte Neumann? Davies has an outstanding cup record and in 1992 raised morale in the first singles match by reaching the long par-5 first green in two enormous blows. Before Laura, no woman golfer had got within 80 yards of the hole in two.

For the Solheim Cup to remain a contest when these two are no longer involved depends on new talent arising, especially from the European mainland countries. Sweden's scintillating Annika Sorenstam proves it is possible.

Despite its short history, the Solheim Cup is already providing moments that will live in golfing legend.

When the underdogs from Europe comprehensively outplayed America to win at Dalmahoy in 1992, it proved the doubters, who believed the whole competition to be a mismatch, wrong.

LEFT: Catrin Nilsmark is swamped by her teammates after holing the winning putt in 1992. RIGHT: Dottie Pepper is a fearsome competitor.

There were great emotional scenes when Catrin Nilsmark sank her putt to win the vital match on the 16th. She was immediately enveloped by her ecstatic teammates. Unseen, her opponent Meg Mallon picked up the forgotten ball out of the hole and presented it to Nilsmark later as a lasting memento.

The greatest shot probably belongs to American Brandie Burton. Playing the short par-3 16th at St Pierre in her singles match with Lisa Hackney, she hit her tee shot far to the right. Hackney was on the green with her tee shot and confidently looking to get back level from one down. It was not to be as Burton chipped in from way off the green, putting the final nail in the European coffin.

In 1994 the impetuous Dottie Pepper breached golfing etiquette in the most unladylike manner. Playing in a fourball against Europe's strong pairing of Laura Davies and Alison Nicholas, she cheered when Davies missed a birdie putt. Davies could only stand still in amazement. Pepper compounded her behaviour by refusing Davies a gimme for a 12-inch putt.

Also in 1994 some of the American players complained about Europe's

Brandie Burton's miracle chip shot dispatched of Lisa Hackney at St Pierre in 1996.

Swedish contingent conversing in their mother tongue. They insisted that they talk in English so it was clear they were not planning anything underhand.

Such incidents illustrate that, in the players' minds at least, the Solheim Cup, like the Ryder Cup, is becoming close to a matter of life and death. With the support of the public, there are exciting years ahead. Long may it continue.

Ricky Leaver

THE
MAGIC PLUS FOURS

A STORY BY P.G. WODEHOUSE

'After all,' said the young man, 'golf is only a game.' He spoke bitterly and with the air of one who has been following a train of thought. He had come into the smoking-room of the clubhouse in low spirits at the dusky close of a November evening, and for some minutes had been sitting, silent and moody, staring at the log fire.

'Merely a pastime,' said the young man.

The Oldest Member, nodding in his armchair, stiffened with horror, and glanced quickly over his shoulder to make sure that none of the waiters had heard these terrible words.

'Can this be George William Pennefather speaking!' he said, reproachfully. 'My boy, you are not yourself.'

The young man flushed a little beneath his tan: for he had had a good upbringing and was not bad at heart.

'Perhaps I ought not to have gone quite so far as that,' he admitted. 'I was only thinking that a fellow's got no right, just because he happens to have come on a bit in his form lately, to treat a fellow as if a fellow was a leper or something.'

The Oldest Member's face cleared, and he breathed a relieved sigh.

'Ah! I see,' he said. 'You spoke hastily and in a sudden fit of pique because something upset you out on the links today. Tell me all. Let me see, you were playing with Nathaniel Frisby this afternoon, were you not? I gather that he beat you.'

'Yes, he did. Giving me a third. But it isn't being beaten that I mind. What I object to is having the blighter behave as if he were a sort of champion condescending to a mere mortal. Dash it, it seemed to bore him playing with me! Every time I sliced off the tee he looked at me as if I were a painful ordeal. Twice when I was having a bit of trouble in the bushes I caught him yawning. And after we had finished he started talking about what a good

game croquet was, and he wondered more people didn't take it up. And it's only a month or so ago that I could play the man level!'

The Oldest Member shook his snowy head sadly.

'There is nothing to be done about it,' he said. 'We can only hope that the poison will work its way out of the man's system. Sudden success at golf is like the sudden acquisition of wealth. It is apt to unsettle and deteriorate the character. And, as it comes almost miraculously, so only a miracle can effect a cure. The best advice I can give you is to refrain from playing with Nathaniel Frisby till you can keep your tee-shots straight.'

'Oh, but don't run away with the idea that I wasn't pretty good off the tee this afternoon!' said the young man. 'I should like to describe to you the shot I did on the –'

'Meanwhile,' proceeded the Oldest Member, 'I will relate to you a little story which bears on what I have been saying.'

'From the very moment I addressed the ball –'

'It is the story of two loving hearts temporarily estranged owing to the sudden and unforeseen proficiency of one of the couple –'

'I waggled quickly and strongly, like Duncan. Then, swinging smoothly back, rather in the Vardon manner –'

'But as I see,' said the Oldest Member, 'that you are all impatience for me to begin, I will do so without further preamble.'

To the philosophical student of golf like myself (said the Oldest Member) perhaps the most outstanding virtue of this noble pursuit is the fact that it is a medicine for the soul. Its great service to humanity is that it teaches human beings that, whatever petty triumphs they may have achieved in other walks of life, they are after all merely human. It acts as a corrective against sinful pride. I attribute the insane arrogance of the later Roman emperors almost entirely to the fact that, never having played golf, they never knew that strange chastening humility which is engendered by a topped chip-shot. If Cleopatra had been outed in the first round of the Ladies' Singles, we should have heard a lot less of her proud imperiousness. And, coming down to modern times, it was undoubtedly his rotten golf that kept Wallace Chesney the nice unspoiled fellow he was. For in every other respect he had everything in the world calculated to make a man conceited and arrogant. He was the best-looking man for miles around; his health was perfect; and, in addition to this, he was rich; danced, rode, played bridge and polo with equal skill; and was engaged to be married to Charlotte Dix. And when you saw Charlotte Dix you realized that being engaged to her would by itself have been quite enough luck for any one man.

But Wallace, as I say, despite all his advantages, was a thoroughly nice, modest young fellow. And I attribute this to the fact that, while one of the keenest golfers in the club, he was also one of the worst players. Indeed, Charlotte Dix used to say to me in his presence that she could not understand why people paid money to go to the circus when by merely walking over the brow of a hill they could watch Wallace Chesney trying to get out of the bunker by the eleventh green. And Wallace took the gibe with perfect good humour, for there was a delightful camaraderie between them which robbed it of any sting. Often at lunch in the clubhouse I used to hear him and Charlotte planning the handicapping details of a proposed match between Wallace and a non-existent cripple whom Charlotte claimed to have discovered in the village - it being agreed finally that he should accept seven bisques from the cripple, but that, if the latter ever recovered the use of his arms, Wallace should get a stroke a hole.

In short, a thoroughly happy and united young couple. Two hearts, if I may coin an expression, that beat as one.

I would not have you misjudge Wallace Chesney. I may have given you the impression that his attitude towards golf was light and frivolous, but such was not the case. As I have said, he was one of the keenest members of the club. Love made him receive the joshing of his fiancée in the kindly spirit in which it was meant, but at heart he was as earnest as you could wish. He practised early and late; he bought golf books; and the mere sight of a patent club of any description acted on him like catnip on a cat. I remember remonstrating with him on the occasion of his purchasing a wooden-faced driving-mashie which weighed about two pounds, and was, taking it for all in all, as foul an instrument as ever came out of the workshop of a clubmaker who had been dropped on the head by his nurse when a baby.

'I know, I know,' he said, when I had finished indicating some of the weapon's more obvious defects. 'But the point is, I believe in it. It gives me confidence. I don't believe you could slice with a thing like that if you tried.'

Confidence! That was what Wallace Chesney lacked, and that, as he saw it, was the prime grand secret of golf. Like an alchemist on the track of the Philosopher's Stone, he was forever seeking for something which would really give him confidence. I recollect that he even tried repeating to himself fifty times every morning the words, 'Every day in every way I grow better and better.' This, however, proved such a black lie that he gave it up. The fact is, the man was a visionary, and it is to auto-hypnosis of some kind that I attribute the extraordinary change that came over him at the beginning of his third season.

You may have noticed in your perambulations about the City a shop bearing above its door and upon its windows the legend:

COHEN BROS.
SECOND-HAND CLOTHIERS

a statement which is borne out by endless vistas seen through the door of every variety of what is technically know as Gents' Wear. But the Brothers

Cohen, though their main stock-in-trade is garments which have been rejected by their owners for one reason or another, do not confine their dealings to Gents' Wear. The place is a museum of derelict goods of every description. You can get a second-hand revolver there, or a second-hand sword, or a second-hand umbrella. You can do a cheap deal in field-glasses, trunks, dog collars, canes, photograph frames, attaché cases, and bowls for goldfish. And on the bright spring morning when Wallace Chesney happened to pass by there was exhibited in the window a putter of such pre-eminently lunatic design that he stopped dead as if he had run into an invisible wall, and then, panting like an overwrought fish, charged in through the door.

The shop was full of the Cohen family, sombre-eyed, smileless men with purposeful expressions; and two of these, instantly descending upon Wallace Chesney like leopards, began in swift silence to thrust him into a suit of yellow tweed. Having worked the coat over his shoulders with a shoe-horn, they stood back to watch the effect.

'A beautiful fit,' announced Isidore Cohen.

'A little snug under the arms,' said his brother Irving. 'But that'll give.'

'The warmth of the body will make it give,' said Isidore.

'Or maybe you'll lose weight in the summer,' said Irving.

Wallace, when he had struggled out of the coat and was able to breathe, said that he had come in to buy a putter. Isidore therefore sold him the putter, a dog collar and a set of studs, and Irving sold him a fireman's helmet: and he was about to leave when their elder brother, Lou, who had just finished fitting out another customer, who had come in to buy a cap, with two pairs of trousers and a miniature aquarium for keeping newts in, saw that business was in progress and strolled up. His fathomless eye rested on Wallace, who was toying feebly with the putter.

'You play golf?' asked Lou. 'Then looka here!'

He dived into an alleyway of dead clothing, dug for a moment, and emerged with something at the sight of which Wallace Chesney, hardened golfer that he was, blenched and threw up an arm defensively.

'No, no!' he cried.

The object which Lou Cohen was waving insinuatingly before his eyes was a pair of those golfing breeches which are technically known as Plus Fours. A player of two years' standing, Wallace Chesney was not unfamiliar with Plus Fours - all the club cracks wore them - but he had never seen Plus Fours like these. What might be termed the main motif of the fabric was a curious vivid pink, and with this to work on the architect had let his imagination run free, and had produced so much variety in the way of chessboard squares of white, yellow, violet, and green that the eye swam as it looked upon them.

'These were made to measure for Sandy McHoots, the Open Champion,' said Lou, stroking the left leg lovingly. 'But he sent 'em back for some reason or other.'

'Perhaps they frightened the children,' said Wallace, recollecting having heard that Mr McHoots was a married man.

'They'll fit you nice,' said Lou.

'Sure they'll fit him nice,' said Isidore, warmly.

'Why, just take a look at yourself in the glass,' said Irving, 'and see if they don't fit you nice.'

And, as one who wakes from a trance, Wallace discovered that his lower limbs were now encased in the prismatic garment. At what point in the proceedings the brethren had slipped them on him, he could not have said. But he was undeniably in.

Wallace looked in the glass. For a moment, as he eyed his reflection, sheer horror gripped him. Then suddenly, as he gazed, he became aware that his first feelings were changing. The initial shock over, he was becoming calmer. He waggled his right leg with a certain sang-froid.

There is a certain passage in the works of the poet Pope with which you may be familiar. It runs as follows:

> 'Vice is a monster of so frightful mien
> As to be hated needs but to be seen;
> Yet seen too oft, familiar with her face,
> We first endure, then pity, then embrace.'

Even so it was with Wallace Chesney and these Plus Fours. At first he had recoiled from them as any decent-minded man would have done. Then, after a while, almost abruptly he found himself in the grip of a new emotion. After an unsuccessful attempt to analyse this, he suddenly got it. Amazing as it may seem, it was pleasure that he felt. He caught his eye in the mirror, and it was smirking. Now that the things were actually on, by Hutchinson, they didn't look half bad. By Braid, they didn't. There was a sort of something about them. Take away that expanse of bare leg with its unsightly sock-suspender and substitute a woolly stocking, and you would have the lower section of a golfer. For the first time in his life, he thought, he looked like a man who could play golf.

There came to him an odd sensation of masterfulness. He was still holding the putter, and now he swung it up above his shoulder. A fine swing, all lissomness and supple grace, quite different from any swing he had ever done before.

Wallace Chesney gasped. He knew that at last he had discovered that prime grand secret of golf for which he had searched so long. It was the costume that did it. All you had to do was wear Plus Fours. He had always

hitherto played in grey flannel trousers. Naturally he had not been able to do himself justice. Golf required an easy dash, and how could you be easily dashing in concertina-shaped trousers with a patch on the knee? He saw now - what he had never seen before - that it was not because they were crack players that crack players wore Plus Fours: it was because they wore Plus Fours that they were crack players. And these Plus Fours had been the property of an Open Champion. Wallace Chesney's bosom swelled, and he was filled, as by some strange gas, with joy - with excitement - with confidence. Yes, for the first time in his golfing life, he felt really confident.

True, the things might have been a shade less gaudy: they might perhaps have hit the eye with a slightly less violent punch: but what of that? True, again, he could scarcely hope to avoid the censure of his club-mates when he appeared like this on the links: but what of that? His club-mates must set their teeth and learn to bear these Plus Fours like men. That was what Wallace Chesney thought about it. If they did not like his Plus Fours, let them go and play golf somewhere else.

'How much?' he muttered, thickly. And the Brothers Cohen clustered grimly round with notebooks and pencils.

In predicting a stormy reception for his new apparel, Wallace Chesney had not been unduly pessimistic. The moment he entered the club-house Disaffection reared its ugly head. Friends of years' standing called loudly for the committee, and there was a small and vehement party of the left wing, headed by Raymond Gandle, who was an artist by profession, and consequently had a sensitive eye, which advocated the tearing off and public burial of the obnoxious garment. But, prepared as he had been for some such demonstration on the part of the coarser-minded, Wallace had hoped for better things when he should meet Charlotte Dix, the girl who loved him. Charlotte, he had supposed, would understand and sympathize.

Instead of which, she uttered a piercing cry and staggered to a bench, whence a moment later she delivered her ultimatum.

'Quick!' she said. 'Before I have to look again.'

'What do you mean?'

'Pop straight back into the changing-room while I've got my eyes shut, and remove the fancy-dress.'

'What's wrong with them?'

'Darling,'said Charlotte,'I think it's sweet and patriotic of you to be proud of your cycling-club colours or whatever they are, but you mustn't wear them on the links. It will unsettle the caddies.'

'They are a trifle on the bright side,' admitted Wallace. 'But it helps my game, wearing them. I was trying a few practice-shots just now, and I couldn't go wrong. Slammed the ball on the meat every time. They inspire me, if you know what I mean. Come on, let's be starting.'

Charlotte opened her eyes incredulously.

'You can't seriously mean that you're really going to play in - those? It's against the rules. There must be a rule somewhere in the book against coming out looking like a sunset. Won't you go and burn them for my sake?'

'But I tell you they give me confidence. I sort of squint down at them when I'm addressing the ball, and I feel like a pro.'

'Then the only thing to do is for me to play you for them. Come on, Wally, be a sportsman. I'll give you a half and play you for the whole outfit - the breeches, the red jacket, the little cap, and the belt with the snake's-head buckle. I'm sure all those things must have gone with the breeches. Is it a bargain?'

Strolling on the club-house terrace some two hours later, Raymond Gandle encountered Charlotte and Wallace coming up from the eighteenth green.

'Just the girl I wanted to see,' said Raymond. 'Miss Dix, I represent a select committee of my fellow-members, and I have come to ask you on their behalf to use the influence of a good woman to induce Wally to destroy those Plus Fours of his, which we all consider nothing short of Bolshevik propaganda and a menace to the public weal. May I rely on you?'

'You may not,' retorted Charlotte. 'They are the poor boy's mascot. You've no idea how they have improved his game. He has just beaten me hollow. I am going to try to learn to bear them, so you must. Really, you've no notion how he has come on. My cripple won't be able to give him more than a couple of bisques if he keeps up this form.'

'It's something about the things,' said Wallace. 'They give me confidence.'

'They give me a pain in the neck,' said Raymond Gandle.

To the thinking man nothing is more remarkable in this life than the way in which Humanity adjusts itself to conditions which at their outset might well have appeared intolerable. Some great cataclysm occurs, some storm or earthquake, shaking the community to its foundations; and after the first pardonable consternation one finds the sufferers resuming their ordinary pursuits as if nothing had happened. There have been few more striking examples of this adaptability than the behaviour of the members of our golf-club under the impact of Wallace Chesney's Plus Fours. For the first few days it is not too much to say that they were stunned. Nervous players sent their caddies on in front of them at blind holes, so that they might be warned in time of Wallace's presence ahead and not have him happening to them all of a sudden. And even the pro was not unaffected. Brought up in Scotland in an atmosphere of tartan kilts, he nevertheless winced, and a startled 'Hoots!' was forced from his lips when Wallace Chesney continued day by day to make the most extraordinary progress in his play.

As I have said before, and I think you will agree with me when I have told you what happened subsequently, it was probably a case of auto-hypnosis. There is no other sphere in which a belief in oneself has such immediate effects as it has in golf. And Wallace, having acquired self-confidence, went on from strength to strength. In under a week he had ploughed his way through the Unfortunate Incidents - of which class Peter Willard was the best example - and was challenging the fellows who kept three shots in five somewhere on the fairway. A month later he was holding his own with ten-handicap men. And by the middle of the summer he was so far advanced that his name occasionally cropped up in speculative talks on the subject of the July medal. One might have been excused for supposing that, as far as Wallace Chesney was concerned, all was for the best in the best of all possible worlds.

And yet ...

The first inkling I received that anything was wrong came through a chance meeting with Raymond Gandle who happened to pass my gate on his way back from the links just as I drove up in my taxi; for I had been away from home for many weeks on a protracted business tour. I welcomed Gandle's advent and invited him in to smoke a pipe and put me abreast of local gossip. He came readily enough - and seemed, indeed to have something on his mind and to be glad of the opportunity of revealing it to a sympathetic auditor.

'And how,' I asked him, when we were comfortably settled, 'did your game this afternoon come out?'

'Oh, he beat me,' said Gandle, and it seemed to me that there was a note of bitterness in his voice.

'Then He, whoever he was, must have been an extremely competent performer,' I replied, courteously, for Gandle was one of the finest players in the club. 'Unless, of course, you were giving him some impossible handicap.'

'No; we played level.'

'Indeed! Who was your opponent?'

'Chesney.'

'Wallace Chesney! And he beat you playing level! This is the most amazing thing I have ever heard.'

'He's improved out of all knowledge.'

'He must have done. Do you think he would ever beat you again?'

'No. Because he won't have the chance.'

'You surely do not mean that you will not play him because you are afraid of being beaten?'

'It isn't being beaten I mind —'

And if I omit to report the remainder of his speech it is not merely because it contained expressions with which I am reluctant to sully my lips, but because, omitting these expletives, what he said was almost word for word what you were saying to me just now about Nathaniel Frisby. It was, it seemed, Wallace Chesney's manner, his arrogance, his attitude of belonging to some superior order of being that had so wounded Raymond Gandle. Wallace Chesney had, it appeared, criticized Gandle's mashie-play in no friendly spirit; had hung up the game on the fourteenth tee in order to show him how to place his feet; and on the way back to the club-house had said that the beauty of golf was that the best player could enjoy a round even with a dud, because, though there might be no interest in the match, he could always amuse himself by playing for his medal score.

I was profoundly shaken.

'Wallace Chesney!' I exclaimed. 'Was it really Wallace Chesney who behaved in the manner you describe?'

'Unless he's got a twin brother of the same name, it was.'

'Wallace Chesney a victim to swelled head! I can hardly credit it.'

'Well, you needn't take my word for it unless you want to. Ask anybody. It isn't often he can get anyone to play with him now.'

'You horrify me!'

Raymond Gandle smoked a while in brooding silence.

'You've heard about his engagement?' he said at length.

'I have heard nothing, nothing. What about his engagement?'

'Charlotte Dix has broken it off.'

'No!'

'Yes. Couldn't stand him any longer.'

I got rid of Gandle as soon as I could. I made my way as quickly as possible to the house where Charlotte lived with her aunt. I was determined to sift this matter to the bottom and to do all that lay in my power to heal the breach between two young people for whom I had a great affection.

'I have just heard the news,' I said, when the aunt had retired to some secret lair, as aunts do, and Charlotte and I were alone.

'What news?' said Charlotte, dully. I thought she looked pale and ill, and she had certainly grown thinner.

'This dreadful news about your engagement to Wallace Chesney. Tell me, why did you do this thing? Is there no hope of a reconciliation?'

'Not unless Wally becomes his old self again.'

'But I had always regarded you two as ideally suited to one another.'

'Wally has completely changed in the last few weeks. Haven't you heard?'

'Only sketchily, from Raymond Gandle.'

'I refuse,' said Charlotte, proudly, all the woman in her leaping to her eyes, 'to marry a man who treats me as if I were a kronen at the present rate of exchange, merely because I slice an occasional tee-shot. The afternoon I broke off the engagement' - her voice shook, and I could see that her indifference was but a mask - 'the afternoon I broke off the en-gug-gug-gagement, he

t-told me I ought to use an iron off the tee instead of a dud-dud-driver.'

And the stricken girl burst into an uncontrollable fit of sobbing. And realizing that, if matters had gone as far as that, there was little I could do, I pressed her hand silently and left her.

But though it seemed hopeless I decided to persevere. I turned my steps towards Wallace Chesney's bungalow, resolved to make one appeal to the man's better feelings. He was in his sitting-room when I arrived, polishing a putter; and it seemed significant to me, even in that tense moment, that the putter was quite an ordinary one, such as any capable player might use. In the brave old happy days of his dudhood, the only putters you ever found in the society of Wallace Chesney were patent self-adjusting things that looked like croquet mallets that had taken the wrong turning in childhood.

'Well, Wallace, my boy,' I said.

'Hallo!' said Wallace Chesney. 'So you're back?'

We fell into conversation, and I had not been in the room two minutes before I realized that what I had been told about the change in him was nothing more than the truth. The man's bearing and his every remark were insufferably bumptious. He spoke of his prospects in the July medal competition as if the issue were already settled. He scoffed at his rivals.

I had some little difficulty in bringing the talk round to the matter which I had come to discuss.

'My boy,' I said at length, 'I have just heard the sad news.'

'What sad news?'

'I have been talking to Charlotte –'

'Oh, that!' said Wallace Chesney.

'She was telling me –'

'Perhaps it's all for the best.'

'All for the best? What do you mean?'

'Well,' said Wallace, 'one doesn't wish, of course, to say anything ungallant, but, after all, poor Charlotte's handicap is fourteen and wouldn't appear to have much chance of getting any lower. I mean, there's such a thing as a fellow throwing himself away.'

Was I revolted at these callous words? For a moment, yes. Then it struck me that, though he had uttered them with a light laugh, that laugh had had in it more than a touch of bravado. I looked at him keenly. There was a bored, discontented expression in his eyes, a line of pain about his mouth.

'My boy,' I said, gravely, 'you are not happy.'

For an instant I think he would have denied the imputation. But my visit had coincided with one of those twilight moods in which a man requires, above all else, sympathy. He uttered a weary sigh.

'I'm fed up,' he admitted. 'It's a funny thing. When I was a dud, I used to think how perfect it must be to be scratch. I used to watch the cracks buzzing round the course and envy them. It's all a fraud. The only time when you enjoy golf is when an occasional decent shot is enough to make you happy for the day. I'm plus two, and I'm bored to death. I'm too good. And what's the result? Everybody's jealous of me. Everybody's got it in for me. Nobody loves me.'

His voice rose in a note of anguish, and at the sound his terrier, which had been sleeping on the rug, crept forward and licked his hand.

'The dog loves you,' I said, gently, for I was touched.

'Yes, but I don't love the dog,' said Wallace Chesney.

'Now come, Wallace,' I said. 'Be reasonable, my boy. It is only your unfortunate manner on the links which has made you perhaps a little unpopular at the moment. Why not pull yourself up? Why ruin your whole life with this arrogance? All that you need is a little tact, a little forbearance. Charlotte, I am sure, is just as fond of you as ever, but you have wounded her pride. Why must you be unkind about her tee-shots?'

Wallace Chesney shook his head despondently.

'I can't help it,' he said. 'It exasperates me to see anyone foozling, and I have to say so.'

'Then there is nothing to be done,' I said, sadly.

All the medal competitions at our club are, as you know, important events; but, as you are also aware, none of them is looked forward to so keenly or contested so hotly as the one in July. At the beginning of the year of which I am speaking, Raymond Gandle had been considered the probable winner of the fixture; but as the season progressed and Wallace Chesney's skill developed to such a remarkable extent most of us were reluctantly inclined to put our money on the latter. Reluctantly, because Wallace's unpopularity was now so general that the thought of his winning was distasteful to all. It grieved me to see how cold his fellow-members were towards him. He drove off from the first tee without a solitary hand-clap; and, though the drive was of admirable quality and nearly carried the green, there was not a single cheer. I noticed Charlotte Dix among the spectators. The poor girl was looking sad and wan.

In the draw for partners Wallace had had Peter Willard allotted to him; and he muttered to me in a quite audible voice that it was as bad as handicapping him half a dozen strokes to make him play with such a hopeless performer. I do not think Peter heard, but it would not have made much difference to him if he had, for I doubt if anything could have had much effect for the worse on his game. Peter Willard always entered for the medal competition, because he said that competition-play was good for the nerves.

On this occasion he topped his ball badly, and Wallace lit his pipe with the exaggeratedly patient air of an irritated man. When Peter topped his second also, Wallace was moved to speech.

'For goodness' sake,' he snapped, 'what's the good of playing at all if you insist on lifting your head? Keep it down, man, keep it down. You don't need to watch to see where the ball is going. It isn't likely to go as far as all that. Make up your mind to count three before you look up.'

'Thanks,' said Peter, meekly. There was no pride in Peter to be wounded. He knew the sort of player he was.

The couples were now moving off with smooth rapidity, and the course was dotted with the figures of players and their accompanying spectators. A fair proportion of these latter had decided to follow the fortunes of Raymond Gandle, but by far the larger number were sticking to Wallace, who right from the start showed that Gandle or anyone else would have to return a very fine card to beat him. He was out in thirty-seven, two above bogey, and with the assistance of a superb second, which landed the ball within a foot of the pin, got a three on the tenth, where a four is considered good. I mention this to show that by the time he arrived at the short lake-hole Wallace Chesney was at the top of his form. Not even the fact that he had been obliged to let the next couple through owing to Peter Willard losing his ball had been enough to upset him.

The course has been rearranged since, but at that time the lake-hole, which is now the second, was the eleventh, and was generally looked on as the crucial hole in a medal round. Wallace no doubt realized this, but the knowledge did not seem to affect him. He lit his pipe with the utmost coolness and, having replaced the matchbox in his hip-pocket, stood smoking nonchalantly as he waited for the couple in front to get off the green.

They holed out eventually, and Wallace walked to the tee. As he did so, he was startled to receive a resounding smack.

'Sorry,' said Peter Willard, apologetically. 'Hope I didn't hurt you. A wasp.' And he pointed to the corpse, which was lying in a used-up attitude on the ground.

'Afraid it would sting you,' said Peter.

'Oh, thanks,' said Wallace.

He spoke a little stiffly, for Peter Willard had a large, hard, flat hand, the impact of which had shaken him up considerably. Also, there had been laughter in the crowd. He was fuming as he bent to address the ball, and his annoyance became acute when, just as he reached the top of his swing, Peter Willard suddenly spoke.

'Just a second, old man,' said Peter. Wallace spun round, outraged.

'What is it? I do wish you would wait till I've made my shot.'

'Just as you like,' said Peter, humbly.

'There is no greater crime that a man can commit on the links than to speak to a fellow when he's making his stroke.'

'Of course, of course,' acquiesced Peter, crushed.

Wallace turned to his ball once more. He was vaguely conscious of a discomfort to which he could not at the moment give a name. At first he thought that he was having a spasm of lumbago, and this surprised him, for he had never in his life been subject to even a suspicion of that malady. A moment later he realized that this diagnosis had been wrong.

'Good heavens!' he cried, leaping nimbly some two feet into the air. 'I'm on fire!'

'Yes,' said Peter, delighted at his ready grasp of the situation. 'That's what I wanted to mention just now.'

Wallace slapped vigorously at the seat of his Plus Fours.

'It must have been when I killed that wasp,' said Peter, beginning to see clearly into the matter. 'You had a matchbox in your pocket.'

Wallace was in no mood to stop and discuss first causes. He was springing up and down on his pyre, beating at the flames.

'Do you know what I should do if I were you?' said Peter Willard. 'I should jump into the lake.'

One of the cardinal rules of golf is that a player shall accept no advice from anyone but his own caddie; but the warmth about his lower limbs had now become so generous that Wallace was prepared to stretch a point. He took three rapid strides and entered the water with a splash.

The lake, though muddy, is not deep, and presently Wallace was to be observed standing up to his waist some few feet from the shore.

'That ought to have put it out,' said Peter Willard. 'It was a bit of luck that it happened at this hole.' He stretched out a hand to the bather. 'Catch hold, old man, and I'll pull you out.'

'No!' said Wallace Chesney.

'Why not?'

'Never mind!' said Wallace, austerely. He bent as near to Peter as he was able.

'Send a caddie up to the club-house to fetch my grey flannel trousers from my locker,' he whispered, tensely.

'Oh, ah!' said Peter.

It was some little time before Wallace, encircled by a group of male spectators, was enabled to change his costume; and during the interval he continued to stand waist-deep in the water, to the chagrin of various couples who came to the tee in the course of their round and complained with not a little bitterness that his presence there added a mental hazard to an already difficult hole. Eventually, however, he found himself back ashore, his ball before him, his mashie in his hand.

'Carry on,' said Peter Willard, as the couple in front left the green. 'All clear now.'

Wallace Chesney addressed his ball. And, even as he did so, he was suddenly aware that an odd psychological change had taken place in himself. He was aware of a strange weakness. The charred remains of the Plus Fours were lying under an adjacent bush; and, clad in the old grey flannels of his early golfing days, Wallace felt diffident, feeble, uncertain of himself. It was as though virtue had gone out of him, as if some indispensable adjunct to good play had been removed. His corrugated trouser-leg caught his eye as he waggled, and all at once he became acutely alive to the fact that many eyes were watching him. The audience seemed to press on him like a blanket. He felt as he had been wont to feel in the old days when he had had to drive off the first tee in front of a terrace-full of scoffing critics.

The next moment his ball had bounded weakly over the intervening patch of turf and was in the water.

'Hard luck!' said Peter Willard, ever a generous foe. And the words seemed to touch some almost atrophied chord in Wallace's breast. A sudden love for his species flooded over him. Dashed decent of Peter, he thought to sympathize. Peter was a good chap. So were the spectators good chaps. So was everybody, even his caddie.

Peter Willard, as if resolved to make his sympathy practical, also rolled his ball into the lake.

'Hard luck!' said Wallace Chesney, and started as he said it; for many weeks had passed since he had commiserated with an opponent. He felt a changed man. A better, sweeter, kindlier man. It was as if a curse had fallen from him.

He teed up another ball, and swung.

'Hard luck!' said Peter.

'Hard luck!' said Wallace, a moment later.

'Hard luck!' said Peter, a moment after that.

Wallace Chesney stood on the tee watching the spot in the water where his third ball had fallen. The crowd was now openly amused, and, as he listened to their happy laughter, it was borne in upon Wallace that he, too, was amused and happy. A weird, almost effervescent exhilaration filled him. He turned and beamed upon the spectators. He waved his mashie cheerily at them. This, he felt, was something like golf. This was golf as it should be - not the dull, mechanical thing which had bored him during all these past weeks of his perfection, but a gay, rollicking adventure. That was the soul of golf, the thing that made it the wonderful pursuit it was - that speculativeness, that not knowing where the dickens your ball was going when you hit it, that eternal hoping for the best, that never-failing chanciness. It is better to travel hopefully than to arrive, and at last this great truth had come home to Wallace Chesney. He realized now why pros were all grave, silent men who seemed to struggle manfully against some secret sorrow. It was because they were too darned good. Golf had no surprises for them, no gallant spirit of adventure.

'I'm going to get a ball over if I stay here all night,' cried Wallace Chesney, gaily, and the crowd echoed his mirth. On the face of Charlotte Dix was the look of a mother whose prodigal son had rolled into the old home once more. She caught Wallace's eye and gesticulated to him blithely.

'The cripple says he'll give you a stroke a hole, Wally!' she shouted.

'I'm ready for him!' bellowed Wallace.

'Hard luck!' said Peter Willard.

Under their bush the Plus Fours, charred and dripping, lurked unnoticed. But Wallace Chesney saw them. They caught his eye as he sliced his eleventh into the marshes on the right. It seemed to him that they looked sullen. Disappointed. Baffled.

Wallace Chesney was himself again.

IF THEY PLAY GOLF
IN HEAVEN...

'Augusta is the closest thing to heaven for a golfer —

and it's just as hard to get into.'

Joe Geshwiler, *San Francisco Examiner*

What makes a great golf hole? In the words of Alister MacKenzie, designer of Augusta, the Royal Melbourne and Cypress Point: 'The ideal hole is one that affords the greatest pleasure to the greatest number, gives the fullest advantage for accurate play, stimulates players to improve their game, and which never becomes monotonous ... but the great test should be that as players of all handicaps play golf, a hole should, as far as possible, be ideal for both scratch and long-handicap players.'

We have assembled a selection of the finest holes in the game of golf. Some you may have already battled with; others may one day lay their charms and treacheries open for your pleasure; others, sadly, because of the restrictions imposed by their owners, you will be have to birdie only in your dreams. Inevitably at 19th holes there will be argument whether one or another might make way for a personal favourite; such is the wealth of glorious holes scattered across a golf-loving world. We will not complain; such is the nature of the game.

Assembled with the advice of current tour professionals, with deference to the greatest names in golf history, and with the admiration of those who travel the world writing about the game, the holes selected undoubtedly satisfy the ambitions of Alister MacKenzie. And together they might make up the course that has been laid out to greet us in heaven - the ultimate golf course.

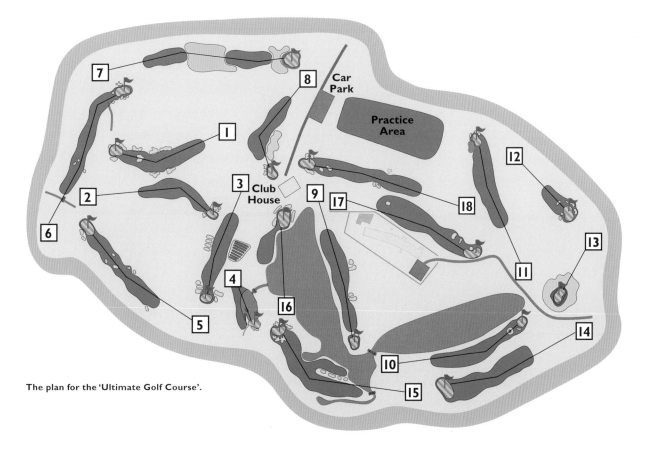

The plan for the 'Ultimate Golf Course'.

CARD OF THE COURSE

Hole	Yards	Par
1	355	4
2	400	4
3	425	4
4	194	3
5	440	4
6	570	5
7	585	5
8	305	4
9	450	4
Out	**3,724**	**37**
10	452	4
11	445	4
12	198	3
13	170	3
14	445	4
15	498	5
16	233	3
17	461	4
18	448	4
In	**3,350**	**34**
Out	**3,724**	**37**
Total	**7,074**	**71**

1. MERION, 355 YARDS PAR-4

Bobby Jones knew the dangers of Merion better than most.

It is fitting to open with the East course at Merion, as it has hosted more United States Golf Association championships than any other course. This is the place where Bobby Jones completed his insurmountable Grand Slam in 1930; where, 19 years later, Ben Hogan defied crippling injuries to win the US Open after a near-fatal car crash. Jones had also led the field at Merion after the first qualifying round of the US Amateur in 1916. 'The kid from Dixie' was only 14 years old. Designed by the Scottish émigré Hugh Wilson, and formerly affiliated with its older brother, the Merion Cricket Club, it sits in the chic and exclusive Main Line area of Philadelphia.

An opening hole of any course should act as a gentle introduction, before the golfer confronts the more severe tasks lying ahead. Merion's first is the perfect example. It is a fairly short, slight-dogleg-right par-4 needing only a long iron from the tee but a perfectly executed chip to hit and stay on the small green and avoid the three greenside bunkers. The approach shot is made more difficult by the fact Merion uses tall red wicker baskets instead of flags to mark the hole – making it far trickier to judge the wind speed and direction. The green itself has many borrows, allowing for several challenging pin positions, and, like all the greens at Merion, it is extremely fast. Putting is key at Merion. Bobby Jones once putted clear off the green into a brook.

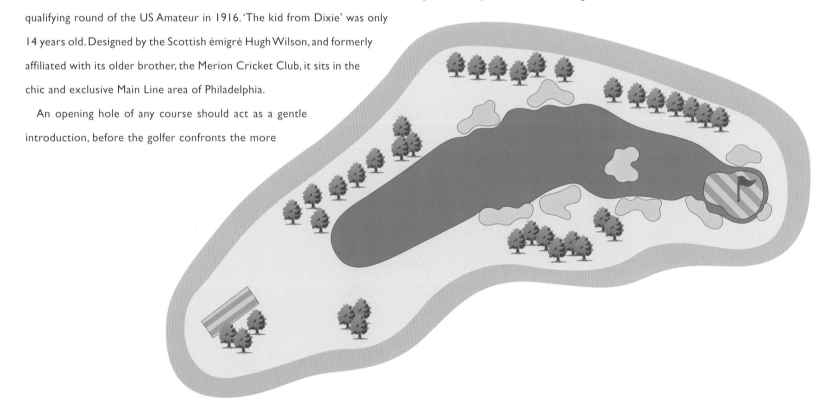

2. VALDERRAMA, 400 YARDS PAR-4

With the imposing Sierra Blanca mountains as the backdrop, the beautifully manicured Valderrama is considered by many to to be the 'Augusta of Europe'. The brainchild of the Spanish industrialist Jamie-Ortiz Patino, it was transformed in 1985 to its present state by the master golf architect Robert Trent Jones, who believes it to be one of his finest works. As well as being the venue for the 1997 Ryder Cup, it has traditionally been the staging post for Europe's end-of-term tournament and biggest prizewinner, the Volvo Masters.

Robert Trent Jones.

Ronan Rafferty is in no doubt about Valderrama's class: 'It is more difficult than any other course in Europe ... You are always looking for pars; birdies are a bonus.'

The second hole exemplifies the unforgiving nature of the whole course. A tight fairway is bordered by clusters of cork and olive trees and lush Bermudan rough. This is made even more hazardous by the positioning of a tree in the centre of the fairway. It is best to drive to the left in order to get a clear view of the green with the second shot. The plateau green itself is a difficult target, but its many contours can bring unexpected embarrassment for the unwary putter.

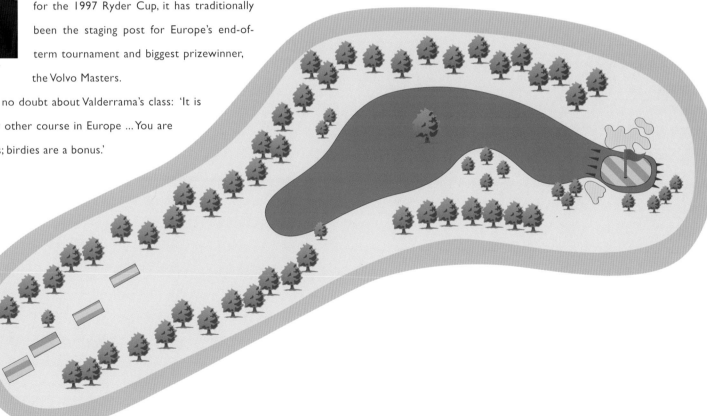

3. OAKMONT, 425 YARDS PAR-4

Standing at the foot of the Allegheny Mountains outside Pittsburgh, Oakmont is one of America's toughest courses. Designed and constructed by Henry Fownes in 1904, it is alternately hailed and cursed the world over for possessing the quickest greens – which regularly defeat even the greatest golfers. Bobby Jones could not break 76 over four rounds when he competed in the 1927 US Open.

Even today, with modern equipment, the course rarely yields to par when hosting major tournaments. Nick Faldo hails it as 'really the most demanding course I have ever seen. The greens are unbelievable. But you've got to get to them first.'

The third hole at Oakmont is famed for its famous Church Pews bunker which unerringly swallows the hooked drive from the tee. Sixty yards long by 40 yards wide, it is an unnerving series of parallel sandy trenches with grassy tops. Once in, a splash shot out sideways is the only real escape and a bogey is the best that can be hoped for.

If the Church Pews are avoided, the hole is certainly birdieable, as proved by Johnny Miller in the 1973 US Open when he struck an amazing 63 in the last

The Church Pews bunkers await the soul who strays.

round. Beware the five bunkers flanking the green and of course the green itself, which is swift as ice. Even so, this is a course to enjoy and it has been said that 'most people have fun here ... even when they're lining their fourth putt.'

4. BALTUSROL, 194 YARDS PAR-3

Breathtaking, inviting and treacherous.

Baltusrol in Springfield, New Jersey, is unquestionably another of America's great courses, and has deservedly hosted the US Open six times. It first laid itself open to the unsuspecting golfer in the 1890s as a small nine-holer, not taking its present shape until it was expanded and redesigned in 1922 by the golf architect, A.W. Tillinghast.

Under the aegis of Robert Trent Jones, the course underwent further alterations in readiness for the 1954 US Open. The main change he made was to transform the fourth hole into the complete water hazard – every inch of the hole is over water from the end of the tee to the front edge of the green, which is fronted by a stone wall.

Like the short 12th at Augusta, the green is wide but not at all deep.

Club selection is all important – not enough club means a watery grave; too much and bunkers at the back of the green await. Many of the club members protested that the hole was too difficult. In an effort to placate them, Trent Jones played the hole with the club pro, Johnny Farrell. Jones struck the perfect iron; the shot landed a few feet from the flag and rolled gently into the hole for an ace. He turned to the members with a patient smile and said: 'As you can see, gentlemen, this hole is not too tough.'

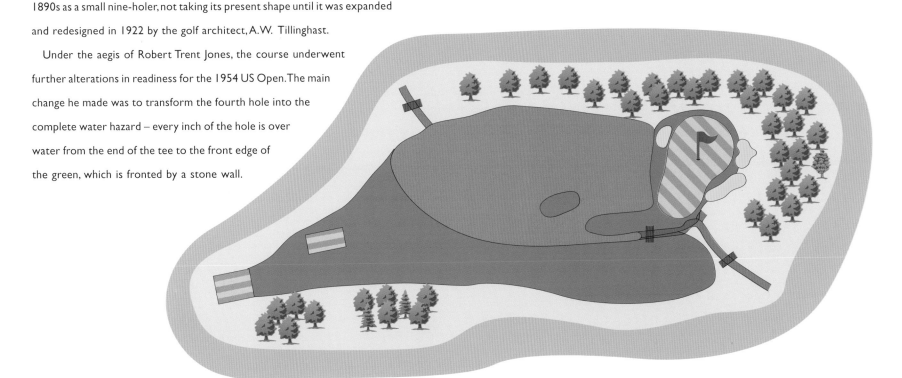

5. ROYAL COUNTY DOWN, 440 YARDS PAR-4

Can there be many more beautiful spots than Royal County Down, in Northern Ireland, which lies in the curve of Dundrum Bay with the majestic Mountains of Mourne as a dramatic backdrop? The course has been described as 'exhilarating even without a club in your hand'.

Created in 1889, it was, according to the club's minutes, designed by Old Tom Morris for the very reasonable sum of £4. Tom Watson believes that the first 11 holes are 'the finest consecutive 11 holes of links golf that I have ever played.'

Of those magnificent holes, the fifth is perhaps the finest, rewarding pure ball-striking and punishing severely the errant shot. The drive has to carry a large area of scrub to reach the fairway, which runs diagonally left to right towards the green. The stronger hitters can shorten the hole by driving further right over a heathery hillock. The green, protected by towering dunes and bunkers fringed with whispy grass, is still far away and requires a precisely hit long iron or even fairway wood. Any player who records a par on this hole will know that his or her long game is in particularly good order.

A spectacular location – whether you have a club in your hand or not.

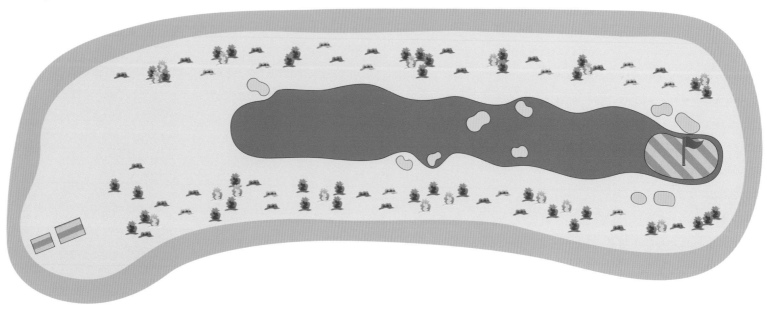

6. CARNOUSTIE, 570 YARDS PAR-5

Another course laid out by Old Tom Morris, although later redesigned by James Braid in the 1920s, Carnoustie is a giant among the links courses of Great Britain and Ireland, and is thought by many to be the best and (with the wind blowing) the most fearsome of them all. Ernie Els is a great admirer − even though he could manage rounds of only 76 and 77 in the 1996 Scottish Open: 'What a course,' he enthused, 'the best I've ever played. It brought me to my knees, that's for sure. I felt like a ten-handicapper out there but I'm glad I came.'

It is deservedly back on the Open roster and will host the 1999 championship. It has also been a great nursery for developing golfing talent. At the beginning of the century more than a hundred young men set out from Carnoustie to take their chance in the world by plying their golfing trade in America, among them the famous Smith brothers, Willie, Alex and MacDonald.

The sixth at Carnoustie is a classic par-5, where brain rather than brawn is needed to achieve satisfaction. With an out-of-bounds fence running the whole left side of the hole, most drivers naturally will favour the right side of the fairway. However, they have to make a decision, inevitably influenced by the prevailing wind direction, whether to fly the two bunkers in the middle of the

fairway or lay up short.

For the second shot, Jockie's Burn, which runs diagonally into the right side of the fairway one hundred yards short of the green, has to be taken into

View from the long sixth, beyond the fifth green.

consideration. Do you take a chance to play over, or lay up? Ben Hogan, when he won the British Open in 1953, showed exactly how it should be played on the final two rounds. Having hit a drive safely over the fairway bunkers, he twice hit the perfect brassie (three wood) over the burn to 30 yards short of the green. Each time he chipped and single-putted for a birdie 4. But only one of the greatest golfers ever could make this hole look relatively easy.

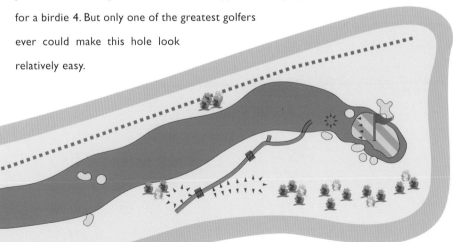

7. PINE VALLEY, 585 YARDS PAR-5

The view from the tee. Hell's Half Acre can be seen in the far distance.

Pine Valley in Clementon, New Jersey, was created by the hotelier George Crump, who originally spotted the sight for his dream course while travelling by train from Philadelphia to Atlantic City. Completed in 1919, it has a fearsome reputation and members have a standing bet with any players that they cannot beat 80 shots in their introductory round. Arnie Palmer, in his amateur days in the early 1950s, put his money where his mouth was and

took many of the members on. 'I was getting married and desperate for the money,' he later recalled. He carded 68. Most other players, however, never see their money again even though they might have played only a few bad shots. The course really is a monster.

The long seventh illustrates perfectly the problems faced at Pine Valley. Looking out from the tee, the player is presented with a view of two island fairways amidst a sea of unraked sand and scrub. The drive must find the first island but cannot be hit too hard as the fairway ends at 285 yards. The second shot must now negotiate Hell's Half Acre, a carry of at least 150 yards over unkempt sand to the second island fairway and from them a chip or medium iron to the third island, the green. Little wonder that the green has never been reached in two shots – though that may change when Tiger Woods graces the course.

8. ROYAL MELBOURNE, 305 YARDS PAR-4

Royal Melbourne can justly claim to be the best course in the southern hemisphere. The golf writer Henry Longhurst believed that the course 'sifts champions from mediocre players' and like all great courses it certainly requires finesse, judgement and great skill. The championship course, a regular venue for the Australian Open, is an amalgamation of the East course designed by Alex Russell, and the West course designed by Alister Mackenzie, who later helped Bobby Jones construct Augusta. Opened in 1926, it is a duneland course with many links characteristics and it boasts very true and extremely fast putting surfaces.

The eighth hole is one of the best short par-4s in the world. It pleads with the big hitter to reach the green in one, to set up a chance of a birdie or even an eagle. To do this, the drive must carry a long cavernous bunker on the left, descend into a large gully and hopefully trickle on to the green, which is

Alister MacKenzie.

slightly raised. If the drive is slightly hooked, it will be lost in the trees; if it is mishit, it will find the large bunker and a shot will be lost. Alternately the safe line is to drive to the right and hit across to the pin with a short iron — but this is never easy as the pitch has to be hit precisely to avoid the greenside bunkers directly ahead and hit with enough backspin to stay on the green. However the hole is played, it is a very serious a challenge.

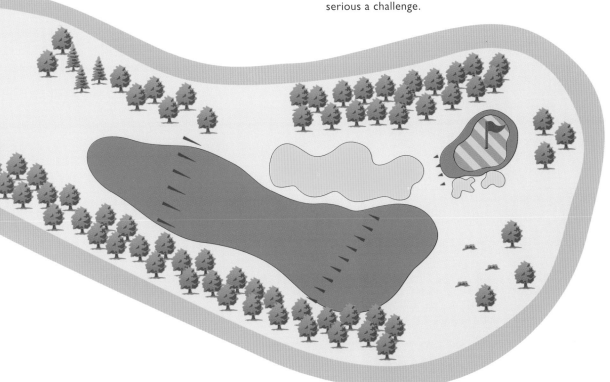

9. PEBBLE BEACH, 450 YARDS PAR-4

If you know golf, you will know of Pebble Beach; it is breathtaking and it is dramatic. Seven of its holes sit hard against the Californian cliffs of the Monterey Peninsula – once described by Robert Louis Stevenson as the world's 'greatest meeting place of land and water'. Situated 120 miles due south of San Francisco, Pebble Beach was the inspiration of two amateur golfers, Jack Neville and Samuel Morse, who opened their masterpiece in 1919. Jack Nicklaus is a big fan: 'If I had only one more round of golf to play, I would choose to play at Pebble Beach,' he said. 'It's a superb championship test.'

The ninth hole is known as 'The Old Heartbreaker' as so many have ruined their card by landing on the beach (Dale Douglass took 19 shots to complete the hole in the Bing Crosby National Championship in 1963).

'The greatest meeting place of land and water'. The ninth and tenth holes at Pebble Beach are inspiring but terrifying to play.

The drive is usually played to the left away from the sea, although a small headland does offer protection against the sliced or pushed shot.

It is the second shot, however, that presents the problems. With the jagged cliffs biting into the fairway and the prevailing wind – always a factor at Pebble Beach – blowing in from the right, the daring golfer will take a chance on aiming 10 or even 20 yards out to sea with their long iron or even wood and hope that the ball will draw round and find the distant and rather small green. The meek (or wise) will fire the ball left well away from the sea and settle for a bogey.

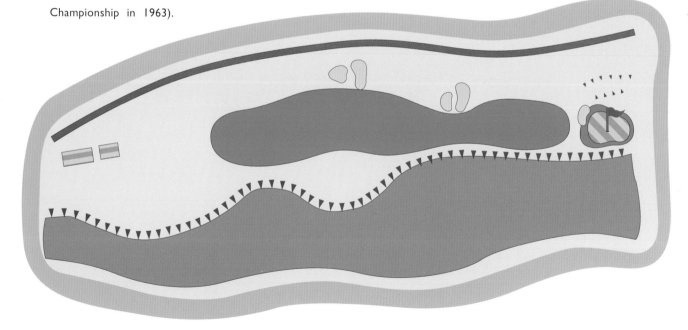

10. TURNBERRY, 452 YARDS PAR-4

One of the newer Open venues, Turnberry quickly became a favourite among the players. Lee Trevino, playing on a perfect summer morning at the first day of the 1994 Open, was moved to say: 'I tell you, if Heaven's any better than this, take me tomorrow.' Although built in the early part of the century, it was extensively damaged in World War II when many of the greens and fairways were razed to build an airfield base for Liberator bombers.

After the war it was brought back to life by the designer MacKenzie Ross, and those who play here will be forever in his debt. On a cloudless day with the sea at its bluest, the lighthouse on the headland, the famous Turnberry hotel on the hill above the clubhouse, and the dramatic island Ailsa Crag rising vertically out of the Irish Sea, there is surely no more beautiful setting in golf

Of all the holes on the Open roster, the 10th at Turnberry is closest to the sea. Here John Daly was doing so well in the 1994 Open until one of his wild drives was hooked and lost on the beach. He eventually took 7.

The drive from just under the lighthouse should, if possible, veer towards the left of the fairway and on to the flat plateau from where the golfer can address a long second shot from an even stance. The approach shot to green has to carry over a large bunker with an island of turf and avoid another sand trap close to the right-hand side of the green. Once on the green one has to concentrate hard, for it is too easy to be lulled into a false sense of security by the inspiring view back to the lighthouse.

Once used as a wartime airfield, the famous Turnberry links have been reborn.

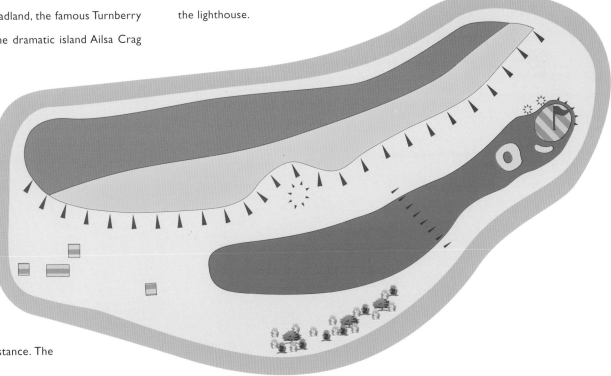

11. AUGUSTA, 445 YARDS PAR-4

The hole is enclosed by white dogwood shrubs.

Augusta is the ultimate strategic golf course; it is extremely beautiful; and best of all, it demands and inspires the most dramatic and unbelievable golf year after year.

Ben Crenshaw, twice winner of the Green Jacket, describes the fine line between glory and failure: 'Augusta is the most tempting golf course I've ever seen. It goads you into trying different shots because there's so much to gain. If you're right on your game and you live dangerously for a day and you can just skirt the trouble here and there, you can come off with a brilliant score. But if you're not, that's when it's really punishing.'

The 11th is the first of the 'Amen Corner' holes and needs careful thought, which is why it is so effective as a play-off

hole. Gary Player always insisted that it was best to drive down the left side of fairway, leaving a longer approach to the green – possibly a four iron rather than six iron – but bringing the advantage of hitting the ball away from the pond on the left rather than towards it. Ben Hogan was scared enough of the water to deliberately aim wide of the green and settle for a chip and a putt for par: 'If you see me on the eleventh green in two, you'll know I missed my second shot,' he would say. Nick Faldo is particularly fond of the 11th – in the 1989 play-off against Scott Hoch he sank a long birdie putt in near darkness to win his first Green Jacket, and won again the next year when Ray Floyd hit his approach shot into the pond. Larry Mize has also reason to be thankful to the 11th, chipping in from 30 yards in 1987 to snatch victory from the luckless Greg Norman.

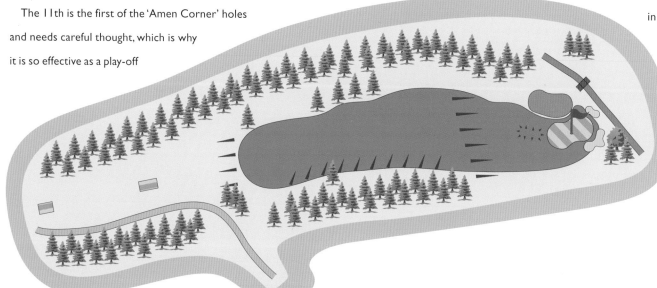

12. ROYAL LYTHAM, 198 YARDS PAR-3

Founded in 1886, and designed by Herbert Fowler, Royal Lytham is the most unromantic of the Open venues. The sea is nowhere to be seen and the course is bounded by a railway line to one side and by housing to the rest. But it is savage. Bernard Darwin summed up the general feeling: 'It has beautiful turf, but not much else of beauty. It is a beast but a just beast.' It places heavy emphasis on good driving and iron-play, and demands genuine expertise from sand; the 17th hole alone has 18 bunkers.

The 12th is a long par-3 that is particularly difficult to judge. The tee is sheltered within a small copse and it can be easy to underestimate the strength of the wind. Seve Ballesteros, in his amazing last round of 65 to win the Open in 1988, chose the wrong club. He hit a four iron that came up short of the raised green leaving him a difficult chip to

pin and a subsequent bogey – his only mistake in a near faultless round. A good long iron is required and Tom Lehman hit the perfect shot in the last round in the 1996 Open to be pin high. He holed the putt for his only birdie of the round and gave himself a valuable cushion over the

Bernard Darwin (left) admired Lytham's toughness.

chasing pack of Faldo, Els and McCumber. But it is easy to come unstuck: in 1974 Johnny Miller was mounting a challenge to the leader Gary Player until he hit a tee shot too hard and nearly went out of bounds behind the hole. He eventually took 6.

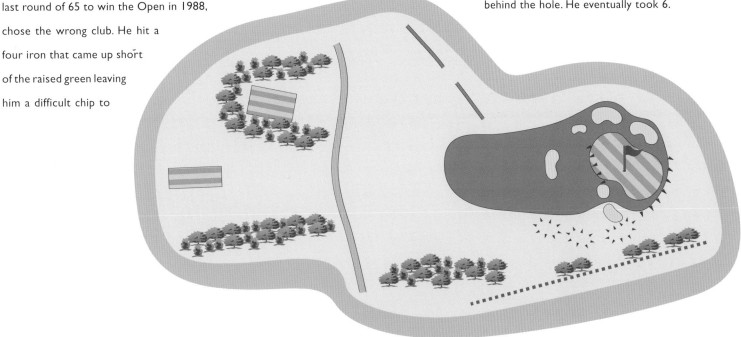

13. CASA DE CAMPO CAJUILES, 170 YARDS PAR-3

Cajuiles – the Spanish for cashew – was built in 1970 when the holiday-resort owner Alvaro Carta asked the architect Pete Dye to construct 'a special course' for the Dominican Republic. Dye, now today's premier golf course architect, was quick to accept the challenge and described his task as 'a chance of a lifetime to create a seaside course where so much of the sea – almost three miles of it – came into play'.

Built among coconut, sea grape and cashew trees, the course is famous for its imaginative par-3s. The 13th is one of the great fun holes of the world – a real death-or-glory shot. Nicknamed the Doughnut, and surrounded by four trees and a huge expanse of sand, it takes a fine shot to land on the green. Club selection is all important. On a still day a six or possibly seven iron will do. More often, however, a cooling breeze is blowing off the

Pete Dye saw Cajuiles as one of his greatest challenges.

Caribbean and straight into the golfer's face. Then a four or three iron is required to get home.

It is a tough but enticing hole – holidaymakers have been known to extend their vacation until they have been successful in mastering it.

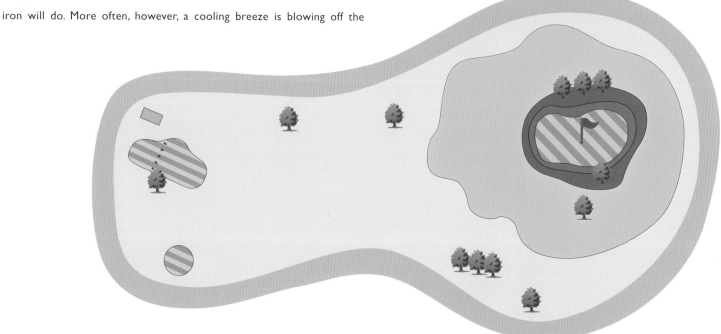

14. ROYAL DORNOCH, 445 YARDS PAR-4

For many years, Dornoch was a special golfing secret known only to the few. It was formed in 1877, although there are records of golf being played up to 300 years ago in the ancient Sutherland town. It is by far the most northerly of all the great links courses in Britain, and its inaccessibility has prevented the course being chosen as a venue for the Open. Now, it has been discovered by the most determined of the great players, many of whom have flown up there prior to the Open to get in some much-needed practice on tough linksland. Tom Watson hails the course as 'a natural masterpiece'.

The 14th, known as 'Foxy' because it is so tricky to play, is the most natural hole of them all. It has no bunkers but requires two very good shots to find the green. The drive must be long and must avoid the heavy rough on the left and the large dune to the right. The approach shot calls for a well-struck iron or wood to find a green that is raised four or five feet from the fairway.

Miss the green and you have to choose between the bump and run and shot up the bank or a floated chip that will be hit high and stop quick. Either way the shot has to be hit precisely and judged perfectly. And it is why sixes and sevens are common on this hole. The raised green here has been much

imitated in newer courses around the world and shaped much of Dornoch-born Donald Ross's thinking when designing his masterpiece, Pinehurst No. 2.

A perfect training ground for the most dedicated.

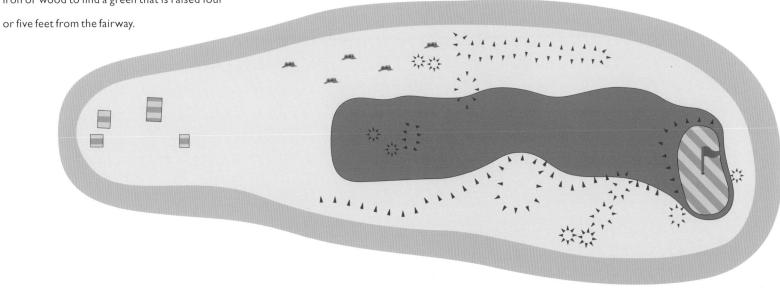

15. SEMINOLE, 498 YARDS PAR-5

Donald Ross.

Donald Ross was also responsible for Seminole – named after the local native American Indian tribe – in Palm Beach, Florida. Designed in the boom years of the early 1920s, Seminole is a formidable challenge to any golfer. Its main defences against a good score are its huge army of bunkers – there are over 200 – and the brisk wind that blows in straight from the Atlantic Ocean. The course was a particular favourite of Ben Hogan, who used to practice long and hard at Seminole every year prior to the Masters at Augusta: 'If you can play well there, you can play well anywhere,' he declared.

The dogleg right par-5 15th can be played in two ways. The adventurous or longer hitters can go the direct route, aiming for the thin strip of right-hand fairway that is bounded by a string of bunkers on the left and a lake on the right.

If the fairway is safely found, the green is reachable in two and birdies can be made, but the encroaching water will catch the mishit or sliced approach. The conservative or shorter hitters will take the safer but much longer route of the left-hand fairway, which arcs round the palm trees to the distant green – but this will take three or possibly four good hits. Then, in the hallmark of all Donald Ross courses, the green is raised and difficult to hit and contains many hidden borrows.

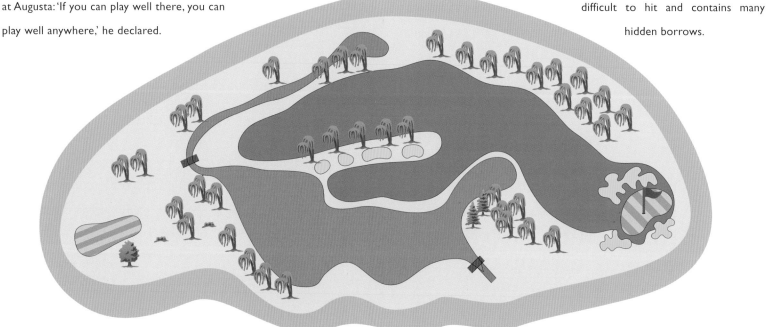

16. CYPRESS POINT, 233 YARDS PAR-3

The very private Cypress Point – it has only 250 members – was designed by Alister MacKenzie and opened in 1928. Situated in the foothills of the Santa Luca mountains, it is often compared to its near neighbour, Pebble Beach. Many judges think it is better; the twice US Open champion Julius Boros claimed: 'Pebble Beach has six great holes – all those that lie on the coastline. Cypress Point has eighteen of them, whether they lie on the coast or not.' It is a beautiful mixture of three types of course – heathland, woodland and links – and is often called 'the Sistine Chapel of golf'.

The 16th is a true death-or-glory hole. It's usually played into a brisk wind, and a driver is the only club to use. The direct route from tee to green is all carry and the slightest mishit or slice means oblivion in the Pacific Ocean. If you're not confident of reaching the green, it is best to

aim left – still a formidable carry – and play the hole as a par-4. Even the pros can be made to look like weekend hackers and it's no wonder that the hole is

Cypress Point – the Sistine Chapel of golf.

statistically the hardest on the USPGA tour. That fanatical amateur Bing Crosby is among the few who have holed in one.

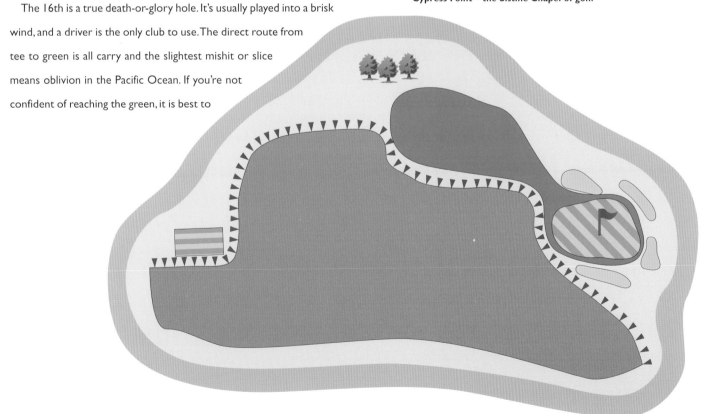

17. ST ANDREWS (OLD COURSE), 461 YARDS PAR-4

The most romantic venue in all golf.

This small grey university town is the Mecca of golf, where the great game began, with records of play going back to 1552. The course is unique: only 40 yards wide along its whole shepherd's-crook length, it ends and begins right in the middle of the old town with the last hole hard against shops, hotels and student digs. It features huge double greens; and it has many small, often hidden, bunkers that are just big enough, said Henry Longhurst, for 'an angry man and his niblick'.

Tony Lema, winner of the 1964 Open, aptly says: 'It's like going to Scotland and visiting your sick grandmother. She's old and she's crochety and she's eccentric. But look real close and, my, isn't she dignified and elegant? I sincerely believe anyone who doesn't fall in love with her is totally lacking in imagination.'

The 17th, or Road Hole as it is known, puts more fear into tournament pros than any other on the Open roster. Seve Ballesteros

calls it 'the hardest hole in championship golf'. It starts with a blind tee shot over old railway sheds. Slice, and the ball will go out of bounds into the grounds of the Old Course Hotel; hook and it will sink deep into thick rough on the left. The ideal drive is to go as far right as you dare, opening up the green with the second shot.

Now for the most difficult shot in golf. Go centre or left with the approach and the ball will be caught by the fearsome Road bunker that protects the flag in the middle of the green. Many call it the Sands of Nakajima after Tommy Nakajima took five shots to get out in 1978. Hit the approach too hard and the ball will fly over the green on to the road. Many opt to play short and right with their approach and aim to chip and putt for par, risk misjudging the pitch (or putt) up the narrow green and end up in the very Road bunker which all along they have been trying to avoid.

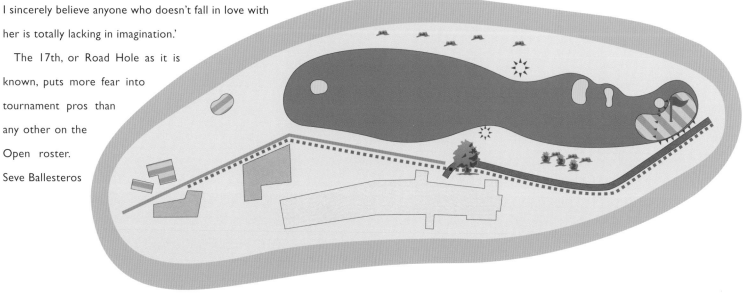

18. MUIRFIELD, 448 YARDS PAR-4

Muirfield, in the small East Lothian town of Gullane, was formed in 1891 when the Honourable Company of Edinburgh Golfers decided to forsake Musselburgh and find less cramped facilities outside the Scottish capital. Once dismissed by the famous pro Andrew Kirkaldy as 'an old water meadow', the Harry Colt-designed links is now perennially voted the Best Course in Britain and Ireland. Its amazing roll of Open winners – Vardon, Braid, Hagen, Cotton, Nicklaus, Trevino, Watson and Faldo – illustrates how it brings out the best in the best, and it is very popular with the players.

Jack Nicklaus says: 'It is not the toughest course I have ever played, but what makes it such a great course is the variety of shots it makes you play.' It certainly taught the young, brash Nicklaus a few valuable lessons when he first came across it in the 1959 Walker Cup: 'What I discovered was that you always had to temper distance with accuracy. You must put the ball in the right place. It was the first time that I really understood the meaning of the shot value of a course.'

An island of turf in a sea of trouble.

The 18th is a wonderful finishing hole, and anyone who makes a par there to win a tournament can feel justly proud. As with all the holes at Muirfield, the the drive is narrow, and it requires accuracy, length and a good deal of nerve to hit the drive beyond the bunkers flanking the fairway. The second shot normally requires a long iron that must fly a series of bunkers short of the green and also avoid the strange bunker with an island of turf on the right. That just leaves a green armed with a myriad humps and hollows, making judging the correct pace of the putt an art in itself. It is a fine hole which demands perfection in every facet of a golfer's game.

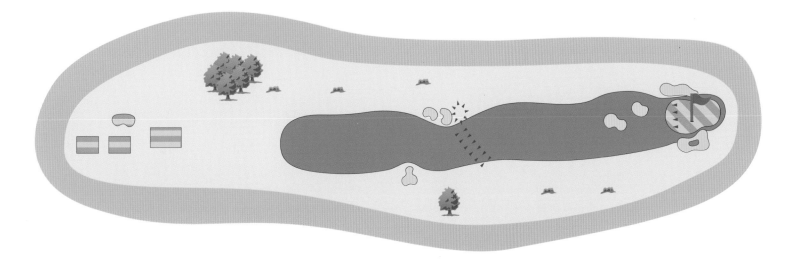

A CURIOUS GAME

'A CADDIE IS SOMEONE WHO ACCOMPANIES A GOLFER

AND DIDN'T SEE THE BALL EITHER.'

Anon

In his 1932 dystopian novel *Brave New World*, Aldous Huxley created a series of disturbing possibilities for the future of mankind.

He conjured up a cruel world without love or heroism; where synthetic babies were decanted from bottles and conditioned at every stage of development for the work that awaited them. It was a world in which the children of the poor were reared en masse in hygienic nurseries and taught by electric shock to curb their interest in flowers, pictures, and other seductive objects.

It was a world that was shallow, promiscuous, dehumanized, and society was pacified by television, scent organs, and ... golf.

Golf?

Who knows, he could be right. He wasn't far off the mark with promiscuity, test-tube babies and the influence of television, and today golf is the addictive passion for a staggering 27 million people in the United States alone.

It's a game that the richest pay fortunes to play, and Bill Clinton, the most powerful man in the world, centres his election campaigns around, playing classic courses in between speeches.

It is the visionary game played by the blind – a game for the common man that is rife with discrimination and elitism. A game that gives one player an incredible high and brings calm to another. Golf is a curious game.

Take, for example the challenge that took place in 1912 when Guy Livingstone, secretary of the Chelsea Golf School, wrote to the London *Daily Mail* that it wasn't strictly necessary to keep your eye on the ball when playing golf.

He was swamped by a tidal wave of angry responses including one from the former Open champion J. H. Taylor, who doubted 'anything so heretical' had ever been said about the game.

It prompted a Mr Toogood, pro at the Chelsea, to an extraordinary challenge. Believing the argument that keeping your head still was more important that keeping your eye on the ball, he practised for days on end to play blindfold against Tindal Atkinson at Sunningdale.

Toogood's driving and putting, even blindfold, was extraordinarily good and his approach shots were remarkably accurate, but he would have been pushing his luck, even with his eyes open.

Tindal Atkinson played off scratch – and he knew every blade of grass at Sunningdale.

At the first tee, Toogood carefully addressed his ball, settled himself in position, then said, 'All right.' An assistant then tied a purple handkerchief tightly over his eyes, and Toogood drove off.

The report at the time said: 'Toogood's first drive was a fairly long one under the trying conditions, but slightly sliced. Mr Tindal Atkinson pulled his tee shot a little. It was a trying ordeal for the amateur, since he had everything to lose and little to gain in this match with a blindfolded player. Toogood's second shot, however, practically settled the game. The ball was lying fairly clear, but Toogood "snatched" at the ball and sliced it badly. Indeed, it passed within a foot of a too-daring photographer who was snapping the shot, and had it not been badly topped it would have gone far out into the rough.

'This was Toogood's chief fault throughout the match. He always appeared to "snatch" at the ball and nearly always sliced it a little. Moreover, when putting he was nearly always to the right of the hole.

'It must be stated, however, that just lately he had had a nasty fall off his bicycle and hurt his side; consequently every stroke yesterday caused him considerable pain and doubtless affected his play.'

Even then, injured, in pain, blindfolded and playing against a scratch opponent although he did not win any holes, he managed to halve the ninth and tenth. Tindal Atkinson won by 8 up and 7 to play.

Former British Ryder Cup captain Charles Whitcombe fell victim to play-daze:
'My mind just went blank. I was in a haze.'

How good a player was Toogood? Three times during the match he was bunkered. Blindfolded and without grounding the club, he got out in two every time.

In the 1930s golf was the source of a new medical condition, quaintly dubbed play-daze. Described as a form of mental blackout owing to over-concentration, play-daze was thought to be an increasing problem in the world of competitive sport – notably with the decision of Harry Bentley, the British Walker Cup player, to take a complete rest from the game.

'My doctor will not let me take part in the Lancashire County Championship at Formby next week,' he said. 'As soon as I got back from Deal my nerves seemed to be all wrong and I felt terrible. My doctor told me to put my clubs away for a while.'

The week before at Southport Charles Whitcombe, the British Ryder Cup captain, had fallen victim to play-daze. His ball became embedded behind a bush. Four times he hacked at it, then threw it across the green, disqualifying himself. 'My mind just went blank,' he said afterwards. 'I was in a haze.'

Funnily enough, while overplaying can create havoc with the nerves, it is often to the golf course that those who are under most pressure turn for peace of mind. Golf soothes away the most awful trauma. After all, Mary Queen of Scots resorted to a few holes after the murder of her husband.

In 1936 a man with a revolver tried to assassinate Edward VIII during a royal review of the troops on Constitution Hill in central London. A sharp-eyed police officer knocked the man to the ground before the gun could be fired. While the whole world hastened to send messages of congratulations to the King on his escape, he spent the afternoon regaining his composure by playing golf alone at Coombe Hill.

In earlier days – 1603 to be precise – King James I of England showed that golf had long been a royal priority. Within a week of ascending to the throne

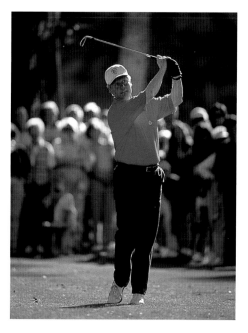

LEFT: Edward VIII who often played golf to escape from pressure.
CENTRE: US president **Bill Clinton** is still improving as a golfer.
RIGHT: John F. Kennedy, the most talented of the presidential golfers.

he had appointed his own personal clubmaker. Affairs of state came later.

But then golf is an instant remedy for overworked men and women. American presidents, above all, are noteworthy proponents of the calming effects of wielding the irons. Bill Clinton worked out a solution to the Bosnian crisis on the putting green at the White House. He's the only president in history who has managed to reduce his handicap while in office. But some say he cheats so much that it is hard to work out just what his handicap is.

The White House green was built by President Eisenhower, who was found on the links by aides in 1960, when US-Soviet relations took a turn for the worse after an American U-2 spy plane was shot down.

President Wilson played a full round before declaring war on Germany in 1917. John F. Kennedy played off seven, but tried to keep his love of the game a secret lest it make him look elitist. And he would sometimes put opponents off by mentioning water hazards as they addressed the ball.

Vice-President Dan Quayle plays superbly, prompting his wife to say: 'Dan would rather play golf than have sex any day.'

President Bush demanded 'gimmes' on the grounds of 'respect for my high office'. Richard Nixon was once caught throwing his ball out of a bush.

Gerald Ford, once a 12-handicapper, developed a habit of hitting spectators while playing at pro-ams. When Clinton, Bush and Ford played together Ford struck a woman on the hand with his second shot, and Bush sliced a drive into the face of a 71-year-old woman, who required ten stitches.

Calvin Coolidge once took 11 on a par-3. President Taft, elected in 1908, refused to meet the president of Chile, saying: 'I'll be damned if I will give up my game of golf!'

Presidents are just about the most powerful players you can get, but there are others, more powerful, who are asked for help. The Findhorn Foundation in Moray, Scotland, is launching a programme called 'Fairway to Heaven' which is aimed at showing golfers how to come into closer communion with God while in trouble on the course.

Hopefully it will be done with a little more respect than was displayed by the golf writer Bernard Darwin, who is alleged to have called for guidance while stuck beneath the towering face of a bunker. 'God help me. By the way, this is serious; don't send the lad. Better come yourself.'

Golf can create a high for those who you'd have thought would have had the chance to try just about every kind of high there is.

Dennis Hopper is one of the movie world's coolest, strangest guys. If the part is weird, crazed and dangerous, then Hopper's probably the actor playing it. This is the man whose image has been linked to drugs, non-conformity

LEFT: Dennis Hopper in *Blue Velvet*. (De Laurentiis)
TOP RIGHT: Jack Nicholson as private eye Jake Gittes in *Chinatown*. (Paramount Pictures)

and complete hatred of the establishment. He plays golf? Yes, and he plays with Bob Dylan!

Could all those peace-loving hippies really have done all that revolutionary, bomb-banning, free-love-protesting stuff only to see their icons dressed in check sweaters pootling around the fairways in a golf cart? Sorry, sixties, that's the way it is with golf.

Hopper — a member of the Riviera Country Club where the joining fee is around $580,000 — Dylan and Neil Young are regular partners. Jack Nicholson wants to build his own course — Willie Nelson has already built one.

Victor McLaglen (right) in the John Ford-directed classic *She Wore a Yellow Ribbon*. (RKO Radio Pictures Inc)

Bob Dylan in Sam Peckinpah's *Pat Garrett and Billy the Kid*. (MGM)

You'd think that actors, world-famous musicians and celebrities would generally be welcomed with open arms at most places, but golf isn't like that. Hopper tells of one course that turned down his $225,000 application fee. 'Then there's Hillcrest and the Los Angeles Country Club: one's Jewish and one's WASP – no Jews, no blacks, and no actors either.'

According to Hopper, Victor McLaglen, the giant Irish former wrestler who appeared as the tough guy in a string of classic John Wayne movies, applied to join the LA Country Club.

They said: 'We're sorry, Mr McLaglen, but we don't accept actors here.'

And he said: 'Actors? Nobody ever accused me of being an actor before.'

Kevin Costner, star of *Tin Cup*, the world's first popular golf movie (and everybody thought that you could never make a popular golf movie), was a non-player who learned the game solely in order to look convincing on screen, and he ended up with a middle-order handicap. But as always with life, the truth was more curious than the fiction. During the film Costner plays a round using a rake, a baseball bat and a shovel – a novel incident in the film, and one that is better for being based on a true story.

That incident happened in 1937 when big-spending John Montagu of the

How John Montagu beat Bing Crosby – LEFT TO RIGHT: 'driving' the ball with his baseball bat; carrying his 'clubs' to the first tee; 'putting' with his rake.

But Montagu was more than just that. Newspaper reports of the match were read by a Los Angeles detective who recognized the golfer as Laverne Moor, a bandit wanted for a roadside hold-up seven years earlier. 'We believed that Moor would one day reveal himself – he was always a real good golfer,' said the delighted sleuth.

Crosby himself was a fine player. He is one of only six amateurs to have made a hole-in-one at the 16th at Cypress Point, perhaps the most spectacular tee shot in the world.

While the many of the US courses, such as Lakeside, have astronomical membership fees, Alan Shepard, commander of the Apollo 14 space ship, was the first to play golf literally out of this world.

In 1971 he played two shots on the surface of the moon using an iron clubhead on an improvised shaft.

One shot flew 200 yards, the other was a shank. He returned to Earth to find a telegram from the Royal and Ancient: 'Warmest congratulations to all of you on your great achievement and safe return. Please refer to Rules of Golf section on etiquette, paragraph 6, quote – before leaving a bunker a

hugely expensive Lakeside Club in Beverly Hills played against Bing Crosby for a $20 wager. Crosby had a full set of clubs while Montagu had only three clubs, plus the rake, shovel and baseball bat.

He 'drove' off by throwing up the golf ball and hitting it full swing with the bat – straight down the fairway for 300 yards. He actually sank a 30-foot putt with the rake. Crosby said: 'I am never playing Montagu for big money. The man is a magician.'

player should carefully fill up all holes made by him therein – unquote.'

But then secretaries are sticklers for the rules. It's the same story at the distinguished Royal Lytham St Anne's, one of the great Open courses. It was there that the golfer Donald Beaver thinned his ball out of a bunker and found it stuck in the ivy growing on the clubhouse windowsill.

The knowledgeable Mr Beaver realized that the ball was still in play. He also realized that spikes could not be worn in the clubhouse. He removed his shoes, walked upstairs and played back out on to the 18th green. It was ingenious, skilful, and all to no avail. The club secretary, who had held the post for more than 40 years, disqualified Beaver for leaving the course without having completed his round.

Still, at least the ordinary golfer has a chance of playing at Royal Lytham. There is no chance of the common man or woman playing at Augusta, home of the Masters. How much does that worry most golfers? Not much. How much did it worry Texans Denis Wilkerson, Barron Jacobsen and Jim Williams? A heap. They wanted to play Augusta – and the other great courses of America – and realized that they would have no chance, so they decided to build a replica course.

Using aerial photographs processed into 3-D graphics by computer they drew the contours of the holes and then copied them exactly, importing vegetation to complete the job. Amen Corner took 2,000 azaleas, 400 myrtles, 400 dogwoods and liberal quantities of pine needles from Georgia so the players could feel the authentic crunch underfoot.

One player who didn't feel anything underfoot – he was walking on air at the time – was Eric Fiddian, a 23-year-old Stourbridge golfer playing in the Irish Open Amatuer Championship on the links at Royal County Down in 1933.

He scored a hole-in-one at the 128-yard seventh, then another at the 205-yard fourteenth.

But he lost his match three and two. It is a curious game.

Tim Steveson

The old walking stick at last gets replaced by something more useful.

ANY OLD IRON...

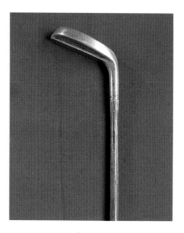

DESPITE THE OLD CHESTNUT ABOUT GOLF BEING A DULL GAME FOR DULL

PEOPLE, IT HAS LONG INSPIRED SOME STUNNINGLY CREATIVE ARTISTS —

AND BEEN THE GODSEND OF THE SHARP-EYED ADVERTISING MAN.

Do not throw this book away! Guard it with your life. It may not improve your swing, but one day it might make your descendants fabulously rich. It might not, of course, but will you be prepared to take that risk when you have taken a look at the curious world of golf memorabilia?

Many believe you would need great courage, a touch of madness, or a pot-load of money voluntarily to turn out on a golf course dressed like Payne Stewart. They say you need all three to be a golf collector.

Of all the strange practices surrounding the game – and a close look at the rules will reveal a fair few curiosities – the collecting of golf memorabilia is up there with the best of them.

Not that the ancient game hasn't drawn its fair share of tributes in the form of brilliant artistry, elegant chinaware and some pretty memorable humour – but would you pay out your good money for a second-hand box of wooden tees?

The avid collector does, and will rush to snap up a dog-eared copy of the *Radio Times* of 30 June 1933 simply because it has a picture of Gene Sarazen on the cover.

When the long-dead Thomas Mattison penned *The Goff* – the first book on the game – in 1743, he started a collectors' boom that sees museums fighting

Old Tom Morris and the 14th hole at St Andrews depicted on a tin of mint-flavoured drops.

over the stuff and many of the world's top players scouring curious market stalls in far-flung lands.

Since Mattison's 24-page primer – reprinted twice before his death – rafts of golf books have become collectors' items.

Anthology, architecture, greenkeeping, club histories, fiction, humour, poetry, autobiographical, history, annuals and year books – there's no end to the catalogue of golf books.

Worse – there are books about collecting golf books. By 1910 Harry B. Wood's epic *Golfing Curios and the Like* documented 500 worthy tomes. Cecil Hopkinson assembled the thrilling *Collecting Golf Books 1743–1938*, and in the late 1960s Joseph S.F. Murdock put out *The Library of Golf 1743–1946* with a supplement on card covers in 1978. (And don't forget that to the average collector anything made as recently as 1978 is the equivalent of last week.)

At the time, the book was scorned by an ungrateful public who, unimpressed by its elegant title and dismissive of its ripping plot, weren't prepared to fork out the eight pounds it cost for a pristine copy. But if you find even a tatty one in a junk shop these days you'll have earned yourself at least £300.

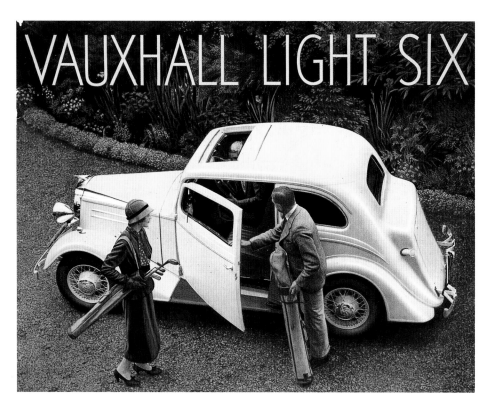

FAR LEFT: Advertising has produced a rich source for collectors, in this case a 1930s promotion for Vauxhall cars.

LEFT: Today golf and music might seem an unlikely mix, but not in 1900.

BOTTOM LEFT: Advertisers would associate a pretty girl swinging a club with any new product.

BELOW: The title page for Thomas Mattinson's *Goff* – the first book on golf.

Like anything that attracts the fan or fanatic, the range of golf collectables can be split into categories. There are those that are desired for their rarity, others for their beauty and yet more for their historic associations.

Almost anything to do with Bobby Jones is sought after, especially his vellum-bound book *Down the Fairway*, which is worth £1,000 a copy.

When it comes to art almost anything goes, with prints, etchings, lithographs, aquatints, mezzotints, steel engravings and photogravure all commanding high prices.

The earliest paintings were mainly the result of golf societies commissioning portraits of their captains and officers. The first known painting is of William Innes, captain of the Royal Blackheath Golf Club in 1790, an original oil by Lemmel Francis Abbot. A few years ago a portrait in oils of the 1823 Royal and Ancient captain John Whyte-Melville was sold for £165,000. Unsurprisingly, most of the original art is owned by the Royal and Ancient Golf Club, Royal Blackheath GC and the United States Golf Association.

The curious thing is that despite the old chestnut about golf being a dull game for dull people, it has long inspired some stunningly creative artists – and been the godsend of the sharp-eyed advertising man.

New cars, holidays, books, calendars, food, drink, tobacco, magazines and some truly awful clothes – you could sell anything if you stuck a pretty girl with a golf club on the packaging. Who cared if the link between golf and product was tenuous? Hand a creative copywriter a picture of a smiling face and a well-clipped fairway and you had customers queuing halfway down the street.

'The Scotch Lassie, like her English sister, revels in a Game of Golf and does the course with zest, knowing that her Sphere Suspenders will keep her ever trim and neat'!

There was even a time when the game was considered so generally appealing, decent and – dare one say it? – upright that one company used the image of a rugged golfer to sell contraceptives!

With the expansion of the railways and spread of tourism came a flood of colourful posters encouraging people to travel – and golf was a key temptation. They promised fun, cost little to produce and were an eye-catching way to spread the word. Few survived once they had outlived their purpose, torn down or pasted over to make way for the latest thing, which is why one of the original seaside posters would fetch over £3,000 these days.

Ceramics are one of the most popular forms of collecting golfiana, and before World War II golfing porcelain and stoneware was given as prizes. String together a few good rounds and you'd be halfway to a complete Royal Doulton dinner service.

As for silver – the display cabinets of the world are littered with the stuff, thanks to the heady days when society trophies were made of the real thing and didn't come on little plastic stands.

Championship winners went home clutching anything from golf clubs

FAR LEFT: A record cover for *That's Amoré*. The song won *The Caddy* an 1953 Oscar nomination for Best Song.
LEFT: Proof at last that golf is a sport for 'He-men'!

overlaid with silver to loving cups and solid silver plates. Early medals were made of silver and gold with intricate design – as opposed to today's fake bronze roundel glued on a wooden plaque.

The successful turn-of-the-century husband and wife golfers could have furnished a home with an array of silver objects, including jewellery, cruet sets, vases, tape measures, clocks, inkwells, blotters and buttons.

Silver spoons are popular. Typical is a pair, each 3¾ inches tall, showing a male and female golfer. The female spoon shows the back view of the lady with a driver at the top of her swing, the club lying across her back. She is wearing a long skirt, small button-up shoes, a fitted jacket with cuffs, gloves and a beret on a mop of very curly hair. Turn it over and there is a detailed front view. Made in 1910 in Birmingham, the pair will fetch well over £500. And there are butter knives, wine-tasting spoons, pickle forks, toasting forks, eggcups, knife rests, toast racks and on and on.

All this domestic booty allowed the proud (or guilty) golfer the opportunity to arrive home and present the useful bit of silver to his beloved in a victorious gesture – rather in the manner of the caveman hurling down a brontosaurus leg at the cave entrance.

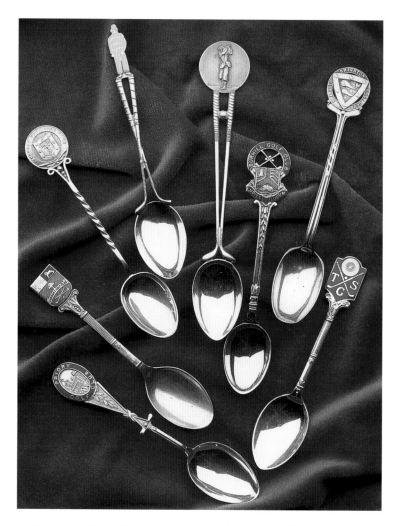

**LEFT: An art nouveau 'golf ball' tea set.
RIGHT: crested silver spoons have long been popular prizes in club competitions.**

Women golfers did not, however, make much effort to repay the compliment. Instead of commissioning essentials like the solid-silver fish slice and tea caddy that were missing from the collection, they chose to award themselves jewellery as society prizes. So much more sensible.

There are candlesticks, serviette rings, menu holders decorated with clubs and balls, not to mention vesta cases (which held matches) in silver, ivory, tortoiseshell or enamel. Here things become hotly competitive, as collectors

LEFT: Willie Park Jnr's Open medal of 1887 could fetch over £30,000 at auction.
RIGHT: Early postcards of Old Tom Morris are great favourites.

of golfiana vie with collectors of 'smoke-iana' (smokers' collectibles). The auctioneer could make a killing if bidding became lively.

Some of the most prized items on the collectors' circuit is the memorabilia from great events. You are hardly likely to end up buying the Claret Jug clutched so proudly by Open winners, but you might end up with one of the medals awarded to the champion. A few Open medals have reached the market and these days you could reasonably expect one to make well over £30,000.

Even Amateur Championship items should not be overlooked. A medal won by Michael Scott at the Royal Liverpool Golf Club in 1933 was auctioned for £14,000. Scott was the oldest winner of the British Amateur, at the age of 55.

Just watching a tournament can put you on the road to a collector's heaven. A first Masters programme from the 'First Annual Invitation Tournament', as it was then called, at the Augusta National Club on 22–25 March 1934 will command up to £7,000.

If it seems surprising that the players' bag tags are sought after, take note that there is even a trade in notable golf parking permits!

Collecting clubs is a speciality in itself and has become so popular that the marketplace is littered with forgeries. Jamie Ortiz-Patino, owner of the

Ryder Cup host course Valderrama, paid over £90,000 for a seventeenth century 'rake' iron to put in his personal museum.

Early clubs were made of beech, ash or thornweed, and often apprentices would mould a club which they felt was not good enough for playing with into a walking stick or an umbrella – still highly prized. Women came to covet parasols with golfing handles, often in silver, gold or ivory.

Finding early postcards of the great players is proving more difficult these days, and a rare postcard of Tom Morris Snr, Open winner in 1861, 1862, 1864 and 1867, can now cost up to £120.

Greeting cards have become one of the most popular areas for devotees at prices around £25. They include Christmas cards in all shapes and sizes, merit cards given to schoolchildren as prizes at a Sunday School, Easter cards, leap year

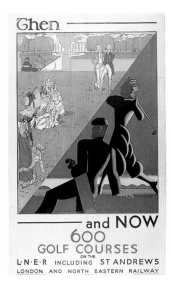

BELOW: Colourful posters encouraged travel on the newly expanded rail network.

ABOVE: A golfing Valentine from World War I.
LEFT: Tobacco companies were quick to associate themselves with golf through cigarette cards and shop displays.

day, Thanksgiving and New Year cards and even Valentines with surprisingly immodest messages:

> 'Golf is a dandy game, I think.
>
> At pretty girls I always wink.
>
> Love is the Game that suits me to a Tee.
>
> Come Dear Valentine, come and play with me.'

Then there are books. The US tour player Ben Crenshaw has amassed a wonderful collection, is a great friend of many of the specialist sellers, and is particularly proud of his rare acquisitions. But few of the big-name players are major collectors, although many have a small amount of cherished equipment.

One of the latter is Mark Roe, one of Europe's top professional players. Consistently a leading money-winner on the PGA European tour (1992 Lancome Trophy, 1994 French Open); he has represented England in the

European tour professional Mark Roe is a keen collector of golfing memorabilia.

Dunhill Cup at St Andrews and was the best European finisher in the 1995 US Open. His interest in golfing memorabilia was sparked 15 years ago when he was an assistant professional at Arrowe Park golf club just outside Birkenhead and members occasionally brought in old sets of clubs to be valued.

He says: 'I am one of the most enthusiastic collectors and I am very fond of some of the things I have picked up, like my porcelain golfer and caddie figurines painted by the famous artist John Hassall.'

Mark's first love is a collection of old golf balls. He can trace the evolution of the golf ball starting with a feathery from 1840, going on to the various gutta-percha balls of the second half of the nineteenth century, through to the development of the Coburn-Haskell-designed 'modern' rubber-cored ball such as the lattice and bramble-patterned variety. All very different from the ultra-modern Top-Flite Strata ball that he uses today for tournament play.

ABOVE (left to right):
A pair of Swiss porcelain figurines – the clubs are made of wood.
Books by Bobby Jones are much sought after.
LEFT: Mark Roe is particularly fond of his collection of old golf balls.
ABOVE: Old ball boxes, especially ones as rare as Zodiac Zome, are now in vogue.

'The expression "Oh, you bounder!" comes directly from the Haskell golf ball,' he said. 'The Haskells, when first invented in 1904, were known as "Bounding Billys" because of the extra distance they travelled when hit, and players who had the advantage of using the new balls were immediately dubbed "Bounders".

'I would like to be able to try out the effectiveness of the old clubs and balls, but unfortunately most collectors have their old equipment so highly insured that you just don't get the opportunity. The only time I did get the chance I was allowed to hit only a couple of shots, and you could immediately feel the difference.

'At impact there was nothing like the same "ping" you get from modern equipment, and the ball travelled only half the distance I would expect to get. It must have been quite exhausting and very difficult. I don't know how long it would take to master backspin with them!

'I've also got a long-nosed "play" club used by the three-times British Open winner Jamie Anderson, and a "mid-spoon" and "baffie-spoon" manufactured by the clubmaker Douglas McEwan.

These long-nosed clubs are made of hard woods such as beech, thorn, tulip and pear with lead inserted at the back of the clubhead to give extra weight and ram's horn at the bottom to protect the sole. The shafts are of hickory and the grips of calfskin.'

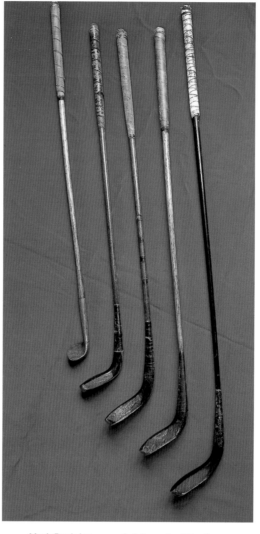

Mark Roe's long-nosed clubs and rutting iron are a far cry from the equipment he uses on the PGA tour.

Shop carefully and you can find a large range of weird and wonderful clubs from the turn of the century – a time of great experimentation for clubmakers. All seemed designed for special occasions. The tiny-headed rutting iron that was used for hitting balls out of cart ruts; a giant niblick, with a face the size of a man's hand, was used for extra height while chipping; a 'rake' iron was considered helpful when getting out of heavy rough; and the friend to all golfers was the anti-shanking iron.

More useful, perhaps, was the Urquhart adjustable-headed iron. A golfer, armed with just a small coin, could change the elevation of the clubhead from a wedge to a one iron or even a straight face for putting. R. Johnston played the 1906 British Open at Muirfield with a single club similar to this and managed to ace the par-3 14th. Putters, too, come in all shapes and sizes, reflecting golfers' eternal (and desperate) search for the putter that will give them the killer touch on the greens. Most noticeable is the centre-shafted Schenectady putter, used so notoriously by the American Walter Travis when winning the British Amateur title in 1904.

And if your junk-shop patrols bring you across a Harry Busson four wood, you are on to a small fortune. Busson was an incomparable clubmaker based at Walton Heath from the 1930s to the 1950s, and his streamlined clubs with

Rocket metal shafts are certain to reach £2,000. Is it not only the seriously old material that is worth money. Clubs from the 1960s, like a Julius Boros MacGregor keyhole wood, will sell for as much as £800.

Tees and balls are worth money these days, too. The golfer whose forefathers lost so few balls that they were able to hand down a few old favourites is fortunate indeed. But mint-condition items, too, are extremely valuable: an unused feathery golf ball could fetch £12,000. And balls still wrapped and in their original boxes are the centre of a booming collecting area. With the first golf ball box issued in 1895 by Silvertown, there are plenty of them out there.

The international auctioneers and valuers Sotheby's reflect the boom in collectables with a sale of golf memorabilia every six months. So next Christmas, when you win the tin of biscuits that's seventh prize in the golf club raffle, don't be disheartened. Check to see if there is a golfer painted on the side or the top – if there is, leave the wrapper on, stick it in the attic and start counting the pennies. Better than that new set of clubs any day.

Tim Steveson

The turn of the century saw great experimentation in club making: (clockwise from the bottom) Forgan centre-shafted chipper, Spalding spring-faced iron, Mills Duplex aluminium-headed iron, Spalding cleek with wooden-faced insert, Urquhart adjustable headed iron, giant niblick, Jack White elliptical mid iron, rake iron and anti-shank iron.

INSTRUCTION

'NEVER TRY TO KEEP MORE THAN **300** SEPARATE THOUGHTS

IN YOUR MIND DURING YOUR SWING.'

Henry Beard

TOM LEHMAN

In most sports there is somebody who stands out as both a brilliant talent and as a shining example of decency. Arthur Ashe was everything the game of tennis could have dreamed of; in soccer Pele was close to Mr Perfect. In golf, there isn't a better combination of outright skill and sheer likeability than in the shape of Tom Lehman.

The Minnesotan is as modest and amiable off the course as he is tough and highly competitive on it. Churchgoer, charity fundraiser, family man; great golfer.

But the way in which Lehman kept Nick Faldo, Ernie Els and company at bay on the scorching final day of the 1996 Open at Royal Lytham St Annes proved his steel and his class.

And it put an end to the doubters who had dogged his earlier career saying: 'Nice guys never win — and that rules out Lehman.'

His is a classic rags-to-riches story: he struggled for years to make ends meet and almost gave up golf for good. When he won his first big pay cheque of £180,000 — he went shopping for new clothes but wouldn't buy trousers for £90 because he worried that it was too much money to spend on pants.

Yet when he won the Open, the first $20,000 of his winnings was apportioned to go to a rehabilitation centre for juvenile delinquents.

With his quality all-round game, his grit, and his temperament there's no reason why Lehman's Open success shouldn't be followed by a series of majors — and a series of gifts that will go a long way to helping young people out of trouble.

Tom has many golfing qualities but probably the most outstanding is his ability to hit the ball straight; his poise and skill with a mid-iron, perhaps the most reliable and potent weapon in his armoury, rarely lets him down in the heat of battle, and he's particularly deadly with a five iron in his hands.

'I let the loft of the club get the ball in the air, as you don't need to be helping it gain flight — that's something you do with the hands or body.

'I just go ahead and swing the club, keeping my head steady and turning around my spine, ensuring I prevent my spine from moving either laterally or vertically.

'It's like a machine — you want to have as few moving parts as possible in order to avoid breaking down.

- Keep your head steady
- Maintain a steady spine position
- Turn round spine on way back and through
- The ball gets in the way of the clubhead and away she goes!
- Don't try to swing too hard
- Hit within yourself, using 80 per cent of your power.

'To be honest, I don't think of technique at all — all I think about is picking a target out, visualizing the shot and swinging the club. I feel where the clubhead is. Basically it's all down to intuition; I play by feel.

'Golf is a game you play and is similar to, say, an artist who is creating something. You don't do it in stages but bit by bit — it's all in one big picture. If you can get the big picture in your head, you're on the way.

'My advice is to be as natural as possible and just let it happen. Even if you're struggling badly with your game, then you may only need to think about one or two swing thoughts at the most, such as a full shoulder turn, shifting your weight properly or keeping your head steady. Don't make the game too complicated.'

SWING SEQUENCE

To win the USPGA Tour Order of Merit not only requires talent, determination and endurance: it also calls for the ability to hit consistently good shots week in, week out. Topping the 1996 Order confirmed that Tom Lehman has that ability, thanks to a golf swing which, while very individual, is also as sound as it is powerful.

The Lehman action is something of a throwback to the swings of the 1950s and 1960s, and there are parts of Tom's swing, especially his position at the top and his action through impact, where he resembles the legendary Arnold Palmer at his peak. And who knows? With a great temperament and a truly competitive nature, Tom Lehman has all the credentials required to follow in the great man's footsteps.

(1) Hitting solid and accurate golf shots first and foremost requires a sound platform from which to swing the club and Tom Lehman's address position is perfect. Tom's set-up is completely free of tension, with his feet solidly planted a comfortable shoulder-width apart, his arms hanging freely at a natural angle from his shoulders and his legs nicely flexed. Note also how Tom holds his head up, keeping his chin well clear of his chest.

(2) Tom starts the club back smoothly with his hands and arms and there is little or no body movement in the early stage of his backswing.

(3) Only as the club approaches waist height in the backswing do the hips start to turn slightly. Note, too, how the clubface appears slightly hooded, rather than fanned open at this point, which is due in some degree to Tom's desire to create the maximum backswing extension and take the club almost straight back on a fairly upright swing path.

(4) Approaching the top of the backswing and that straight left arm indicates Tom has continued to build that wide swing arc which will become a major factor in creating the great power he is able to generate in his downswing. The hips are still resisting the pull of the upper body created by his shoulders turning and that high chin position has enabled the left shoulder to turn freely across his chest. At this point in his backswing the club is perfectly in plane, with the back of the left hand mirroring the angle of the clubface and shaft.

(5) It is at this point that Tom Lehman makes a move which is unique to his swing. Just as the club reaches the top of the backswing, Tom arches his left wrist slightly and this has the effect of closing the face of the club just a fraction. Although the shaft of the club is well short of being parallel to the ground to the top of his backswing, Tom has still created a huge amount of coil by winding the top half of his body against the resistance created in the lower half, through a restricted hip turn.

(6) Because there has been very little foot action in the backswing, Tom has no problems returning his weight smoothly back on to his left side at the start of his downswing, as he pulls the club back down powerfully towards the ball with his left arm. With an upright backswing path, there is always the danger of the club coming over the top as it starts back down and creating an out-to-in downswing path. However, that slight 'arching' of the left wrist at the top helps ensure that Tom's right elbow is tucked well into his right side as he starts down, enabling him to attack the ball with the club moving on a slightly flatter in-to-out swing path.

(7) This is an extremely powerful position which highlights Tom's great physical strength. At this point in the downswing, most amateur golfers would have allowed the right arm to straighten. However, Tom's strength enables him to hold back the clubhead release to the last possible moment, to ensure maximum clubhead speed through impact. Note how the arched left wrist position has also been maintained, ensuring the left wrist won't collapse through the hitting area.

(8) All the power generated in Lehman's downswing has now been released through impact, yet he is still in full control of his swing. His head has stayed down and his weight has been transfered smoothly on to his left side. Unlike many players, he doesn't produce a fast cross-over of the hands through impact. Instead, Lehman's action through impact is one of a physically strong man and there is no attempt to 'flick' the ball away off the turf. The right hand hits through under the left, driving the clubface straigh through impact along the target line; which is one of the reasons why Lehman is one of the most accurate iron players in the modern game.

(9) Despite the great power and clubhead speed generated through impact, Tom finishes his swing perfectly balanced. His hips have fully cleared, the belt buckle on his trousers is facing directly towards the target and yet another five-iron shot is flying straight at the flag.

Kevin Brown

MARIE-LAURE DE LORENZI

Marie-Laure de Lorenzi took to golf at an early age. At the age of seven she was caddying for her mother, and by the time she was nine she was beating teenage boys in local competitions in her home town of Biarritz, in south-western France.

Marie-Laure joined the Women's Professional Golf European Tour in 1987 and immediately won the title of Rookie of the Year. The following year she utterly dominated the tour by winning seven times, still a tour record a full decade later.

She has won 18 tour titles, twice represented Europe in the Solheim Cup, and her calm under pressure has earned her the nickname of 'Mademoiselle Cool'.

Calmness, she says, is a key to lower handicaps. 'Most weeks I play with men in Pro-Am events. They are generally reasonable golfers, but they all want to hit the ball further than me because I am a woman.

'Mostly they can't do it in any case, but the harder they try, the worse they get. Their problem is that they get tense and try to use pure force to blast the ball as far as possible. It is about the worst thing you could do.

'You don't need to be particularly strong to regularly hit the ball well over 200 yards – and if the average club golfer could do that from the tee, he or she would see their handicap come down.

'For me the rhythm of the swing is the most important thing. I take it slowly and just release my hands through the ball. Just concentrate, relax and swing – and then see the ball sail into the distance.

'If you want proof that you don't have to be big and strong to get good distance off the tee, watch Alison Nicholas. She's one of the best women golfers in Europe, who has won in the US, and who stands just five feet in her golf spikes.

SWING SEQUENCE: THE SET-UP

'Don't be tense. Don't try to just hammer the ball. And, most of all, don't worry. Often people in **Pro-Ams** are so nervous that they top the ball, or worse, they play an air shot. Remember, at the end of the day, golf is a game to be enjoyed. Perhaps if you are playing in a club competition, then a few nerves can be good to get you focused - but if you are too nervous you will not play well.

'Your first shot is as important as your last, so you want to make it a good one. As I address the ball, I hover the club just off the ground, which helps me to stay smooth. Imagine you are sweeping it off the tee instead of trying to smack it into oblivion. Let your arms hang loosely.'

THE BACKSWING

'A good shoulder turn is important, but impossible if you are tense. Many golfers seem to have a good swing yet their shoulders face forward all the time and they find themselves making nice contact but not getting a great distance. That's such a shame because they are very close to really hitting the ball well. It is something that needs to be practised at the driving range.

'You may feel you are turning too much, or not enough, and start hooking or slicing. And when you concentrate too much on a shoulder turn, you concentrate less on hitting the ball. Relax; just because you turn your shoulders, don't suddenly feel you want to hit the ball harder. Your body will do that for you.

'My left arm is never stiff, which enables me to swing back perfectly smoothly. Keep your legs free from tension, to help you turn better. If you only swing with your upper body you are not swinging to your full potential – and apart from playing poorly, you could injure yourself.

'If you get it right, you can get into a very powerful position at the top of your backswing, yet you have actually done nothing that in itself uses brute force. A nice smooth swing, with a good turn and help from your legs, leaves you coiled at the top of the swing, ready to release.'

DOWNSWING THOUGHTS

'Accelerate down smoothly. Don't punch at the ball. Don't apply the power until your hands are around your right hip. If you do it earlier you will swing too quickly and there is more chance of a mis-hit.

'Keep your head back and watch your hands sweep through. Don't crouch over the ball or stand slumped. Stand tall.

'Whatever you do, don't hit the ball as hard as you can. You may be very strong, but that's not the key thing here. Keep it smooth; timing is everything. Keep your swing within yourself.

'Find a rhythm you can repeat. Then you can do it over and over again. As you hit the ball swing through it. Don't just punch it, which is something I see often. A myth is that you should keep your head down, but that isn't the case. In fact that does more harm than good. As your body comes through the shot, let it bring your head up with it naturally. Let your arms go through the shot, hold your hands high and, with your head up, watch the ball sail away.'

Simon Cainey

SWING SEQUENCE

Because Jones learned to play the game during the hickory shaft era, his backswing was slightly longer than might be considered ideal in the modern game. However, that long backswing was also a major factor in helping him develop the exquisite rhythm and timing which was to epitomise his swing through his comparatively short but spectacular career.

(1) Jones' shoulders and arms start the club back with the classic low and wide backswing, so typical of all long and accurate hitters.

BOBBY JONES

The phrase 'grace under pressure' could have been penned to describe the swing of Robert Tyre Jones Jnr. Jones was without question one of the greatest golfers the game has ever seen; and his swing, considering he played during the era of the often unpredictable hickory shaft, was good enough, as one critic put it, 'to enable him to have played successfully with a stair rod'.

He had that rare ability which allowed him to combine tremendous power with superb balance. The end result was a smooth and seemingly effortless swing which sent the ball rocketing into the far distance, usually with unerring accuracy.

Although he became one of the great statesmen of the game, and was hailed as an example of calm concentration, as a young man Jones had a fiery temper which at times threatened to derail his progress on the fairways. In fact on his first visit to the Old Course at St Andrews, a course and town which he later came to love, he played so badly that he tore up his card and marched off the course, vowing never to return.

His was a unique and natural talent. His teacher and life-long golfing mentor Stewart Maiden said: 'I taught Bobby as little as possible. I knew it was a mistake to confuse him with too many things.'

So technically good was Jones' swing that with only a few minor alterations to compensate for the change from hickory to steel shafts, he would not have looked out of place on the practice tee at a modern tour event.

In a brief but spectacular international career, which really started in 1923 when he won the US Open and ended seven years later with his remarkable Grand Slam victory, Jones played in only 52 tournaments but won 23 of them; a record which will surely never be matched.

Not only the greatest player of his era, Bobby Jones was also one of the most highly educated men to play the game of golf, holding degrees in law, literature and engineering – all of which gave him both the technical insight and command of language to write eloquently and succinctly about the game to which he gave so much.

(2) The club has moved well away from the ball, yet note how low to the ground the clubhead has remained, as Jones begins to extend his arms to create as wide an arc as possible.

(3) As his weight starts to move on to his right leg, Jones begins to coil his shoulders, while the straight left arm, which he believed was one of the keys to both accuracy and power, maintains the width of his arc.

(4) Jones now has his weight fully established on his right side, his shoulder turn is approaching 90 per cent and his hips are also being pulled around by the coiling action of his shoulders.

(5) With the shaft now parallel to the ground, his shoulders coiled almost to the maximum and that left arm still ramrod straight, Jones has built up a tremendous store of power in his backswing.

(6) Now, as he prepares to unleash all that power, Jones' first move as he starts the club back down is to plant his left foot firmly down on the ground. This not only starts his weight moving back on to his left side, but also provides a firm and stable platform through which to pour on the power in the downswing.

(7) That straight left arm continues to be a dominant factor in Jones' downswing, as he pulls the club down firmly with his left hand towards the hitting area. Note how his right elbow has remained tucked into his right side, helping to keep the club on the desired in-to-out swing path.

(8) Check the height of his head against the bunkers in the distance and note how it has remained steady. A classic position: head well behind the ball and a firm left side at impact. The hips have now cleared to the left, creating space for the arms to swing through the target line.

(9) The sheer speed and power of his swing is pulling Jones' hands and arms on and up, but only now does he allow his head to come up and follow the flight of the ball. He looks so poised and relaxed, but the ball is moving like a bullet.

(10) Perfectly balanced, Jones' momentum virtually pulls his body to a perfect follow-through position with hands high, chest facing the target and the club lying naturally across his shoulders, still perfectly in plane. An unforgettable image, as close to perfection as you will get.

Bill Robertson

JOYCE WETHERHEAD (Lady Heathcoat-Amory)

This rare and remarkable swing sequence shows admirably why Joyce Wetherhead was such a magnificent player.

Unquestionably one of the finest women golfers ever to grace the fairways, and perhaps the best, Joyce Wetherhead had a swing which was described by Bobby Jones as 'the best swing of either man or woman' ever seen. 'I have never played golf with anyone, man, or woman, who has made me feel so utterly outclassed.'

Born into a golfing family – her brother Roger Wetherhead was one of the best amateur golfers of his generation – Joyce didn't develop a serious interest in the game until the family acquired a holiday home close to the world-famous links at Dornoch in Scotland.

A modest and shy girl, Joyce was 18 before she played in her first competitive event; and she entered the 1920 Ladies' English Amateur championship – which she won – only in order to accompany a friend. Cecil Leitch, another legendary figure in women's golf, highlighted Joyce's amazing powers of concentration by recalling an incident when a train roared by as Joyce was standing over an important putt. So intense and complete was her concentration that, when asked about the incident later, Joyce admitted that she had not even heard the train pass.

However, Joyce, while seemingly cold and clinical on the golf course, was by nature a nervous person who was often physically sick before an important match. By 1925 the strain of striving to remain at the pinnacle of the women's game was beginning to tell and at the age of only 26 she announced her retirement from competitive golf. She did make a brief return three years later to defeat the top American Glenna Collett 3 and 1 in the final of the 1929 Ladies' Championship at St Andrews, but, perhaps feeling that she now had nothing left to prove, Joyce retired for a second time.

(1) Joyce Wetherhead adopts the wide stance which was the norm for this period, with the ball positioned slightly farther back in her stance than the accepted modern-day address position.

(2) The swing starts with the club appearing to be pushed back from the ball with the left arm, rather than pulled away with the right hand; and the straight left arm ensures the clubhead remains low to the ground at the initial stage of the backswing. The left-hand grip looks fairly strong. However, there has been no attempt to 'fan' the clubface open too early in the backswing.

(3) At this point Joyce still has her weight evenly distributed between both feet and as yet there is no indication of any major weight shift on to her right side. Her wrists still show no signs of cocking and this, combined with her straight left arm, is helping to create a wide swing arc. Joyce looks beautifully balanced and in complete control of the club; and there is not the slightest suggestion of any tension, apart from the natural initial coiling action of her upper body.

(5) If this were a 1990s swing, the club would now have reached the top of the backswing. The shoulders have turned through 90 degrees, pulling the left heel up well off the ground. Joyce has now transferred her weight on to her right side, her hips have been pulled around by the powerful coiling action of the upper body and that left arm has remained almost perfectly straight.

(4) As the club passes waist height, Joyce allows her wrist to cock. Her left heel is just starting to lift off the ground as the swing of her arms starts to move her weight across to her right side. Note, too, how at this point her hips are still resisting the pull from her shoulders, encouraging that all-important coiling action which helps to build up power in the backswing. The left arm has remained straight, yet Joyce still looks relaxed and there is no sign of any physical strain in her swing.

(6) In this frame, you can see how Joyce has carried her hands that extra few inches higher and by doing so squeezed an extra few degrees of coil into her upper body. As a result, the club shaft has dipped past the horizontal but Joyce still looks composed, well balanced and in total control of her swing.

(7) This magnificent position highlights just why Joyce Wetherhead was such a wonderful golfer. As that left arm starts to pull the club down, Joyce has planted her left foot firmly back down on the ground and her weight is already established once again on her left side. Although of slim build, Joyce has created a very powerful movement to start to her downswing, but such is her talent and superb balance that she accomplishes this without any part of her swing appearing hurried in any way.

(9) The position of the tree just to the left of Joyce's head reveals how still she has kept her head, both in the backswing and the downswing. Even with her weight now almost completely transferred back on to her left side and her hips clearing to the left, Joyce's head is rock-steady and her height remains constant.

(8) As that straight left arm continues to pull down strongly on the handle of the club, note how Joyce's legs have already started to drive the bottom half of her body laterally towards the target. At this point in the downswing many less talented golfers would have allowed the wrists to uncock. However, Joyce retains that critical angle between her left wrist and the club shaft, storing up power to be released through impact.

(10) Centrifugal force has finally uncocked Joyce's wrists at the optimum moment and her hands are being whipped through impact at tremendous speed, thanks to the 'flail' action created by the straight left arm and the hinge created by her wrists. Joyce has fully cleared her left side, her right knee is now driving through and the clubhead is powering straight down the target line through impact. Even when the clubhead is travelling at great speed and generating a degree of power which would appear to be well beyond the physical capabilities of such a slim frame, Joyce retains superb balance, as she sends yet another tee shot rifling down the centre of the fairway.

Bill Robertson

THE
EQUIPMENT GUIDE

'SOCCER IS A SIMPLE-MINDED GAME FOR SIMPLE PEOPLE; GOLF IS

MERELY AN EXPENSIVE WAY OF LEAVING HOME.'

Michael Parkinson

When it comes to the equipment you choose, the legendary Harry Vardon put it all into perspective in an article he penned during World War I. His words bear an embarassing veracity today.

'Very many golfers handicap themselves for more than they imagine by using implements which come into their possession in a more or less promiscuous way. They walk into the stores; see a club which takes their fancy; they emerge five minutes later with what they fondly regard as a treasure, but which ultimately proves to be a traitor.'

And with the proliferation of bigger, better, lighter, tougher, whippier clubs that are honed, dedicated, reinforced, finessed and all the rest of it, it is easy to get confused. I know one young player who stumped up nearly £300 for a new driver at a club dinner auction – only to realize when he got home that he already had one.

The selling of golf equipment these days involves massive amounts of cash. Premium brand price points have risen as new technology has been introduced into the market, but the amount of money spent by manufacturers in research and development of new products, and then of marketing the end result, has grown to immense proportions.

In the field of research and development, golf has leapt into the future to harness the latest technologies being developed by space exploration.

Callaway, makers of Big Bertha golf equipment, opened a state of the art R&D and testing centre in Carlsbad, California, housing robotic testing machines, ultra high-speed cameras and computers.

It has what is probably the best driving range in the world, with different types of grasses in use on various greens, bunkers with a range of different types of sand textures, and even sensors underneath the grass to detect the exact spot that a ball lands. In 1995 Callaway spent over $8.5 million on research and development alone.

Peanuts! The really big money isn't spent until we get to product marketing, which focuses around two areas: player endorsement and advertising.

Cobra Golf, for example, heralded the launch of their 1996 titanium wood range by spending £1 million just on their stand and display at a single American trade show! The Cobra iron for 1997, the King Cobra II, is being backed by a $40 million worldwide campaign.

As for player endorsement, logic dictates that the better you are, the more media exposure you will gain for a product; so

LEFT: Callaway's testing centre in Carlsbad, California. RIGHT: No expense is spared in selling the King Cobra II iron.

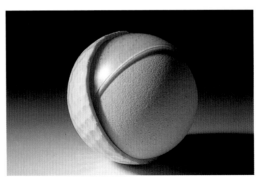

the better golfers can demand more for endorsing a particular product on the circuit with its related TV coverage.

World number one golfer, Greg Norman, reputedly picks up £8 million a year just in product endorsement. When he signed a multi-year deal to endorse the new Maxfli XS golf ball, as well as to help research new product, the signing-on fee was reported to be between £10 million and £20 million.

The brilliant Tiger Woods only turned professional in 1996, but he jumped straight into the world league when it came to endorsement deals. Before he had even struck a ball as a professional, Tiger had netted a five year $40 million deal with shoe and sportswear manufacturer, Nike. And he signed a five year agreement with Titleist to play their balls and clubs in a deal with a potential value of $20 million.

Product endorsement and high profile exposure is vital for the manufacturers. If they get a hot product on the professional Tours it will invariably lead to good sales.

For example, in 1995 in every tournament on the five major professional Tours in Europe and the USA, Callaway had nearly one in three players using a Big Bertha driver. As a result, so many lesser players saw the products in use on television that the company's net sales topped $550 million, making a gross profit approaching $300 million.

LEFT: The conventional wound ball with a rubber core. ABOVE: The new Top-Flite multi-layer Strata ball. RIGHT: Greg Norman earns millions for endorsing the Maxfli XS.

But the best deal of 1996 was probably done by youthful putter manufacturer Odyssey, who persuaded Nick Faldo to try one of their newly developed products. Faldo liked it: then he won the Masters using it. Odyssey estimate that his win added a cool $5 million to their sales. In return they paid Faldo a mere $700 from their bonus pool!

STARTING OUT

Of course, it is essential that the beginner and the high handicapper shouldn't get carried away. Buying a Big Bertha may improve your game, but it won't make you a great player.

The Rules of Golf state that 'the maximum number of clubs a golfer shall be allowed to carry on the course is 14'. Take any more than that number in your bag during a competition and you can be docked four shots in a medal round.

As a beginner, it would be unwise to set foot on a course for the first time with a full compliment of clubs over your shoulder, it is simply not necessary.

Most beginners start out with a few odd clubs, usually supplied by the club professional they have turned to for lessons. This is fine, as far as it goes.

Golf is not a cheap game to start out in, and many are the tales of would-be Nick Faldos splashing out excessive amounts of cash on clubs right from the off, only to discover that they do not get on with the game. The best advice is to start out with just a couple of clubs on the practice range. When you feel you are ready to make a commitment to the game, that is the best time to start considering which weapons will work best for you.

When it comes to buying that first set of clubs, there are several options. The first is to buy a half-set of clubs – for example, a three wood, four, six, and eight irons, pitching wedge, sand wedge and putter. This is a cheap way of starting out, and as you get more proficient at the game you can always add clubs to your bag one at a time.

Some people say that starting out with a half-set is limiting your chance of playing the game to your best level, because you may not have the right club for a certain shot. Ignore them.

If you're just starting out it is best not to overcomplicate things. Furthermore, take a tip from Seve Ballesteros, arguably the most versatile shot maker in the history of golf. Seve learned the game with just one club, a three iron, and he could play almost any shot in the book with it.

RIGHT: Perimeter-weighted, cavity-backed irons are much more forgiving than traditional bladed clubs.

If you really would rather carry the full set of clubs from the off, then make the first set of clubs you buy a reasonably priced one. Less than £300 can buy you a perfectly reasonable set of new clubs or you might buy a bigger brand name second-hand. (When buying second-hand look out for things like worn grips, because these will need replacing at extra cost.)

The combination of clubs you carry comes down to personal choice. The last couple of years have seen a high rise in popularity of utility woods, very lofted woods for use from tee, fairway or rough. The advantage and appeal in such clubs is that they are much easier to hit than the longer irons, therefore the utility woods have particularly found popularity with the higher handicapped players.

At the better end of the playing scale on the other hand, more advanced golfers have a whole host of specialist

wedges to choose from, clubs which will help them save shots around the green. It is commonplace for professional golfers to carry four different wedges in their bag, and amateurs are fast catching on to the benefits of utility wedges. When people like Tiger Woods or John Daly can reach a 500-yard hole with a driver and a pitcher, they don't need many long irons to carry round.

MADE TO MEASURE

Once you reach the stage where you feel you have some natural aptitude for the game, you'll probably be thinking about investing some serious money in your clubs. It's a natural progression, start the game with the cheaper equipment, then invest

One in three tournament professionals use Big Bertha woods.

more money when you feel the time is right.

With some sets of irons costing in excess of a thousand pounds these days, and the premium brand woods retailing at around £300 and above, buying the best clubs for your game is a crucial decision.

There are two ways in which you can approach buying a new set of clubs – in much the same way as you would go and buy a new suit.

You could just go and buy a set of clubs straight off the rack. As with an off the peg suit, you could browse the shops and have a closer look at a few that take your fancy, before finally settling on one. It is the way in which golf clubs have been bought for years.

But consider this statistic from a University of Tokyo study: 88 per cent of golfers are non-standard when it comes to clubs. That is why more and more players are having their clubs custom fitted. Just as you'll feel more comfortable in a made to measure suit, so golf clubs that are designed to fit your build and swing quirks will serve you better.

There are several elements of a golf club which can be custom fit. One of the most overlooked elements is ensuring that your clubs have a grip that is the correct size. Having a good hold on the golf club is one of the absolute fundamentals for success. An incorrectly sized grip will prejudice your hold on the club and therefore significantly reduce your chances of hitting a good shot.

Not all golfers are the same height, but beware the fallacy that because a player is above standard height he necessarily requires longer golf clubs, or vice versa for the shorter player. Lengthening or shortening golf clubs may be the correct procedure in some cases, but it can also be detrimental. For example, giving a short player shorter than standard clubs means he will not have as great a swing arc, and therefore may suffer a reduction in power, so it is always best to approach an expert first.

Most clubfitters will prefer to adjust the lie angle of the golf club to suit a player's height. This is the angle which allows the club to sit properly, and squarely at address. If, at address, the toe of your club is in the air, then the club is too upright and you will probably find your shots flying left of the target (for a right-hander). Conversely, if you find that the toe of the club tends to dig in the ground at impact, then the lie angle of the club is too flat, and will result in shots flying to the right of the target.

Simply ensuring that the grip size, length and lie angle of your clubs are the best for your game will ensure that you have a better chance of hitting a good golf shot.

The really key area of the golf club, though, is the shaft, and this is where things get a little more complicated.

Most golfers will tend to base their buying decision about a new set of clubs on the cosmetics of the head. The shaft is one of the most overlooked components of a club, and it is also one of the most important. If you are not using a club with the right shaft for your game, then you are not hitting the best golf shots that you possibly can. That is a fact.

Choosing the right shaft is a matter of trial and error, preferably under the watchful eye of an expert PGA professional. At its most basic level: if you have a shaft that is too flexible for your swing, then you will have trouble controlling shots and will more than likely hook the ball; if you have a shaft that is too stiff, then you will more often than not hit a slice or fade.

Given that there are no industry standards to shaft specification, the importance of discussing the selection of a shaft with an expert cannot be overstated. Shaft flexes are generally categorized in the following way: XS (extra stiff), S (stiff or firm), R (regular), A (senior) and L (ladies).

Take note: the fact that you may have played great golf using one brand of shafts labelled 'regular' does not necessarily mean that when you switch to another brand, that 'regular' will still be the correct flex for you. Flex classifications vary from company to company, and one brand's regular shaft could be another brand's ladies' flex.

THE VOGUE

From the early part of the twentieth century up until the 1970s, golfers would use woods with heads that were made of either persimmon or maple laminate, and blade irons that were made from forged steel.

Things began to change in the early 1970s when Karsten Solheim, maker of Ping golf equipment, pioneered the process of investment casting of irons, a process which allowed him to introduce a new head design – the perimeter-weighted, cavity-back club.

These days, by far the majority of irons sold are of a cavity-back design, the old forged blade is now a club only for purists and those who play at the very top level. The perimeter weighting of the cavity-back generates more forgiveness in the club-head if the ball is hit off-centre – perfect for the amateur golfer.

Like tennis racquets, irons have followed the trend of moving to oversize, with head sizes 10–20 per cent bigger than the traditional standard. Oversize iron technology also allows the development of a club that offers greater forgiveness to mis-hits, and also greater ease of play than the old blades.

The days of the wooden-headed wood are also numbered. At the end of the 1970s Taylor Made pioneered the way for new club-head materials by introducing a wood that used a stainless steel head. As well as being much easier and cheaper to manufacture, the metal head, like its cavity-back iron counterpart, allowed club designers to spread the weight around the head to make them more forgiving. These days, metal woods account for some 90 per cent of sales in the 'wood' market.

Club designers, since the introduction of stainless steel for wood heads,

ABOVE AND RIGHT: Taylor Made's Bubble shaft helps increase swing speed to give more power.

WELCOME TO THE SPACE AGE

The search for new and greater club-head materials to make titanium obsolete will undoubtedly be high on the agenda of club designers. But further development in the golf shaft is top of their priorities.

Although there were experiments with steel shafts more than 100 years ago, it wasn't until the 1920s that steel supplanted hickory. While it had been popular in the United States for several years, it wasn't until 1929 that the Royal and Ancient golf club formally accepted the steel shaft as legal. Although the decision was inevitable and the diehard objectors were few, they were pretty much forced to accept steels as legal when the Prince of Wales turned up to play at St Andrews with a full set in his bag.

Their introduction was one of the greatest advances in golf club technology ever, and helped set a standard of club design which was to remain largely unaltered for a full 50 years.

A competitor to the steel shafts – graphite – first hit the headlines in the 1970s, notably when American golfer Johnny Miller won the 1976 Open Championship at Royal Birkdale using graphite-shafted clubs.

Those early products were, however, notorious for their inconsistency, and players could find two clubs in the bag, with supposedly the same shaft, behaving in radically different ways.

The prime advantage of graphite was its weight. Standard steel shafts tipped the scales around 200 grams, but standard graphite shafts were around 30 grams lighter, and today's ultralight shafts, which are the focal point of product development, are as light as 50 grams.

Graphite consistency has improved since those early days, and the strength

have not stopped looking for its successor, and titanium is the next revolution in golf club technology.

As strong as steel, but 45 per cent lighter, the advanced properties of titanium were put to rigorous test by the aviation and aeronautic industries, and the metal features prominently in the construction of the Voyager interplanetry spacecraft. It gives club designers a large margin of weight distribution to experiment with in producing clubs that are even more forgiving to play with.

The new material has also pushed premium brand prices upwards, a top end titanium-headed driver will cost you anything between £250 and £500. Given the fact that there are now very few manufacturers that do not offer a titanium 'wood' and several are pushing irons with either pure titanium or titanium insert heads, it is fair to say that club design has already stepped into the next millennium.

and lightness of the material means club designers have more leeway for changing the weight distribution of a golf club to enhance performance. This was the theory behind the development of Taylor Made's Bubble shaft, which was launched in 1995 to wide acclaim and has helped Taylor Made to double its business in two years.

The Bubble pioneered the way for the changing shape of the graphite shaft. Five years in development, it is the product of rocket science meeting golf – Taylor Made has a team of 20 engineers in its design team, and one former aerospace specialist working fulltime on the professional Tours to get feedback from Taylor Made players.

The concept of reducing the weight at the grip end of the club and shifting it down towards the head, the aim of the Bubble, means a player can generate greater swing speed, which means more power, without extra effort. It is his incredible swing speed that enables Tiger Woods to outdrive all-comers. The other key benefit being pushed by the manufacturers, is greater stability for the club through impact.

Not surprisingly, Taylor Made is not alone in developing products with these twin goals. 1996 saw the launch of the Muscle shaft, developed by Fenwick and being used in Top-Flite clubs. The Muscle, like the Bubble, also features a bulge in the shaft, but is positioned lower down and can be repositioned from club to club, depending on the length and flexpoint of the club required.

Companies like Lynx and Cobra are using wide-tipped shafts for greater stability at impact. Lynx's Flare shaft uses a tip which is 20 per cent wider than standard, while Cobra's new IQ shaft is strengthened to be stiff towards the head and flexible towards the grip for greater shot control.

Goldwin Golf and shaft manufacturer Unifiber have recently combined to offer a golf club, the Goldwin AVDP XL driver, which weighs a mere 265 grams,

the shaft contributing just 55 grams. This means virtually all the weight is in the head, creating greater swing speed and generating greater power.

One consequence of 'super light', is that clubs can be made super long. Golf clubs are getting longer – already the accepted industry standard length of a driver has crept up an inch or so to 45 inches. Some in the industry believe that this will soon extend to 46 or even 47 inches. Whether the extraordinary levels attained by Jarmo Sandelin, the Swedish professional, become the norm is in doubt. Sandelin uses a Top-Flite driver that is 54 inches long to power his balls out from the tee, and he has been know to use one that is 58 inches long in practice.

There are two schools of thought about longer shafts in golf clubs. One says that for the amateur the longer shaft will be harder to control, so any

A custom-built 54-inch driver standing head and shoulders above the others in Jarmo Sandelin's bag.

benefits of extra distance will be lost in accuracy. The other argues that because modern technology ensures there is no extra weight in the longer shaft, a couple more inches on the club can instead be a blessing for players. Teachers who support this theory say that the longer club promotes a wider swing arc and a better swing plane, particularly for amateurs, which will lead to more consistent shots.

Even then: they are billions of dollars away from making the game easy.

Mike Wood

THE HEART OF
THE GAME

Etiquette underpins the spirit of the game of golf. It is

a fair game, predominantly self-ruling, and should be

played in a considerate frame of mind.

In the hot summer of 1900, one of the more bizarre golfing matches on record took place on the streets of Pittsburgh.

A group of wealthy members of the Alleghany Club, in a state of wild enthusiasm, wagered four thousand dollars that a golf ball could be driven four and a half miles in less than 150 strokes. Through the middle of the city.

William Patten, a scratch player with as much nerve as he had ability, was selected to carry out the test.

Aware that he was unlikely to be entirely popular with the local citizens, and mindful of the need to get a fair light to chart his course (there are many unnerving hazards in the city centre) he selected an early time to tee off outside the front door of the imposing Alleghany Club en route to the equally impressive Pittsburgh clubhouse.

Selecting his club with more than usual care, he took his first stroke at 5 a.m. under an overcast sky, accompanied by 25 golfers in full costume, some of them perhaps not perfectly sober or attentive to the tradition of quiet at such an hour.

The first mile proved the most difficult. Nerves, a failure to warm up and the raucous cheering of his supporters did much to unsettle the dedicated Patten. Nor was he used to allowing horse-drawn delivery vehicles to play through, so it took a full 50 strokes to cover the mile and, with a third of his shots gone in under a quarter of the course, absolute dedication was called for. He rose to the task with enormous skill.

However, in a momentary lapse he drove a wayward slice through the bedroom window of a prominent citizen (unsurprisingly causing, as the papers recorded, 'a great disturbance'). A mile further on he sent another through the window of an early-morning tram car and came close to receiving direct retribution from the passengers.

Yet despite these distractions, Patten finished by landing a perfect chip clean through the (closed) window of the Pittsburgh clubhouse with 31 strokes to spare.

Three balls were lost, three clubs were broken, and about £100 worth of damage (about £6,500 by today's prices) was done.

Unfortunately, although Patten's backers won their bets, even the most generous commentator would not regard the episode as being in accordance with the one timeless, international absolute in the game - Etiquette.

Max Faulkner, British Open Champion of 1951, summed up what it means to have a grasp of golfing etiquette.

What any player should strive for, he said, was to be described as 'a nice

William Patten (left) with referee Mr O.D. Thompson.

LEFT: The starting point, Alleghany Country Club.

ABOVE RIGHT: A workman hit by the ball wanted to have a fight.

BELOW: The crossing over the Alleghany river.

LEFT: The ball struck a tram car much to the annoyance of the conductor.

RIGHT: A high bridge over woods. Perhaps the most difficult obstacle.

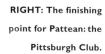

RIGHT: The finishing point for Pattean: the Pittsburgh Club.

chap to play with. If you are thus described, you will never seek in vain for a game.'

Etiquette underpins the spirit of the game of golf. It is a fair game, predominantly self-ruling, and should be played in a considerate frame of mind.

This is not to say that golf is not competitive, because it can plainly be one of the most ferocious of games, mentally if not physically. Yet even at the very height of intense combat on the golf course, even under the pressure of competition for hundreds of thousands of dollars in prize money and millions more in endorsements, all players from the bottom up should retain the dignity and spirit of fair play.

The spirit of decency is built into the game - so much so that in the Rules of Golf, Section One sets out the considerations that every player should bear in mind on the course.

In truth, much of golfing etiquette is based on common sense, but at a time when there have been attacks, fights and even a death as a result of a fracas on the greens, the modern golfer is in more need than ever to be aware of the spirit that underpins the game.

If you are one those players who manage to abide by most or all of the following, then you shouldn't have any trouble finding a game.

The basic premise for etiquette starts with consideration for other players, not just the ones you are playing with, but on the rest of the course. Your opponent or your

By C. Dana Gibson.   From "Snap-Shots." Copyright.
ADVICE TO CADDIES.—You will save time by keeping your eye on the ball, not on the player.

playing partners should suffer no distractions caused by you when playing their shots. And equally golfers around the course should not be disturbed by shouts of anguish or curses over a missed putt, or, the very worst *faux pas*, a club thrown in anger.

Golf is a game that should be played at a brisk pace, so always be aware if you are being followed by a faster group - it is only polite to let them play through. A group of four players should really not take any longer than four hours to complete 18 holes. Unfortunately, in the modern era golf has become a slower game, thanks largely to the poor example set by professional golfers who more than occasionally have to be reminded that it is rather nice to have the entire tournament field complete the round before darkness. Amateurs should not let themselves slip into such poor practices.

The second basic article of golf etiquette is care for the course. Remember, you are not the only golfer who has the pleasure of playing the course, and that it will be there for other golfers long after you have hung up your spikes.

Any damage you cause to the terrain in the process of playing your shot should be carefully repaired so that the course remains in good condition and also so that players following you are not hindered. Remember what it is like to find your own ball in a bad lie because a player in front hadn't bothered to cover his or her tracks.

So if you find yourself in a bunker, rake it after playing. If you take a divot, repair it to the best of your ability - likewise if your ball leaves a pitchmark where it lands on the green, or if you accidentally drag a spike and cut the turf up.

Etiquette, the spirit of fair play and the Rules of Golf are the three pillars that form the strength of the game and protect its largely clean image.

The qualities of golf are exceptional, too, in that we are expected to call penalty on ourselves if we infringe the rules.

Yes, there are referees in professional golf tournaments, but they are only called upon for an explanation of a ruling, or to judge a situation at the player's request. So the etiquette of self-policing is an inherent discipline for the game.

And surprisingly, it is when the game is played at the highest levels that the standards of self-regulation are at their most finely honed. It is a fair bet that most amateurs have not been entirely rigorous on occasion over strict application of the laws. So it is all the more refreshing when we are given a reminder of the strict need for honour.

Take, for example, the unfortunate incident that happened in 1996 to the then world number-one player Greg Norman.

At the Canon Greater Hartford Open in June, the Great White Shark disqualified himself from the tournament at the halfway stage, despite still being in contention for the top prize money.

The reason behind his withdrawal was a mix-up over the balls he used. His sponsor, Maxfli, inadvertently filled his locker with balls labelled XS-9, not the XS-90 the Australian normally used.

Although the XS-9 was identical in every way to the XS-90, its name had not been registered and approved with the golfing authorities. It was, therefore, an illegal ball. A minor technicality, but an illegal ball, nonetheless.

Trivial as it may seem to the average player, Norman felt it only right to disqualify himself. In a phrase that should haunt the golf-course cheat,

Nicklaus and Jacklin at the end of their titanic singles battle at 1969 Ryder Cup.

Norman explained it simply: 'Each of us is our own judge, jury and executioner.'

The great joy of etiquette and fair play is that these ideals can elevate even the most ordinary of games into something that will be remembered for years to come by those who experienced or witnessed the gesture.

One of the great moments of sporting etiquette and fair play was played out between two of the game's great rivals when they were at the peak of their powers.

Nothing is more competitive than the Ryder Cup. International rivalry, professional determination and usually vociferous and jingoistic crowds can put pressure on the strongest heart.

So it was all the more tense when, in the 1969 Ryder Cup at Royal Birkdale, the entire match result rested on the singles being fought out between the legendary Jack Nicklaus and Britain's Tony Jacklin, then playing some of the best golf of his career.

It couldn't have been closer - the two were all square going up the last hole. Nicklaus then holed a four-foot putt for a birdie, leaving Jacklin the awful pressure of a three-foot putt, with the world watching - to halve and save the match. As one of the British team remarked at the time, there isn't a more difficult shot in the whole of golf.

But before Jacklin could even address the putt, Nicklaus picked up the Englishman's marker, put his arm around his shoulder and said almost casually: 'I know you won't miss that putt, Tony, so I'm not going to give you the opportunity.' Try that one Saturday morning and see how it feels.

However, the game's brave endeavours to stand out as a pillar of deportment and fair play doesn't mean that an element of gamesmanship fails to creep on to the links.

As cricket has its sledging of the batsman and rugby has the indelicate words exchanged by opposing front rows in the scrum, golfers are able to stretch etiquette to a point where the line between what is and isn't acceptable becomes just a touch blurred.

Few golfers will not have experienced a bit of jovial banter with their colleagues on the course; it is perfectly acceptable as long as it does not overstep the mark of etiquette which says you should not distract your opponent or partner when he is playing a shot.

But, and this is a very debatable but, there is nothing wrong with putting thoughts into your opponent's mind.

Sam Snead's particular subtlety, often used to make a few extra dollars in friendly games, was to tell opponents that they were reaching a great position at the top of the backswing. On the one hand a compliment, on the other a psychological killer as the unknowing victim focused on achieving that 'great position' at the expense of other fundamentals. Guaranteed disaster.

When golf and the spirit of fair play do part company, the result always leaves a bitter taste.

A prime example was the disturbing 1991 Ryder Cup match held at Kiawah Island, USA - dubbed the War On The Shore.

The game completely lost contact with its traditional roots. The crowd behaviour was more akin to what you could see at a boxing match, and some of the players were not much better. They memories that linger in the mind are not of the Nicklaus-Jacklin type, rather of Corey Pavin cavorting grotesquely wearing a US military Desert Storm baseball cap, and a huge row involving Seve Ballesteros.

The red-hot European pairing of Ballesteros and Jose-Maria Olazabal ran into controversy during their foursomes match with Paul Azinger and Chip

Best of enemies: Ballesteros and Azinger at Kiawah Island in 1991.

Beck. The Spaniards noticed that the Americans had changed from a 100 compression ball to a 90 compression ball during the round - which was against the rules. A row ensued, and the Americans were told they had flouted the rule of law, but no penalty could be applied in a matchplay game.

Meanwhile, Beck and Azinger had become increasingly irritated at what they saw as deliberate coughing by Ballesteros. Once again, the officials had to be involved, and after the match Azinger branded Ballesteros as 'the king of gamesmanship'.

Thankfully, Pavin has matured since his unfortunate display, Azinger and Ballesteros have long since patched up their differences, and the Ryder Cup, thanks to the dignity of the players and captains since Kiawah, has re-established itself as the pinnacle event in team competition.

Amateur golf, on the other hand, has seen its reputation as the bastion of fair play hugely dented by several high-profile incidents. In 1994 a libel case was brought by the golfer John Buckingham against two fellow players who had accused him of cheating. Buckingham took on the expense of going to court with the aim of defending his reputation against the smear of dishonesty - and lost his case.

Inevitably the running of large and efficient clubs requires organizations, and, unfortunately, organizations need committees. And while the game of golf has committee members who are among the most fair-minded, decent, affable and respected souls on this earth, it also has a particularly strong set of officials who are insufferable prigs. It isn't the game's fault, it is just that its relatively affluent social nature attracts a disproportionate share of small-minded bureaucrats with an inflated sense of self-esteem. It is one of the

Keep your eye on the Ball

A humorous golfing postcard by Scottish caricaturist Cynicus.

reasons why sexism and racism still undermine the game.

Sadly, even normally sane officials can be overwhelmed by the letter, rather than the spirit, of the law, to the detriment of the game's image.

A public-relations disaster is the only good description of the controversy that surrounded Mrs Audrey Briggs and her son Laurie in 1996. The pair found themselves excluded from the Family Foursomes tournament held at Burhill GC near Walton-on-Thames - because someone pointed out to the rules committee that only blood relations could enter, and that 13-year-old Laurie was adopted. After making inquiries, officialdom at the club held that the boy was ineligible!

This display of staggering stupidity provoked outrage, and fortunately sanity was restored a week or so later when the rules were 'clarified' to allow Laurie and his mother to play in the tournament in future years. Mrs Briggs showed admirable dignity by saying she and her son would be happy to go back to Burhill to compete.

The game has also had to acknowledge the birth of two phenomena in recent years - litigation and 'golf rage'.

Litigation, a particularly North American habit, has included the case of a woman who drove off the ladies' tee only for her ball to hit a railway line and rebound into her face. She successfully sued the club for not telling her in advance that the metal obstacle was there.

And there is the wife who is suing a club after her husband died when he fell out of his golf cart. The club says he was full of the joys of spring (and alcohol); the wife says that is the club's fault.

Even for the best of them, golf is a frustrating game, and it is not uncommon for a player to slam a club into the ground, or chastise himself in industrial language, and more than a few bemused pet dogs have felt the aftermath of a missed two-footer on a crucial green.

But Valerie Leathley may have taken things too far after playing what she described as the worst round of golf in her life. She smashed up her Toyota car with her clubs.

The incident of golf rage experienced by Andrew Durban in the summer of 1996 was anything but funny. Putting out on one of the greens at the London Golf Centre, he noticed a golf ball from the group behind land too close for comfort. Mr Durban quite rightly pointed out this breach of etiquette to the pair, who in return assaulted him, first verbally, and then physically.

Since then, in the United States, we have even had a death on the course as a result of a golfing dispute.

What is vital is that golfers don't just dismiss these things as inevitable signs of the times we live in, because until now, golf has always risen above the unpleasant. With care, it will continue to do so. For while golf has its faults - and never forget that it is, after all, only a game - the foundations upon which it is built, the etiquette of consideration for people and for the environment, are fine lessons for life itself.

Bobby Jones lost the US Open play-off many years ago. There wouldn't have been a play-off, he would have won outright, if he hadn't penalized himself one stroke for accidentally moving his ball a fraction of an inch. Nobody else had seen it happen.

Asked why he did it, Jones said: 'There is only one way to play the game.' He dismissed congratulations for his act by saying: 'You might as well praise a man for not robbing a bank.'

Cheating has become endemic, and once the golfer starts cheating the game allows him to cheat more and more in all sorts of ways.

Accidentally move the ball a fraction of an inch, so what? Then you improve your lie on a few shots, then every shot. You move live branches in the woods, stamp down grass for a better lie and so on.

And how many people reading this think: 'Hey, that's not really cheating, it's not as if we were playing for prizes'? See how far cheating is becoming the norm. Some courses now have installed video cameras on short par-3 holes because of golfers lying about getting a hole-in-one.

In parts of America it not unusual for players to 'walk the doggie' - nudge the ball from behind a tree or a bush to give yourself a clear shot at the green. In other areas 'mulligans' are the norm, where players replay a poor shot with no penalty. Then the player claims he scored a par when it should be a double-bogey.

Etiquette is self-imposed. To play the game correctly, have no hesitation, no second thoughts, no prevarication. Believe in your heart that Bobby Jones was right.

Mike Wood

A guide for those unsure of correct golfing etiquette.

DREAM RESORTS

WHAT REALLY SETS THE SPORT APART IS THE INFINITE

VARIETY OF COURSES AND PLAYING CONDITIONS

THAT ARE OPEN TO THE ORDINARY PLAYER.

The range of pleasures that can be derived from golf is probably far greater than in any other sport. That each outing is an individual struggle with one's own skills is not a quality unique to golf. Nor is the challenge of overcoming an opponent, or the camaraderie of playing for a team.

That the determined golfer *can* play in weather conditions that would frustrate a rugby player or baseball fan is an attraction that one may not wish to call upon: the fact that the golfer can play in ten degrees of frost does not necessarily mean that the golfer actually *wants* to.

But what really sets the sport apart is the infinite variety of courses and playing conditions that are open to the ordinary player.

Nine-hole courses, par-3 courses, links courses, woodland courses; tees on clifftops, greens on plateaux, pins surrounded by lakes or swamp; views over mountains, towns, rivers, oceans and deserts.

Eighteen holes that you have mastered time and again can suddenly play like a course in a different world if the wind changes.

There is that enormous sense of pride in just being allowed to pit one's wits against the famous courses that reflect the game's long history; there is a masochistic pleasure in taking on the holes that you have seen so closely on television; there is even an enjoyable admission of fallibility, mingled with unending awe, as you go bogey 3 on a hole you have seen the Tour pros birdie time after time. When you successfully chip out of a precipitous bunker renowned for dashing the hopes of some of the game's greats, the thrill is almost unending (as is your account of the incident).

But courses do not have to be famous or historic to give pleasure. Many mingle brilliant course design with spectacular settings and luxurious accommodations. Any golfer can find a limitless diversity of resorts where sport walks hand in hand with indulgence.

Here **Malcolm Campbell**, one of the game's most respected writers, selects a handful of golfing havens which are outstanding for this combination of fine golf and sheer opulence.

Penina

THE MERIDIEN PENINA GOLF & RESORT HOTEL, PORTUGAL

OPPOSITE: The ninth hole – from mud flats to magnificence. BELOW: The fifth is one of many spectacular holes at Cotton's masterpiece.

The late Sir Henry Cotton, three times winner of the Open Championship, built the Penina golf course on what was once a flooded rice paddy more than 30 years ago.

It was the first course on the Portuguese Algarve and the catalyst for the golf boom that has transformed this glorious stretch of European coastline. Alas the great man is no longer there, but his presence can still be felt along the fairways and on the practice ground where he imparted so much of his golfing wisdom to great champions and to golf rabbits alike.

For Sir Henry the creation of Penina was the culmination of a great career and it was the place where he would find peace and contentment for his retirement years. But he had been presented with a singularly unpromising piece of real estate when he was asked to design the course. The land was perfectly flat, and was flooded when he first saw it, but he so fell in love with the area that he conjured up a vision of a golf course that would be his masterpiece.

The result was nothing less than a magnificent tribute to his skills, and the big names from the world of golf, from entertainers to statesmen, made their way to play this beautiful course and sit at the court of the man they called 'Maestro'. The endearing Cotton welcomed them with open arms.

Now owned and operated by the Forte Hotels group, the five-star hotel and golf course have recently been given a facelift, but the character of Sir Henry's original layout has been retained and is central to the redevelopment of the resort.

The hotel has been brought up to the highest standard and a golf academy has been added to the major redevelopment of the course to keep Penina very much in the forefront of the great golf resorts of the world.

Grand Traverse

GRAND TRAVERSE RESORT, MICHIGAN, USA

OPPOSITE: The daunting 15th, with humps and hollows, deep bunkering and large contoured greens, is typical of Nicklaus' 'Bear Course'.
BELOW: The 18th hole at Spruce Run, the first course built at Traverse.

A longside the sparkling waters of Grand Traverse Bay on the shores of Lake Michigan lies a golf resort that has won numerous awards as one of the finest in the United States.

The Grand Traverse Resort at Traverse City is one of the great golf experiences in the American Midwest, and its Jack Nicklaus Bear Course is rated one of the top resort courses in the country.

But it's not just the golf that makes the Grand Traverse Resort so special. It is an all-year-round destination. Whether during the blossom of spring, the brilliance of summer, the blazing colour of a Michigan autumn or wrapped in the snowy blanket of winter, this is a very special place.

Spruce Run was the original course at Traverse and is a good enough test by any standards, but it is Jack Nicklaus's mighty Bear Course that is the undoubted star of the show.

Home of the Michigan Open, the course is typically Nicklaus in concept and layout. Plateau fairways, clearly defined landing areas, severely bunkered greens and first-class maintenance are all Nicklaus hallmarks. The Bear has them all, plus some particularly interesting terrain with rolling acres, woods, lakes, streams and flatlands.

That it is a wonderful course goes without saying - Jack doesn't build bad ones - but at the Bear he has gone for bigger greens than usual with original and inventive features to hide the pins.

And there are fabulous days ahead. Two new courses, designed by Lee Trevino and Gary Player, are in the pipeline, and will enhance even further the reputation of a resort with world-class amenities, luxurious accommodation and spectacular surroundings.

Atalaya Park

ATALAYA PARK GOLF AND COUNTRY CLUB, SPAIN

OPPOSITE: Magnificent – and that's just the practice green.
BELOW: All rooms overlook the Mediterranean.

There was a time, not so long ago, when a little of the polish had worn off the Atalaya Park Golf and Country Club on Spain's Costa del Sol. A five-year drought had devastated the fine Bernhard von Limburger course, laid out in 1967, and the twin buildings of the popular old hotel were in need of rejuvenation to return the resort to its former glory.

The one-time leading lady of the golf courses of the Costa was losing her fans, but with the installation of a life-saving supply of water, the appointment of a new director and a bold redevelopment plan by the hotel's German owners, the seasoned star is back on centre stage where she rightly belongs. Rave notices are once again being written.

The popular Scot Derek Brown, a veteran of the golf scene in southern Spain, was given the task of restoring the von Limburger course and the newer Rosner layout. With Brown's arrival came not only a commitment to return Atalaya to its former premier position among the great golf resorts of Europe but a determination to develop it into a genuine five-star destination.

With the breaking of the drought, a huge investment in irrigation and a total recovery of the courses, the resort has moved into a new and exciting era. There has already been recognition from the PGA of Europe, who have held their Annual Congress at the resort concurrently with their annual Team Championship. A contract was immediately signed to hold the event at Atalaya for the following five years, reflecting the confidence the PGA of Europe has in the complex.

The hotel is only 13 kilometres from fashionable Marbella, and elegant Puerto Banus is minutes away. There are five restaurants in the complex with the growing reputation of the Don Quixote restaurant's international and local cuisine being richly deserved.

A complete range of sport and leisure facilities is on offer, and hotel guests have access to both courses free of charge.

Le Paradis

LE PARADIS, MAURITIUS

OPPOSITE: Try concentrating on the golf with the Indian Ocean on your doorstep. BELOW: An exotic welcome awaits those lucky enough to visit Le Paradis.

For those in quest of peace and tranquillity there is, in the crystal-clear waters of the Indian Ocean, an island garden that might have been Eden. This is Mauritius; bathed in sunlight, surrounded by golden beaches and blue lagoons and far, far removed from the troubled world.

To set foot on to this island of swaying palms, with its riot of floral colour and stunning scenery, is to take a step back to a time where concern for the visitor and the real spirit of hospitality are an ingrained way of life.

This is an island of irresistible charm where the visitor shares the convivial but simple way of life of the islanders in surroundings such as Le Paradis Hotel.

Built to blend sympathetically with its delicate tropical surroundings, this wonderful retreat nestles on its own private peninsula between the towering majesty of Le Morne Mountain and the warm Indian Ocean.

Le Paradis is a special place, and is one of the world's great resorts in its own right, but has the additional glory of a wonderful golf course. The Paradis course is an exotic excursion around the Le Morne peninsula with some glorious holes, mighty challenges and views as idyllic as can be found anywhere that this captivating game is played.

Le Paradis put Mauritius on to the world's golfing map when it introduced the innovative Paradis Open tournament a few years ago and invited a clutch of European Tour stars to play during the week of the US Masters. For several years it was the only truly open tournament in world golf where the ordinary amateur, gentleman or lady, provided they had an official handicap, could tee off alongside the stars of the professional game. John Bland, Miguel Martin, Jean Van de Velde and Tony Johnstone from Zimbabwe are past winners.

With every conceivable water sport available and a fleet of big-game fishing boats to hunt giant tuna and blue marlin, Le Paradis may be as close to paradise as it is possible to be on this earth.

La Manga

HYATT LA MANGA CLUB RESORT

OPPOSITE: The three courses are tough, dramatic and beautiful. **BELOW:** The most famous course in Spain.

Covering an area larger than the Principality of Monaco, with three superb golf courses and a magnificent hotel, this is the Hyatt La Manga Resort on south-east Spain's Costa Calida, where a whole community has grown up around one of Europe's finest resorts.

Since it was taken over by P & O Ferries in the 1980's, La Manga has flourished with the building of a new £20 million hotel and a major redevelopment of the golf facilities.

The five-star hotel is the centrepiece of the resort; built in Andalusian style with whitewashed walls, terracotta stonework and classic Spanish arches, it is the epitome of refinement, comfort and style. Less formal accommodation is on offer at the Spanish pueblo-style Los Lomas apartments at the Peninsula Club featuring a raft of studios and flats.

American breakfasts on the gigantic scale, excellent food in a variety of restaurants and a mass of tapas bars take care of the nourishment for the hungry golfer, while the fitness centre and international tennis centre will work off any excesses that the golf does not reach.

A major investment in new irrigation for the North and South courses, alterations to the South course layout and a total revamp of the old La Princessa course have pushed La Manga to the forefront of the golf-dependent resorts of Spain. The La Princessa course in its new suit of clothes is now called more aptly the West Course, and offers staggering views and a tough challenge.

Amazing strides forward have been made at La Manga in upgrading facilities in general, but the resort has lost nothing of its special charm. Without question it now stands comparison with anything Europe has to offer.

Pont Royal

PONT ROYAL, PROVENCE, FRANCE

OPPOSITE: Seve Ballesteros has won great praise for his course design.
BELOW: Accommodation in authentic Provençal style.

Provence is unashamedly beautiful. Breathtaking villages perch on rugged mountains, lavender and wild thyme scent the air and olive groves run down to the beaches and fishing villages that border the Mediterranean. It was here, on 450 acres between Avignon and Aix-en-Provence, that Seve Ballesteros chose to build his first golf course outside Spain. It is a magnificent 18 holes overlooking the Durance river with a dramatic backdrop formed by the Luberon hills. Seve's ethos is that if you have done the course design well, you should have the impression that the course has always been there.

Pont Royal offers luxury homes built in authentic Provençal style but also a golf course that offers a serious challenge in a daunting environment. Greens are well protected by lakes and bunkers, and the course is narrow, playing through valleys and densely packed oak woods.

It has already gained a reputation as one of the finest in Europe and its wide range of tees ensures an appeal to the amateur and the tour professional. Under the watchful eye of Patrice Galitzine, the course has gone from strength to strength and hosts a few select tournaments annually.

Le Village de l'Eglise is the first of the villages to be completed and is based around two squares containing a restaurant and café as well as shops.

Properties range from lakeside studios and apartments to townhouses built in clusters around a shared pool. At the top of the range are substantial, individually designed villas with private pools and excellent views over the golf course.

Leisure facilities abound: tennis, swimming, horse riding and field sports, and barely a day goes by without a local market or festival taking place. Pont Royal offers Provence at its best.

Half Moon

HALF MOON GOLF, TENNIS AND BEACH CLUB, JAMAICA

OPPOSITE: The Trent Jones-designed course is a perfect pitch for tropical splendour. BELOW: The dining room at the Half Moon Club.

Five miles east of Montego Bay on the tropical island of Jamaica rests the beautiful and luxurious colonial-style Half Moon Golf, Tennis and Beach Club. Outside the white plantation-style buildings that hug the bay the crystal clear waters of the Caribbean lap almost to the hotel room door while across the way the splendid challenge of the resort's Robert Trent Jones golf course shows off its glorious character. Host to major competitions, enticing, testing, and surrounded by magnificent scenery, this is a course you are proud to have played on.

But then this is one of the truly great resorts at which one can make the most of a huge variety of sporting attractions and take time to relax and while away the day on a perfect beach under a tropical sun.

It is also one of the world's more environmentally aware resorts. Under its managing director Heinz Simonitsch, Half Moon has won a host of awards for its contribution to protecting the environment and encouraging guests to play a significant role in helping to preserve the natural beauty and resources of this luxurious corner of the island.

Simonitsch has been the guiding light at Half Moon for more than 30 years and he has developed the resort with great style and panache.

A major programme of preservation of water and electricity in no way intrudes upon guests' amenities, and the results in terms of conservation have been spectacular. The coral reef which shelters Half Moon's glorious white sandy beach is itself protected. A structure which supports solar panels to generate low-voltage electricity through wire mesh wrapped around the damaged parts of the reef is increasing the growth rate of the exisiting coral and encouraging new formations.

Golfers will find the layout of the course, designed by the prolific and talented Robert Trent Jones, a mighty challenge. It has been home to the Jamaica Open on many occasions since opening in 1961.

Coolum Resort

HYATT REGENCY COOLUM RESORT, AUSTRALIA

OPPOSITE: The sixth has been sculpted out
of unforgiving bushland and rainforest.
BELOW: Coolum is a haven for wildlife.

Picture this. In the shadow of Mount Coolum on Queensland's Sunshine Coast, set among 150 hectares of lush rainforest and bushland and fronting miles of Pacific Ocean beach, is Australia's most outstanding international resort and spa.

The Hyatt Regency Coolum Resort, some 90 minutes' drive north of Brisbane, is nothing short of a spectacular experience. Robert Trent Jones Jnr built the course in 1988 between the beach resorts of Maroochdore and Noosa and left most of the natural landscape and vegetation intact. The swamps, marshes and low bushland around the huge grey rock of Mount Coolum have been transformed into a testing 6,900-yard layout.

Trent Jones has always maintained that his courses are not designed to punish champions, 'just find out who they are'. The philosophy is clearly in evidence at the Coolum Resort.

Pacific breezes blow through the shrubs flanking most of the greens and across fairways winding their way through the native eucalyptus trees. There is charm and great beauty here, making it hard to concentrate on hitting and holding the small and slippery greens – a task made all the more difficult because many of the greens are set so close to ponds or the swamp.

Helping to make any visit here really memorable, of course, are the miles of sandy white beaches, the magnificent Hyatt Regency Hotel with its luxurious spa , excellent food and five-star service and facilities.

Add in a spectacular setting, eight swimming pools, a seven-court tennis centre fringed by natural rainforest, four restaurants and a village square with shops and eateries, and the lure of Coolum is hard to resist.

The golf course is designed primarily for use by hotel guests. Visitors are permitted by invitation only as this is a resort which guards its exclusivity jealously.

Emirates Club

DUBAI, UNITED ARAB EMIRATES

It is hard to think of a golf destination that has captured the imagination so quickly as the United Arab Emirate of Dubai. Not so long ago, while the Bedouin roamed the deserts, only pearl fishermen sustained the local economy of these lands. Then came oil. And while the Bedouin will always remain masters of the desert wastes, in a single generation the flat scrubland and great tracts of rust-coloured sand dunes have been transformed into one of the most developed and elegant new power centres of the world.

Within this vast and helter-skelter advancement, the vision of Sheikh Mohammed Al Maktoum, helped by a little of his oil revenue, has created a golf oasis of staggering imagination and grandeur. Sheikh Mohammed is not himself a golfer: his connection are firmly embedded in horse racing, but he has been quick to understand the value of the royal and ancient game of golf in terms of attracting tourism and the first commercial splash of green grass appeared in the desert in the late 1980s.

The Emirates Golf Club was not the first golf facility in Dubai - that honour belongs to the Dubai Country Club, which for years played on a sand course with 'browns' for greens - but it was the first grass golf course in the Middle East, and spectacular it is too.

Built from scratch in 18 months, the Emirates Club is now a firm favourite with the European Tour and hosts The Desert Classic - one of the leading events - early each year. Two further courses have been added, the Dubai Creek Golf Club and the Dubai Golf and Racing Club, which is now, amazingly, a fully floodlit layout.

The Emirates Club is essentially a members' club but its expansion to 36 holes will ease some of the pressure on a golf course that the whole world seems to want to play. Add to the golf facilities a magnificent choice of some of the finest hotels in the world and it is not difficult to understand Dubai's expanding popularity.

OPPOSITE: Is this the largest clubhouse in the world? BELOW: It is difficult to believe that you're in the desert.

Mount Juliet

THOMAS TOWN, COUNTY KILKENNY, IRELAND

OPPOSITE: The Jack Nicklaus-designed course is nothing short of magnificent.
BELOW: One can always expect great hospitality from the 19th hole.

Mount Juliet at Thomastown in County Kilkenny is one of the last great historic estates in Europe. Set among 1,500 acres of spectacular rolling woodland, this elegant Georgian country house retains its aura of eighteenth-century grandeur and is without question one of the great leisure resorts of the world.

Here is gracious living combined with matchless Irish hospitality and a leisurely pace of life guaranteed to rejuvenate the most troubled soul.

There is a Jack Nicklaus-designed golf course which has hosted the Irish Open on several occasions, a David Leadbetter Golf Academy, fishing, archery, clay-pigeon shooting, tennis and a leisure centre and spa which have established a world-class reputation.

But there is also that indefinable something that makes Ireland so special for golfers from all over the world.

Nature has uniquely endowed this land with magnificent scenery made up of a kaleidoscope of green landscapes and pastures and crystal-clear rivers. And this is, too, a land of people with a unique zest for life.

To play golf in Ireland is always special. To share the fun and humour of the Irish in the 19th hole afterwards is a privilege, and there is no more magnificent 19th hole than at Mount Juliet. The elegance and grandeur of the original 200-year-old mansion, built by the Earl of Carrick, has been painstakingly preserved.

There are 32 bedrooms, each with its own individual character, and Mount Juliet boasts a table of international repute. A menu of classic Irish dishes is offered in the splendid Lady Helen dining room but there is a less formal aspect too. The Hunters Yard, a short walk from the great house, is at the centre of Mount Juliet's many sporting activities and it also offers courtyard bedrooms to provide a more rural contrast to the opulence of the main building.

THE
LETTER OF THE LAW

A Story By P.G. Wodehouse

'FO-O-O-RE!' The cry, in certain of its essentials not unlike the wail of a soul in torment, rolled over the valley, and the young man on the seventh tee, from whose lips it had proceeded, observing that the little troupe of spavined octogenarians doddering along the fairway paid no attention whatever, gave his driver a twitch as if he was about to substitute action for words. Then he lowered the club and joined his companion on the bench.

'Better not, I suppose,' he said, moodily.

The Oldest Member, who often infested the seventh tee on a fine afternoon, nodded.

'I think you are wise,' he agreed. 'Driving into people is a thing one always regrets. I have driven into people in my golfing days, and I was always sorry later. There is something about the reproachful eye of the victim as you meet it subsequently in the bar of the club-house which cannot fail to jar the man of sensibility. Like a wounded oyster. Wait till they are out of distance, says the good book. The only man I ever knew who derived solid profit from driving into somebody who was not out of distance was young Wilmot Byng ... '

The two young men started.

'Are you going to tell us a story?'

'I am.'

'But –'

'I knew you would be pleased,' said the Oldest Member.

Wilmot Byng at the time of which I speak (the sage proceeded) was an engaging young fellow with a clear-cut face and a drive almost as long as the Pro's. Strangers, watching him at his best, would express surprise that he had never taken a couple of days off and won the Open Championship, and you could have knocked them down with a putter when you informed them that his handicap was six. For Wilmot's game had a fatal defect. He was impatient. If held up during a round, he tended to press. Except for that, however, he had a sterling nature and frank blue eyes which won all hearts.

It was the fact that for some days past I had observed in these eyes a sort of cloud that led me to think that the lad had something on his mind. And when we were lunching together in the club-house one afternoon and he listlessly refused a most admirable steak and kidney pudding I shot at him a glance so significant that, blushing profusely, he told me all.

He loved, it seemed, and the partner he had selected for life's medal round was a charming girl named Gwendoline Poskitt.

I knew the girl well. Her father was one of my best friends. We had been at the University together. As an undergraduate, he had made a name as a hammer thrower. More recently, he had taken up golf, and being somewhat short-sighted and completely muscle-bound, had speedily won for himself in our little community the affectionate sobriquet of the First Grave Digger.

'Indeed?' I said. 'So you love Gwendoline Poskitt do you? Very sensible. Were I a younger man, I would do it myself. But she scorns your suit?'

'She doesn't scorn any such dashed thing,' rejoined Wilmot with some heat. 'She is all for my suit.'

'You mean she returns your love?'

'She does.'

'Then why refuse steak and kidney pudding?'

'Because her father will never consent to her becoming my wife. And it's no good saying Why not elope? because I suggested that and she would have none of it. She loves me dearly, she says – as a matter of fact, she admitted in so many words that I was the tree on which the fruit of her life hung – but she can't bring herself to forgo the big church wedding, with full choral effects and the Bishop doing his stuff and photographs in the illustrated weekly papers. As she quite rightly pointed out, were we to sneak off and get married at the registrar's, bim would go the Bishop and phut the photographs. I can't shake her.'

'You ought not to want to shake her.'

'Move her, I mean. Alter her resolution. So I've got to get her father's consent. And how can I, when he has it in for me the way he has?'

He gave a groan and began to crumble my bread. I took another piece and put it on the opposite side of my plate.

'Has it in for you?'

'Yes. It's like this. You know the Wrecking Crew?'

He was alluding to the quartet of golfing cripples of which Joseph Poskitt was a regular member. The others were Old Father Time, The Man With The Hoe, and Consul, the Almost Human.

'You know the way they dodder along and won't let anyone through. There have been ugly mutterings about it in the Club for months, and it came even harder on me than on most of the crowd, for, as you know, I like to play quick. Well, the other day I cracked under the strain. I could endure it no longer. I –'

'Drove into them?'

'Drove into them. Using my brassie for the shot. I took a nice easy stance, came back slow, keeping my head well down, and let fly – firing into the brown, as it were, and just trusting to luck which of them I hit. The man who drew the short straw was old Poskitt. I got him on the right leg. Did you tell me he got his blue at Oxford for throwing the hammer?'

'Throwing the hammer, yes.'

'Not the high jump?'

'No.'

'Odd. I should have said –'

I was deeply concerned. To drive into the father of the girl you love, no matter what the provocation, seemed to me an act of the most criminal folly and so I told him.

He quivered and broke a tumbler.

'Now there,' he said, 'you have touched on another cause for complaint. At the time, I had no notion that he was the father of the girl I loved. As a matter of fact, he wasn't because I had not met Gwendoline then. She blew in later, having been on one of those round-the-world cruises. I must say I think that old buffers who hold people up and won't let them through ought to wear some sort of label indicating that they have pretty daughters who will be arriving shortly. Then one would know where one was and act accordingly. Still, there it is. I gave old Poskitt this juicy one, as described, and from what he said to me later in the changing room I am convinced that any suggestions on my part that I become his son-in-law will not be cordially received.'

I ate cheese gravely. I could see that the situation was a difficult one.

'Well, the only thing I can advise,' I said, 'is that you cultivate him assiduously. Waylay him and give him cigars. Ask after his slice. Tell him it's a fine day. He has a dog named Edward. Seek Edward out and pat him. Many a young man has won over the father of the girl he loves by such tactics, so why not you?'

He agreed to do so, and in the days which followed Poskitt could not show his face in the club-house without having Wilmot spring out at him with perfectos. The dog Edward began to lose hair off his ribs through incessant patting. And gradually, as I had hoped, the breach healed. Came a morning when Wilmot, inquiring after my old friend's slice, was answered not with the usual malevolent grunt but with a reasonably cordial statement that it now showed signs of becoming a hook.

'Ah?' said Wilmot. 'A cigar?'

'Thanks,' said Poskitt.

'Nice doggie,' said Wilmot, pursuing his advantage by administering a hearty buffet to Edward's aching torso before the shrinking animal could side-step.

'Ah,' said Poskitt.

That afternoon, for the first time for weeks, Wilmot Byng took twice of steak and kidney pudding at lunch and followed it up with treacle tart and a spot of Stilton.

And so matters stood when the day arrived for the annual contest for the President's Cup.

The President's Cup, for all its high-sounding name, was one of the lowliest and most humble trophies offered for competition to the members of our club, ranking in the eyes of good judges somewhere between the Grandmother's Umbrella and the Children's All-Day Sucker (open to boys and girls not yet having celebrated their seventh birthday). It has been instituted by a kindly committee for the benefit of the *canaille* of our little golfing world, those retired military, naval and business men who withdraw to the country and take up golf in their fifties. The contest was decided by medal play, if you could call it that, and no exponent with a handicap of under twenty-four was allowed to compete.

Nevertheless, there was no event on the fixture list which aroused among those involved a tenser enthusiasm. Centenarians sprang from their bathchairs to try their skill, and I have seen men with waist lines of sixty doing bending and stretching exercises for weeks in advance in order to limber themselves up for the big day. Form was eagerly discussed in the smoking room, and this year public opinion wavered between two men: Joseph Poskitt, the First Grave Digger, and Wadsworth Hemmingway, better known in sporting circles as Palsied Percy.

The betting, as I say, hovered uncertainly between these two, but there was no question as to which was the people's choice. Everybody was fond of Poskitt. You might wince as you saw his iron plough through the turf, but you could not help liking him, whereas Hemmingway was definitely unpopular. He was a retired solicitor, one of those dark, subtle sinister men who carry the book of rules in their bag, and make it their best club. He was a confirmed hole-claimer, and such are never greatly esteemed by the more easy-going. He had, moreover, a way of suddenly clearing his throat on the greens which alone would have been sufficient to ensure dislike.

The President's Cup was an event which I always made a point of watching, if I could, considering it a spectacle that purged the soul with pity and terror: but on this occasion business in London unfortunately claimed me and I was compelled to deprive myself of my annual treat. I had a few words with Wilmot before leaving to catch my train. I was pleased with the lad.

'You've done splendidly, my boy,' I said. 'I notice distinct signs of softening on our friend's part.'

'Me too,' agreed Wilmot jubilantly. 'He thanks me now when I give him a cigar.'

'So I observed. Well, continue to spare no effort. Did you wish him success for this afternoon?'

'Yes. He seemed pleased.'

'It might be a good idea if you were to offer to caddie for him. He would appreciate your skilled advice.'

'I thought of that, but I'm playing myself.'

'Today?'

I was surprised, for President's Cup day is usually looked on as a sort of Walpurgis Night, when fearful things are abroad and the prudent golfer stays at home.

'I promised a fellow a game, and I can't get out of it.'

'You will be held up a good deal, I am afraid.'

'I suppose so.'

'Well, don't go forgetting yourself and driving into Poskitt.'

'I should say not, ha, ha! Not likely, ho, ho! One doesn't do that sort of thing twice, does one? But excuse me now, if you don't mind. I have an appointment to wander in the woods with Gwendoline.'

It was late in the evening when I returned home. I was about to ring up Poskitt to ask how the contest had come out, when the telephone rang and I was surprised to hear Hemmingway's voice.

'Hullo,' said Hemmingway. 'Are you doing anything tomorrow morning?'

'Nothing,' I replied. 'How did things come out this afternoon?'

'That is what I rang up about. Poskitt and I tied for a low score at a hundred and fifteen. I put the matter up to the Committee and they decided that there must be a play off – match play.'

'You mean stroke play?'

'No, match play. It was my suggestion. I pointed out to Poskitt that by this method he would only have to play the first ten holes, thus saving wear and tear on his niblick.'

'I see. But why was it necessary to refer the thing to the Committee?'

'Oh, there was some sort of foolish dispute. It turned on a question of rubs of the green. Well, if you aren't doing anything tomorrow, will you referee the play-off?'

'Delighted.'

'Thanks. I want somebody who knows the rules. Poskitt does not seem to realize that there are any.'

'Why do you say that?'

'Well, he appears to think that when you're playing in a medal competition you can pick and choose which strokes you are going to count and which you aren't. Somebody drove into him when he was addressing his ball at the eleventh and he claims that that is what made him send it at right angles into a bush. As I told him, and the Committee supported me ...'

A nameless fear caused the receiver to shake in my hand.

'Who drove into him?'

'I forget his name. Tall, good looking young fellow with red hair –'

I had heard enough. Five minutes later, I was at Wilmot's door, beating upon it. As he opened it, I noticed that his face was flushed, his eye wild.

'Wilmot!' I cried.

'Yes, I know,' he said impatiently, leading the way to the sitting-room. 'I suppose you've been talking to Poskitt.'

'To Hemmingway. He told me –'

'I know, I know. You were surprised?'

'I was shocked. Shocked to the core. I thought there was better stuff in you, young Byng. Why, when the desire to drive into people grips you, do you not fight against it and conquer it like a man? Have you no will power? Cannot you shake off this frightful craving?'

'It wasn't that at all.'

'What wasn't what at all?'

'All that stuff about having no will power. I was in full possession of my faculties when I tickled up old Poskitt this afternoon. I acted by the light of pure reason. Seeing that I had nothing to lose –'

'Nothing to lose?'

'Not a thing. Gwendoline broke off the engagement this morning.'

'What?'

'Yes. As you are aware, we went to wander in the woods. Well, you know how you feel when you are wandering in the woods with a girl you adore. The sunlight streamed through the overhanging branches, forming a golden pattern on the green below: the air was heavy with fragrant scents and murmurous with the drone of fleeting insects, and what with one thing and another I was led to remark that I loved her as no one had ever loved before. Upon which, she said that I did not love her as much as she loved me. I said yes, I did, because my love stood alone. She said no, it didn't because hers did. I said it couldn't because mine did.

'Hot words ensued, and a few moments later, she was saying that she never wanted to see or speak to me again, because I was an obstinate, fatheaded son of an Army mule. She then handed back my letters, which she was carrying in a bundle tied round with lilac ribbon somewhere in the interior of her costume, and left me. Naturally, then, when Poskitt and his accomplice held us up for five minutes on the eleventh, I saw no reason to hesitate. My life's happiness was wrecked, and I found a sort of melancholy consolation in letting him have it on the seat of the pants with a wristy spoon shot.'

In the face of the profounder human tragedies there is little that one can say. I was pondering in gloomy silence on this ruin of two young lives, when the door bell rang. Wilmot went to answer it and came back carrying a letter in his hand. There was a look upon his face which I had not seen since the occasion when he missed the short putt on the eighteenth which would have given him the Spring medal.

'Listen,' said Wilmot. 'Cyanide. Do you happen to have any cyanide on you?'

'Cyanide?'

'Or arsenic would do. Read this. On second thoughts, I'll give you the gist. There is some rather fruity stuff in Para One which I feel was intended for my eye alone. The nub is that Gwendoline says she's sorry and it's all on again.'

The drama of the situation hit me like a stuffed eelskin.

'She loves you as of yore?'

'Rather more than of yore, if anything, I gather.'

'And you –'

'And I –'

'Have driven –'

'Have driven –'

'Into –'

'Into old Poskitt, catching him bending –'

'Causing him to lose a stroke and thereby tie for the President's Cup instead of winning it.'

I had not thought that the young fellow's jaw could drop any farther, but at these words it fell another inch.

'You don't mean that?'

'Hemmingway rang me up just now to tell me that he and Poskitt turned in the same score and are playing it off tomorrow.'

'Gosh!'

'Quite.'

'What shall I do?'

I laid my hand upon his shoulder.

'Pray, my boy, that Poskitt will win tomorrow.'

'But even then –'

'No. You have not studied the psychology of the long handicap golfer as I have. It would not be possible for a twenty-four handicap man who had just won his first cup to continue to harbour resentment against his bitterest foe. In the hour of triumph Poskitt must inevitably melt. So pray, my boy.'

A quick gleam lit up Wilmot Byng's blue eyes.

'You bet I'll pray,' he said. 'The way I'll pray will be nobody's business. Push off, and I'll start now.'

At eleven o'clock the following morning I joined Poskitt and Hemmingway on the first tee, and a few minutes later the play-off for the President's Cup had begun. From the very outset it was evident that this was to be a battle of styles. Two men of more sharply contrasted methods can seldom have come together on a golf course.

Poskitt, the d'Artagnan of the links, was a man who brought to the tee the tactics which in his youth had won him such fame as a hammer thrower. His plan was to clench his teeth, shut his eyes, whirl the club round his head and bring it down with sickening violence in the general direction of the sphere. Usually, the only result would be a ball topped along the ground or – as had been known to happen when he used his niblick – cut in half. But there would come times when by some mysterious dispensation of Providence he managed to connect, in which event the gallery would be stunned by the spectacle of a three-hundred-yarder down the middle. The whole thing, as he himself recognized, was a clean, sporting venture. He just let go and hoped for the best. In direct antithesis to these methods were those of Wadsworth Hemmingway. It was his practice before playing a shot to stand over the ball for an appreciable time, shaking gently in every limb and eyeing it closely as if it were some difficult point of law. When eventually he began his back swing, it was with a slowness which reminded those who had travelled in Switzerland of moving glaciers. A cautious pause at the top, and the clubhead would descend to strike the ball squarely and dispatch it fifty yards down the course in a perfectly straight line.

The contest, in short, between a man who – on, say, the long fifteenth – oscillated between a three and a forty-two and one who on the same hole always got his twelve – never more, never less. The Salt of Golf, as you might say.

And yet, as I took my stand beside the first tee, I had no feeling of pleasurable anticipation. To ensure the enjoyment of the spectator of a golf match, one thing is essential. He must feel that the mimic warfare is being conducted in the gallant spirit of a medieval tourney, not in the mood of a Corsican vendetta. And today it was only too plain from the start that bitterness and hostility were rampant.

The dullest mind would have been convinced of this by the manner in which, when Hemmingway had spun a half-crown and won the honour, Poskitt picked up the coin and examined it on both sides with a hard stare. Reluctantly convinced by his inspection that there was no funny business afoot, he drew back and allowed his opponent to drive. And presently Hemmingway had completed his customary fifty-yarder and it was Poskitt's turn to play.

A curious thing I have noticed about golf is that a festering grievance sometimes does wonders for a man's drive. It is as if pent-up emotion added zip to his swing. It was so on the present occasion. Assailing his ball with hideous violence, Poskitt sent it to within ten yards of the green, and a few moments later, despite the fact that Hemmingway cleared his throat both before and during the first, second and third putts, he was one up.

But this pent-up emotion is a thing that cuts both ways. It had helped Poskitt on the first. On the second, the short lake hole, it undid him. With all this generous wrath surging about inside him, he never looked like accomplishing the restrained mashie shot which would have left him by the pin. Outdriving the green by some hundred and seventy yards, he reached the woods that lay beyond it, and before he could extricate himself Hemmingway was on the green and he was obliged to concede. They went to the third all square.

Here Poskitt did one of his celebrated right-angle drives, and took seven to get out of the rough. Hemmingway, reaching the green with a steady eight, had six for it and won without difficulty.

The fourth is a dog-leg. Hemmingway drove short of the bunker. Poskitt followed with a stroke which I have never seen executed on the links before or since, a combination hook and slice. The ball, starting off as if impelled by dynamite, sailed well out to the left, then, after travelling one hundred and fifty yards, seemed to catch sight of the hole round the bend, paused in mid-air and, turning sharply to the right soared on to the green.

All square once more, a ding-dong struggle brought them to the seventh, which Poskitt won. Hemmingway, recovering, secured the eighth.

The ninth brings you back to the water again, though to a narrower part of it, and when Poskitt, with another of his colossal drives, finished within fifty yards of the pin, it seemed as if the hole must be his. Allowing him four approach shots and three putts, he would be down in eight, a feat far beyond the scope of his opponent. He watched Hemmingway's drive just clear the water, and with a grunt of satisfaction started to leave the tee.

'One moment,' said Hemmingway.

'Eh?'

'Are you going to drive?'

'Don't you call that a drive?'

'I do not. A nice practice shot, but not a drive. You took the honour when it was not yours. I, if you recollect, won the last hole. I am afraid I must ask you to play again.'

'What?'

'The rules are quite definite on this point,' said Hemmingway, producing a well-thumbed volume.

There was an embarrassing silence.

'And what do the rules say about clearing your throat on the green when your opponent is putting?'

'There is no rule against that.'

'Oh, no?'

'It is recognized that a tendency to bronchial catarrh is a misfortune for which the sufferer should be sympathized with rather than penalized.'

'Oh, yes?'

'Quite.' Hemmingway glanced at his watch. 'I notice that three minutes have elapsed since I made my drive. I must point out to you that if you delay more than five minutes, you automatically lose the hole.'

Poskitt returned to the tee and put down another ball. There was a splash.

'Playing three,' said Hemmingway.

Poskitt drove again.

'Playing five,' said Hemmingway.

'Must you recite?' said Poskitt.

'There is no rule against calling the score.'

'I concede the hole,' said Poskitt.

Wadsworth Hemmingway was one up at the turn.

There is nothing (said the Oldest Member) which, as a rule, I enjoy more than recounting stroke by stroke the course of a golf match. Indeed I have been told that I am sometimes almost too meticulous in my attention to detail. But there is one match which I have never been able to bring myself to report in this manner, and that is the play off for the President's Cup between Wadsworth Hemmingway and Joseph Poskitt.

The memory is too painful. As I said earlier, really bad golf is a thing which purges the soul, and a man becomes a better and broader man from watching it. But this contest, from the tenth hole – where Poskitt became all square

— onwards, was so poisoned by the mental attitude of the principals that to recall it even today makes me shudder. It resolved itself into a struggle between a great-souled slosher, playing far above his form, and a subtle Machiavellian schemer who, outdriven on every hole, held his own by constant reference to the book of rules.

I need merely say that Poskitt, after a two hundred and sixty yard drive at the eleventh, lost the hole through dropping his club in a bunker, that, having accomplished an equally stupendous stroke at the twelfth, he became two down owing to a careless inquiry as to whether I did not think he could get on from there with a mashie ('seeking advice of one who was not his caddie') and that, when he had won the thirteenth, he became two down once more at the short fourteenth when a piece of well-timed throat-clearing on the part of his opponent caused him to miss the putt which should have given him a half.

But there was good stuff in Joseph Poskitt. He stuck to it manfully. The long fifteenth I had expected him to win, and he did, but I had not been prepared for his clever seven on the sixteenth. And when he obtained a half on the seventeenth by holing out from a bunker, a hundred and fifty yards short of the green, I felt that all might yet be well. I could see that Hemmingway, confident that he would be dormy one, was a good deal shaken at coming to the eighteenth all square.

The eighteenth was one of those objectionable freak holes, which, in my opinion, deface a golf course. Ten yards from the tee the hill rose almost sheer to the table-land where the green had been constructed. I suppose that from tee to pin was a distance of not more than fifty yards. A certain three if you were on, anything if you were not.

It was essentially a hole unsuited to Poskitt's particular style. What Poskitt required, if he was to give of his best, was a great wide level prairie stretching

out before him into the purple distance. Conditions like those of the eighteenth hole put him very much in the position of a house-painter who is suddenly called upon to execute a miniature. I could see that he was ill at ease as he teed his ball up, and I was saddened, but not surprised, when he topped it into the long grass at the foot of the hill.

But the unnerving experience of seeing his opponent hole out from bunkers had taken its toll on Hemmingway. He, too, was plainly not himself. He swung with his usual care, but must have swerved from the policy of a lifetime and lifted his head. He finished his stroke with a nice, workmanlike follow through, but this did him no good, for he had omitted to hit the ball. When he had disentangled himself, there it was, still standing up on its little mountain of sand.

'You missed it,' said Poskitt.

'I am aware of the fact,' said Hemmingway.

'What made you do that? Silly. You can't expect to get anywhere if you don't hit the ball.'

'If you will kindly refrain from talking, I will play my second.'

'Well, don't miss this one.'

'Please.'

'You'll never win at golf if you do things in this slipshod way. The very first thing is to hit the ball. If you don't you cannot make real progress. I should have thought you would have realized that.'

Hemmingway appealed to me.

'Umpire, I should be glad if you would instruct my opponent to be quiet. Otherwise, I shall claim the hole and match.'

'There is nothing in the rules,' I said, 'against the opponent offering genial sympathy and advice.'

'Exactly,' said Poskitt. 'You don't want to miss it again, do you? Very well.

All I'm doing is telling you not to.'

I pursed my lips. I was apprehensive. I knew Hemmingway. Another man in his position might have been distracted by these cracks, but I could see that they had but solidified his determination to put his second up to the pin. I had seen wrath and resentment work a magic improvement in Poskitt's game, and I felt sure that they were about to do so in Wadsworth Hemmingway.

Nor was I mistaken. Concentration was written in every line of the man's face as he swung back. The next moment, the ball was soaring through the air, to fall three feet from the hole. And there was Poskitt faced with the task of playing two from the interior of a sort of jungle. Long grass twined itself about his ball, wild flowers draped it, a beetle was sitting on it. His caddie handed him a niblick, but I could not but feel that what was really required was a steam shovel. It was not a golf shot at all. The whole contract should have been handed to some capable excavation company.

But I had not realized to what lengths an ex-hammer-thrower can go, when armed with a niblick and really up against it. Just as film stars are happiest among their books, so was Joseph Poskitt happiest among the flowering shrubs with his niblick. His was a game into which the niblick had always entered very largely. It was the one club with which he really felt confident of expressing his personality. It removed all finicky science from the proceedings and put the issue squarely up to the bulging biceps and the will to win.

Even though the sight of his starting eyes and the knotted veins on his forehead had prepared me for the effort on the major scale, I gave an involuntary leap as the club came down. It was as if a shell had burst in my immediate neighbourhood. Nor were the effects so dissimilar to those which a shell would have produced. A gasping chasm opened in the hillside.

The air became full of a sort of macédoine of grass, dirt, flowers and beetles. And dimly, in the centre of this moving hash, one perceived the ball, travelling well. Accompanied by about a pound of mixed solids, it cleared the brow and vanished from our sight.

But when we had climbed the steep ascent and reached the green, my heart bled for Poskitt. He had made a gallant effort as ever man made and had reduced the lower slopes to what amounted to a devastated area, but he was lying a full ten feet from the hole and Hemmingway, an unerring putter over the short distance, was safe for three. Unless he could sink this ten-footer and secure a half, it seemed to me inevitable that my old friend must lose the match.

He did not sink it. He tried superbly, but when the ball stopped rolling three inches separated it from the hole. One could see from Hemmingway's bearing as he poised his club that he had no doubts or qualms. A sinister smile curved his thin lips.

'This for it,' he said, with sickening complacency.

He drew back the clubhead, paused for an instant, and brought it down.

And, as he did so, Poskitt coughed.

I have heard much coughing in my time. I am a regular theatre-goer, and I was once at a luncheon where an operatic basso got a crumb in his windpipe. But never have I heard a cough so stupendous as that which Joseph Poskitt emitted at this juncture. It was as if he had put a strong man's whole soul into the thing.

The effect on Wadsworth Hemmingway was disintegrating. Not even his cold self-control could stand up against it. A convulsive start passed through his whole frame. His club jerked forward, and the ball, leaping past the hole, skimmed across the green, took the edge in its stride and shot into the far bunker.

'Sorry,' said Poskitt. 'Swallowed a fly or something.'

There was a moment when all Nature seemed to pause, breathless.

'Umpire,' said Hemmingway.

'It's no good appealing to the umpire,' said Poskitt. 'I know the rules. They covered your bronchial catarrh, and they cover my fly or something. You had better concede the hole and match.'

'I will not concede the hole and match.'

'Well, then, hurry up and shoot,' said Poskitt, looking at his watch, 'because my wife's got a big luncheon party today, and I shall get hell if I'm late.'

'Ah!' said Hemmingway.

'Well, snap into it,' said Poskitt.

'I beg your pardon?'

'I said, "Snap into it".'

'Why?'

'Because I want to go home.'

Hemmingway pulled up the knees of his trousers and sat down.

'Your domestic arrangements have nothing to do with me,' he said. 'The rules allow me five minutes between strokes. I propose to take them.'

I could see that Poskitt was shaken. He looked at his watch again.

'All right,' he said. 'I can manage another five minutes.'

'You will have to manage a little more than that,' said Hemmingway. 'With my next stroke I shall miss the ball. I shall then rest for another five minutes. I shall then miss the ball again …'

'But we can't go on all day.'

'Why not?'

'I must be at that lunch.'

'Then what I would suggest is that you pick up and concede the hole and match.'

'Caddie,' said Poskitt.

'Sir?' said the caddie.

'Go to the club and get my house on the phone and tell my wife that I am unavoidably detained and shall not be able to attend that luncheon party.'

He turned to me.

'Is this five minutes business really right?'

'Would you care to look at my book of the rules?' said Hemmingway. 'I have it here in my bag.'

'Five minutes,' mused Poskitt.

'And as four and a half have now elapsed,' said Hemmingway, 'I will now go and play my third.'

He disappeared.

'Missed it,' he said, returning and sitting down again. The caddie came back.

'Well?'

'The lady said "Oh yeah?"'

'She said what?'

'"Oh yeah?" I tell her what you tell me to tell her and she said "Oh yeah?"'

I saw Poskitt's face pale. Nor was I surprised. Any husband would pale if his wife, in response to his telephone message that he proposed to absent himself from her important luncheon party, replied 'Oh yeah?' And of all such husbands, Joseph Poskitt was the one who might be expected to pale most. Like so many of these big, muscle-bound men, he was a mere serf in the home. His wife ruled him with an unremitting firmness from the day they had stepped across the threshold of St Peter's, Eaton Square.

He chewed his lower lip thoughtfully.

'You're sure it wasn't "Oh, yes" – like that – without the mark of interrogation – as much as to say that she quite understood and that it would be perfectly all right?'

'She said, "Oh yeah?"'

'H'm,' said Poskitt.

I walked away. I could not bear the spectacle of this old friend of mine in travail. What wives do to their husbands who at the eleventh hour edge out of important luncheon parties I am not able, as a bachelor, to say, but a mere glance was enough to tell me that in the Poskitt home, at least, it was something special. And yet to pick up and lose the first cup he had ever had a chance of winning ... No wonder Joseph Poskitt clutched his hair and rolled his eyes.

And so, as I say, I strolled off, and my wandering footsteps took me in the direction of the practice tee. Wilmot Byng was there, with an iron and a dozen balls.

He looked up, as I approached, with a pitiful eagerness.

'Is it over?'

'Not yet.'

'They haven't holed out?'

'Not yet.'

'But they must have done,' said Wilmot, amazed. 'I saw them both land on the green.'

'Poskitt has played three and is lying dead.'

'Well, where's Hemmingway?'

I peered round the bush which hides the eighteenth green from the practice tee.

'Just about to play five from the far bunker.'

'And Poskitt is dead in there?'

'Yes.'

'Well, then ...'

I explained the circumstances. Wilmot was aghast.

'But what's going to happen?'

I shook my head sadly.

'I fear that Poskitt has no alternative but to pick up. His wife, informed over the telephone that he would not be back to lunch, said "Oh yeah?"'

For a space Wilmot Byng stood brooding.

'You'd better be getting along,' he advised. 'From what you tell me, this seems to be one of those matches where an umpire on the spot is rather required.'

I did so, for I could see that there was much in what he said. I found Poskitt pacing the green. Hemmingway climbed out of the bunker a moment later to announce that he had once more been unsuccessful in striking the ball.

He seemed disposed to conversation.

'A lot of wasps there are about this summer,' he said. 'One sang right past my ear just then.'

'I wish it had bitten you,' said Poskitt.

'Wasps', replied Hemmingway, who dabbled in Natural History, 'do not bite. They sting. You are thinking of snakes.'

'Your society would make anyone think of snakes.'

'Gentlemen,' I said. 'Gentlemen!'

Saddened, I strolled away again. Golf to me is a sacred thing, and it pained me to see it played in this spirit. Moreover, I was beginning to want my lunch. It was partly the desire to converse with a rational human being and partly the reflection that he could pop into the clubhouse and bring me out a couple of ham sandwiches that led me to seek Wilmot Byng again. I made my way to the practice tee, and as I came in sight of it I stopped dead.

Wilmot Byng, facing the bunker, was addressing the ball with his iron. And standing in the bunker, his club languidly raised for his sixth, or it may have been his seventh, was Wadsworth Hemmingway.

The next moment Wilmot had swung, and almost simultaneously a piercing cry of agony rang out over the countryside. A magnificent low, raking shot, with every ounce of wrist and weight behind it, had taken Hemmingway on the left leg.

Wilmot turned to me and in his eyes there was the light which comes into the eyes of those who have set themselves a task and accomplished it.

'You'll have to disqualify that bird,' he said. 'He has dropped his club in a bunker.'

Little (said the Oldest Member) remains to be told. When, accompanied by Wilmot, I returned to the green, I formally awarded the match and cup to Poskitt, at the same time condoling with his opponent on having had the bad luck to be in the line of flight of somebody's random practice drive. These things, I pointed out, were all in the game and must be accepted as rubs of the green. I added that Wilmot was prepared to apologize, and Wilmot said, Yes, fully prepared. Hemmingway was, however, none too well pleased, I fear, and shortly afterwards he left us, his last words being that he proposed to bring an action against Wilmot in the civil courts.

The young fellow appeared not to have heard the threat. He was gazing at Poskitt, pale but resolute.

'Mr Poskitt,' he said. 'May I have a word with you?'

'A thousand,' replied Poskitt, beaming on his benefactor, for whom it was plain that he had now taken a fancy amounting to adoration. 'But later on, if you don't mind. I have to run like a ...'

'Mr Poskitt, I love your daughter.'

'So do I,' said Poskitt. 'Very nice girl.'

'I want to marry her.'

'Well, why don't you?'

'You will give your consent?'

A kindly smile flickered over my old friend's face. He looked at his watch again, then patted Wilmot affectionately on the shoulder.

'I will do better than that, my boy,' he said. 'I will formally refuse my consent. I will forbid the match in toto and oppose it root and branch. That will fix everything nicely. When you have been married as long as I have, you will know that what these things require is tact and the proper handling.'

And so it proved. Two minutes after Poskitt had announced that young Wilmot Byng wished to marry their daughter Gwendoline and that he, Poskitt, was resolved that this should be done only over his, Poskitt's, dead body, Mrs Poskitt was sketching out the preliminary arrangements for the sacred ceremony. It took place a few weeks later at a fashionable church with full choral effects, and all were agreed that the Bishop had seldom been in finer voice. The bride, as one was able to see from the photographs in the illustrated weekly papers, looked charming.

IF ONLY I HAD TAKEN UP
GOLF EARLIER...

PELHAM GRENVILLE WODEHOUSE was born on 15 October 1881 at Guildford, Surrey, and died on Long Island on Valentine's Day 1975. During those 93 years he became one of the greatest of all comic writers with a prodigious output of almost a hundred books, in which he created a timeless, idyllic world where it always seemed to be summer.

Yet his own life had its share of darkness. He was living in France when the Nazis invaded and spent a considerable time as an internee in conditions of great deprivation. During this time he was persuaded by his captors to make a series of broadcasts to his fans in America. He felt he was doing his bit to raise morale by playing down the misery of life as a prisoner, and making gentle mockery of his German tormentors. What the naive Englishman – known to his friends as Plum – failed to realize was that his well-meaning words would be used as propaganda and that he would come to be denounced as a traitor by many of his countrymen.

So hurt was he by the reaction at home that Wodehouse never again set foot on British soil. Although his millions of devotees did not doubt his patriotism, others would not forgive his indiscretion. It was only in the New Year Honours of 1975 that he was officially welcomed back into the fold when he was knighted. He died six weeks later, a happy man.

Despite his ordeal during the war, and his subsequent exile, Wodehouse never allowed his personal circumstances to cast a cloud over the sunshine of his work. He will, of course, always be best known for the bumbling Bertie Wooster and his valet Jeeves, the man with the shimmering presence, bulging forehead and answer to any conceivable problem. But Wodehouse lovers reserve a special locker in their heart for the golf stories.

In collections such as *The Heart Of A Goof* and *The Clicking Of Cuthbert*, the Oldest Member spins his yarns in which the course of true love invariably involves 18 holes. It is Wodehouse at his brilliant best, where man golfer takes woman golfer in his arms (generally employing the interlocking grip) and where, when the woman golfer hits her erstwhile soulmate over the head, the wise observer praises her choice of club.

A year before he died, Plum wrote: 'The trouble about reaching the age of 92 is that regrets for a misspent life are bound to creep in, and whenever you see me with a furrowed brow you can be sure

P.G. Wodehouse, 1881–1975.

that what is on my mind is the thought that if only I had taken up golf earlier and devoted my whole time to it instead of fooling about writing stories and things, I might have got my handicap down to under 18. If only they had put a putter in my hands when I was four and taught me the use of the various clubs, who knows what heights I might not have reached. It is this reflection that has always made my writing so sombre, its whole aroma like that of muddy shoes in a Russian locker room.'

He was, as always, joking. And it was, of course, with a typewriter that Wodehouse reached the greatest heights, never more so than in the golfing gems featured in this book.

THE MAJORS:
THE FACTS

'WINNING ISN'T EVERYTHING, BUT WANTING TO IS.'

Arnold Palmer

BRITISH OPEN

Year	Winner	Score	Venue	First prize	Year	Winner	Score	Venue	First prize
1860	W. Park Snr	174	Prestwick	Nil	1882	B. Ferguson	171	St Andrews	£12
1861	T. Morris Snr	163	Prestwick	Nil	1883[†]	W. Fernie	159	Musselburgh	-
1862	T. Morris Snr	163	Prestwick	Nil	1884	J. Simpson	160	Prestwick	-
1863	W. Park Snr	168	Prestwick	Nil	1885	B. Martin	171	St Andrews	£10
1864	T. Morris Snr	167	Prestwick	£6	1886	D. Brown	157	Musselburgh	£8
1865	A. Strath	162	Prestwick	£8	1887	W. Park Jnr	161	Prestwick	£8
1866	W. Park Snr	169	Prestwick	£6	1888	J. Burns	171	St Andrews	£8
1867	T. Morris Snrr	170	Prestwick	-	1889[†]	W. Park Jnr	155	Musselburgh	£8
1868	T. Morris Jnr	157	Prestwick	£6	1890	J. Ball *	164	Prestwick	£13
1869	T. Morris Jnr	154	Prestwick	£6	1891	H. Kirkaldy	166	St Andrews	£10
1870	T. Morris Jnr	149	Prestwick	£6	1892[2]	H. Hilton *	305	Muirfield	£35
1872[1]	T. Morris Jnr	166	Prestwick	£8	1893	W. Auchterlonie	322	Prestwick	£30
1873	T. Kidd	179	St. Andrews	£11	1894	J.H. Taylor	326	St George's	£30
1874	M. Park	159	Musselburgh	£8	1895	J.H. Taylor	322	St Andrews	£30
1875	W. Park Snr	166	Prestwick	£8	1896[†]	H. Vardon	316	Muirfield	£30
1876	B. Martin	176	St Andrews	£10	1897	H. Hilton *	314	Hoylake	£30
1877	J. Anderson	160	Musselburgh	£8	1898	H. Vardon	307	Prestwick	£30
1878	J. Anderson	157	Prestwick	£8	1899	H. Vardon	310	St George's	£30
1879	J. Anderson	169	St Andrews	£10	1900	J.H. Taylor	309	St Andrews	£30
1880	B. Ferguson	162	Musselburgh	£8	1901	J. Braid	309	Muirfield	£30
1881	B. Ferguson	170	Prestwick	£8	1902	A. Herd	307	Hoylake	£30

Year	Winner	Score	Venue	First prize	Year	Winner	Score	Venue	First prize
1903	H. Vardon	300	Prestwick	£30	1930	R. Jones * (USA)	291	Hoylake	£100
1904	J. White	296	St George's	£30	1931	T. Armour (USA)	296	Carnoustie	£100
1905	J. Braid	318	St Andrews	£30	1932	G. Sarazen (USA)	283	Prince's	£100
1906	J. Braid	300	Muirfield	£30	1933[†]	D. Shute (USA)	292	St Andrews	£100
1907	A. Massy (Fr.)	312	Hoylake	£30	1934	H. Cotton	283	St George's	£100
1908	J. Braid	291	Prestwick	£30	1935	A. Perry	283	Muirfield	£100
1909	J.H. Taylor	295	Deal	£30	1936	A. Padgham	287	Hoylake	£100
1910	J. Braid	299	St Andrews	£50	1937	H. Cotton	290	Carnoustie	£100
1911[†]	H. Vardon	303	St George's	£50	1938	R. Whitcombe	295	St George's	£100
1912	E. Ray	295	Muirfield	£50	1939	R. Burton	290	St Andrews	£100
1913	J.H. Taylor	304	Hoylake	£50	1940	*The championship was held in abeyance 1940–5 due to World War II*			
1914[3]	H. Vardon	306	Prestwick	£50	1946	S. Snead (USA)	290	St Andrews	£150
1915	*The championship was held in abeyance 1915–19 due to World War I*				1947	F. Daly (Ir.)	293	Hoylake	£150
1920	G. Duncan	303	Deal	£75	1948	H. Cotton	284	Muirfield	£150
1921	J. Hutchison (USA)	296	St Andrews	£75	1949[†]	A. Locke (SA)	283	St George's	£300
1922	W. Hagen (USA)	300	St George's	£75	1950	A. Locke (SA)	279	Troon	£300
1923	A. Havers	295	Troon	£75	1951	M. Faulkner	285	Portrush	£300
1924	W. Hagen (USA)	301	Hoylake	£75	1952	A. Locke (SA)	287	Lytham	£300
1925	J. Barnes (USA)	300	Prestwick	£75	1953	B. Hogan (USA)	282	Carnoustie	£500
1926	R. Jones * (USA)	291	Lytham	£75	1954	P. Thomson (Aus.)	283	Birkdale	£750
1927	R. Jones * (USA)	285	St Andrews	£100	1955	P. Thomson (Aus.)	281	St Andrews	£1,000
1928	W. Hagen (USA)	292	St George's	£100	1956	P. Thomson (Aus.)	286	Hoylake	£1,000
1929	W. Hagen (USA)	292	Muirfield	£100	1957	A. Locke (SA)	279	St Andrews	£1,000

Year	Winner	Score	Venue	First prize	Year	Winner	Score	Venue	First prize
1958[†]	P. Thomson (Aus.)	278	Lytham	£1,000	1981	B. Rogers (USA)	276	St George's	£25,000
1959	G. Player (SA)	284	Muirfield	£1,000	1982	T. Watson (USA)	284	Troon	£32,000
1960	K. Nagle (Aus.)	278	St Andrews	£1,250	1983	T. Watson (USA)	275	Birkdale	£40,000
1961	A. Palmer (USA)	284	Birkdale	£1,400	1984	S. Ballesteros (Sp.)	276	St Andrews	£55,000
1962	A. Palmer (USA)	276	Troon	£1,400	1985	A. Lyle	282	St George's	£65,000
1963[†]	R. Charles (NZ)	277	Lytham	£1,500	1986	G. Norman (Aus.)	280	Turnberry	£70,000
1964	T. Lema (USA)	279	St Andrews	£1,500	1987	N. Faldo	279	Muirfield	£75,000
1965	P. Thomson (Aus.)	285	Birkdale	£1,750	1988	S. Ballesteros (Sp.)	273	Lytham	£80,000
1966[4]	J. Nicklaus (USA)	282	Muirfield	£2,100	1989[†]	M. Calcavecchia (USA)	275	Troon	£80,000
1967	R. de Vicenzi (Arg.)	278	Hoylake	£2,100	1990	N. Faldo	270	St Andrews	£85,000
1968	G. Player (SA)	289	Carnoustie	£3,000	1991	I. Baker-Finch (Aus.)	272	Birkdale	£90,000
1969	A. Jacklin	280	Lytham	£4,250	1992	N. Faldo	272	Muirfield	£95,000
1970[†]	J. Nicklaus (USA)	283	St Andrews	£5,250	1993	G. Norman (Aus.)	267	St George's	£100,000
1971	L. Trevino (USA)	278	Birkdale	£5,500	1994	N. Price (Zimb.)	268	Turnberry	£110,000
1972	L. Trevino (USA)	278	Muirfield	£5,500	1995[†]	J. Daly (USA)	282	St Andrews	£125,000
1973	T. Weiskopf (USA)	276	Troon	£5,500	1996	T. Lehman (USA)	271	Lytham	£200,000
1974	G. Player (SA)	282	Lytham	£5,500					
1975[†]	T. Watson (USA)	279	Carnoustie	£7,500					
1976	J. Miller (USA)	279	Birkdale	£7,500					
1977	T. Watson (USA)	268	Turnberry	£10,000					
1978	J. Nicklaus (USA)	281	St Andrews	£12,500					
1979	S. Ballesteros (Sp.)	283	Lytham	£15,500					
1980	T. Watson (USA)	271	Muirfield	£25,000					

All players are British unless otherwise stated

* denotes amateur

[†] denotes the winner won after a play-off

[1] T. Morris kept the belt after winning it three times in succession
The championship went into abeyance for one year and continued as the Cup (the now familiar Claret Jug) from 1872

[2] The competition was now extended to 72 holes

[3] Owing to the increasing number of entries from 1914 onwards, a qualifying tournament was set up to narrow down the field to manageable proportions

[4] The tournament is now held over four days

US OPEN

Year	Winner	Score	Venue	First prize	Year	Winner	Score	Venue	First prize
1895	H. Rawlins	173	Newport	$150	1916	C. Evans *	286	Minikahda	$500
1896	J. Foulis	152	Shinnecock Hills	$150	1917	The tournament was held in abeyance 1917–18 due to World War I			
1897	J. Lloyd	162	Chicago	$150	1919[†]	W. Hagen	301	Brae Burn	$500
1898[1]	F. Herd	328	Myopia Hunt	$150	1920	E. Ray (GB)	295	Inverness	$500
1899	W. Smith	315	Baltimore	$150	1921	J. Barnes	289	Columbia	$500
1900	H. Vardon (GB)	313	Chicago	$150	1922	G. Sarazen	288	Skokie	$500
1901[†]	W. Anderson	331	Myopia Hunt	$150	1923[†]	R. Jones *	295	Inwood	$500
1902	L. Auchterlonie	307	Garden City	$200	1924[2]	C. Walker	297	Oakland Hills	$500
1903[†]	W. Anderson	307	Baltusrol	$200	1925[†]	W. MacFarlane	291	Worcester	$500
1904	W. Anderson	303	Glen View	$200	1926	R. Jones *	293	Scioto	$500
1905	W. Anderson	314	Myopia Hunt	$200	1927[†]	T. Armour	301	Oakmont	$500
1906	A. Smith	295	Onwentsia	$300	1928[†]	J. Farrell	294	Olympia Fields	$500
1907	A. Ross	302	Philadelphia	$300	1929[†]	R. Jones *	294	Winged Foot	$1,000
1908[†]	F. McLeod	322	Myopia Hunt	$300	1930	R. Jones *	287	Interlachen	$1,000
1909	G. Sargent	290	Englewood	$300	1931[†]	B. Burke	292	Inverness	$1,000
1910[†]	A. Smith	289	Philadelphia	$300	1932	G. Sarazen	286	Fresh Meadow	$1,000
1911[†]	J. McDermott	307	Chicago	$300	1933	J. Goodman *	287	North Shore	$1,000
1912	J. McDermott	294	Buffalo	$300	1934	O. Dutra	293	Merion	$1,000
1913[†]	F. Ouimet *	304	Brookline	$300	1935	S. Parks	299	Oakmont	$1,000
1914	W. Hagen	290	Midlothian	$300	1936	T. Manero	282	Baltusrol	$1,000
1915	J. Travers *	290	Baltusrol	$300	1937	R. Guldahl	281	Oakland Hills	$1,000

Year	Winner	Score	Venue	First prize	Year	Winner	Score	Venue	First prize
1938	R. Guldahl	284	Cherry Hills	$1,000	1964	K. Venturi	278	Congressional	$17,500
1939[†]	B. Nelson	284	Philadelphia	$1,000	1965[†]	G. Player (SA)	282	Bellerive	$26,000
1940[†]	W. Lawson Little	287	Canterbury	$1,000	1966[†]	W. Casper	278	Olympic	$26,500
1941	C. Wood	284	Colonial	$1,000	1967	J. Nicklaus	275	Baltusrol	$30,000
1942	The tournament was held in abeyance 1942–5 due to World War II				1968	L. Trevino	275	Oak Hill	$30,000
1946[†]	L. Mangrum	284	Canterbury	$1,500	1969	O. Moody	281	Champions	$30,000
1947[†]	L. Worsham	282	St. Louis	$2,000	1970	A. Jacklin (GB)	281	Hazeltine	$30,000
1948	B. Hogan	276	Riviera	$2,000	1971[†]	L. Trevino	280	Merion	$30,000
1949	C. Middlecoff	286	Medinah	$2,000	1972	J. Nicklaus	290	Pebble Beach	$30,000
1950[†]	B. Hogan	287	Merion	$4,000	1973	J. Miller	279	Oakmont	$35,000
1951	B. Hogan	287	Oakland Hills	$4,000	1974	H. Irwin	287	Winged Foot	$35,000
1952	J. Boros	281	Northwood	$4,000	1975[†]	L. Graham	287	Medinah	$40,000
1953	B. Hogan	283	Oakmont	$5,000	1976	J. Pate	277	Atlanta	$42,000
1954	E. Furgol	284	Baltusrol	$6,000	1977	H. Green	278	Southern Hills	$45,000
1955[†]	J. Fleck	287	Olympic	$6,000	1978	A. North	285	Cherry Hills	$45,000
1956	C. Middlecoff	281	Oak Hill	$6,000	1979	H. Irwin	284	Inverness	$50,000
1957	D. Mayer	282	Inverness	$7,200	1980	J. Nicklaus	272	Baltusrol	$55,000
1958	T. Bolt	283	Southern Hills	$8,000	1981	D. Graham (Aus.)	273	Merion	$55,000
1959	W. Casper	282	Winged Foot	$12,000	1982	T. Watson	282	Pebble Beach	$60,000
1960	A. Palmer	280	Cherry Hills	$14,400	1983	L. Nelson	280	Oakmont	$72,000
1961	G. Littler	281	Oakland Hills	$14,000	1984[†]	F. Zoeller	276	Winged Foot	$94,000
1962[†]	J. Nicklaus	283	Oakmont	$17,500	1985	A. North	279	Oakland Hills	$103,000
1963[†]	J. Boros	293	Brookline	$17,500	1986	R. Floyd	279	Shinnecock Hills	$115,000

Year	Winner	Score	Venue	First prize
1987	S. Simpson	277	Olympic	$150,000
1988[†]	C. Strange	278	Brookline	$180,000
1989	C. Strange	278	Oak Hill	$200,000
1990[†]	H. Irwin	280	Medinah	$220,000
1991[†]	P. Stewart	282	Hazeltine	$235,000
1992	T. Kite	285	Pebble Beach	$275,000
1993	L. Janzen	272	Baltusrol	$290,000

Year	Winner	Score	Venue	First prize
1994[†]	E. Els (SA)	279	Oakmont	$320,000
1995	C. Pavin	280	Shinnecock Hills	$350,000
1996	S. Jones	278	Oakland Hills	$425,000

All players are American unless otherwise stated

* denotes amateur

† denotes the winner won after a play-off

[1] The tournament was now played over 4 rounds (72 holes)

[2] Qualifying is introduced for the first time due to the large number of participants

US MASTERS

Held at Augusta National Golf Course

Year	Winner	Score	First prize	Year	Winner	Score	First prize
1934	H. Smith	284	$1,500	1947	J. Demaret	281	$2,500
1935[†]	G. Sarazen	282	$1,500	1948	C. Harmon	279	$2,500
1936	H. Smith	285	$1,500	1949	S. Snead	283	$2,750
1937	B. Nelson	283	$1,500	1950	J. Demaret	282	$2,400
1938	H. Picard	285	$1,500	1951	B. Hogan	280	$3,000
1939	R. Guldahl	279	$1,500	1952	S. Snead	286	$4,000
1940	J. Demaret	280	$1,500	1953	B. Hogan	274	$4,000
1941	C. Wood	280	$1,500	1954[†]	S. Snead	289	$5,000
1942[†]	B. Nelson	280	$1,500	1955	C. Middlecoff	279	$5,000
1943	The tournament was held in abeyance 1943–5 due to World War II			1956	J. Burke	289	$5,000
1946	H. Keiser	282	$2,500	1957[1]	D. Ford	283	$8,750

Year	Winner	Score	First prize	Year	Winner	Score	First prize
1958	A. Palmer	284	$11,250	1981	T. Watson	280	$60,000
1959	A. Wall	284	$15,000	1982[†]	C. Stadler	284	$64,000
1960	A. Palmer	282	$17,500	1983	S. Ballesteros (Sp.)	280	$90,000
1961	G. Player (SA)	280	$20,000	1984	B. Crenshaw	277	$108,000
1962[†]	A. Palmer	280	$20,000	1985	B. Langer (Ger.)	282	$126,000
1963	J. Nicklaus	286	$20,000	1986	J. Nicklaus	279	$144,000
1964	A. Palmer	276	$20,000	1987[†]	L. Mize	285	$162,000
1965	J. Nicklaus	271	$20,000	1988	A. Lyle (GB)	281	$183,800
1966[†]	J. Nicklaus	288	$20,000	1989[†]	N. Faldo (GB)	283	$200,000
1967	G. Brewer	280	$20,000	1990[†]	N. Faldo (GB)	278	$225,000
1968	R. Goalby	277	$20,000	1991	I. Woosnam (GB)	277	$243,000
1969	G. Archer (Can.)	281	$20,000	1992	F. Couples	275	$270,000
1970	W. Casper	279	$25,000	1993	B. Langer (Ger.)	275	$306,000
1971	C. Coody	279	$25,000	1994	J.M. Olazabal (Sp.)	279	$360,000
1972	J. Nicklaus	286	$25,000	1995	B. Crenshaw	274	$396,000
1973	T. Aaron	283	$30,000	1996	N. Faldo (GB)	276	$450,000
1974	G. Player (SA)	278	$35,000	1997	T. Woods	270	$486,000
1975	J. Nicklaus	276	$40,000				
1976	R. Floyd	271	$40,000				
1977	T. Watson	276	$40,000				
1978	G. Player (SA)	277	$45,000				
1979[†]	F. Zoeller	280	$50,000				
1980	S. Ballesteros (Sp.)	275	$55,000				

All players are American unless otherwise stated
* denotes amateur
† denotes the winner won after a play-off
1 A halfway cut is introduced

PGA OF AMERICA

Year	Winner	Score	Venue	First prize	Year	Winner	Score	Venue	First prize
1916	J. Barnes	1 hole	Siwanoy	$500	1938	P. Runyan	8 & 7	Shawnee	$1,000
1917	*The tournament was held in abeyance 1917–18 due to World War I*				1939	H. Picard	1 hole	Pomonok	$1,000
1919	J. Barnes	6 & 5	Engineers	$500	1940	B. Nelson	1 hole	Hershey	$1,000
1920	J. Hutchison	1 hole	Flossmoor	$500	1941	V. Ghezzie	38th hole	Cherry Hills	$1,000
1921	W. Hagen	3 & 2	Inwood	$500	1942	S. Snead	2 & 1	Seaview	$1,000
1922	G. Sarazen	4 & 3	Oakmont	$500	1943	*The tournament was held in abeyance in 1943 due to World War II*			
1923	G. Sarazen	38th hole	Pelham	-	1944	B. Hamilton	1 hole	Manito	$3,500
1924	W. Hagen	2 holes	French Springs	-	1945	B. Nelson	4 & 3	Morraine	$3,500
1925	W. Hagen	6 & 4	Olympia Fields	-	1946	B. Hogan	6 & 4	Portland	$3,500
1926	W. Hagen	6 & 5	Salisbury	-	1947	J. Ferrier	2 & 1	Plum Hollow	$3,500
1927	W. Hagen	1 hole	Cedar Crest	-	1948	B. Hogan	7 & 6	Norwood Hills	$3,500
1928	L. Diegel	6 & 5	Five Farms	-	1949	S. Snead	3 & 2	Hermitage	$3,500
1929	L. Diegel	6 & 4	Hillcrest	-	1950	C. Harper	4 & 3	Scioto	$3,500
1930	T. Armour	1 hole	Fresh Meadows	-	1951	S. Snead	7 & 6	Oakmont	$3,500
1931	T. Creavy	2 & 1	Wannamoisett	-	1952	J. Turnesa	1 hole	Big Spring	$3,500
1932	O. Dutra	4 & 3	Keller	-	1953	W. Burkemo	2 & 1	Birmingham	$5,000
1933	G. Sarazen	5 & 4	Blue Mound	-	1954	C. Harbert	4 & 3	Keller	$5,000
1934	P. Runyan	38th hole	Park Club of Buffalo	-	1955	D. Ford	4 & 3	Meadowbrook	$5,000
1935	J. Revolta	5 & 4	Twin Hills	$1,000	1956	J. Burke	3 & 2	Blue Hill	$5,000
1936	D. Shute	3 & 2	Pinehurst	$1,000	1957	L. Hebert	3 & 1	Miami Valley	$8,000
1937	D. Shute	37th hole	Pittsburgh Field	$1,000	1958[1]	D. Finterswald	276	Llanerch	$5,250

Year	Winner	Score	Venue	First prize	Year	Winner	Score	Venue	First prize
1959	B. Rosburg	277	Minneapolis	$8,250	1982	R. Floyd	272	Southern Hills	$65,000
1960	J. Hebert	281	Firestone	$11,000	1983	H. Sutton	274	Riviera	$100,000
1961[†]	J. Barber	277	Olympia Fields	$11,000	1984	L. Trevino	273	Shoal Creek	$125,000
1962	G. Player (SA)	278	Aronimink	$13,000	1985	H. Green	278	Cherry Hills	$125,000
1963	J. Nicklaus	279	Dallas	$13,000	1986	R. Tway	276	Inverness	$140,000
1964	B. Nichols	271	Columbus	$18,000	1987[†]	L. Nelson	287	PGA National	$150,000
1965	D. Marr	280	Laurel Valley	$25,000	1988	J. Sluman	272	Oak Tree	$160,000
1966	A. Geiberger	280	Firestone	$25,000	1989	P. Stewart	276	Kemper Lakes	$200,000
1967[†]	D. January	281	Columbine	$25,000	1990	W. Grady (Aus.)	282	Shoal Creek	$225,000
1968	J. Boros	281	Pecan Valley	$25,000	1991	J. Daly	276	Crooked Stick	$230,000
1969	R. Floyd	276	NCR	$35,000	1992	N. Price (Zimb.)	278	Bellerive	$280,000
1970	D. Stockton	279	Southern Hills	$40,000	1993[†]	P. Azinger	272	Inverness	$300,000
1971	J. Nicklaus	281	PGA National	$40,000	1994	N. Price (Zimb.)	269	Southern Hills	$310,000
1972	G. Player (SA)	281	Oakland Hills	$45,000	1995[†]	S. Elkington (Aus.)	267	Riviera	$360,000
1973	J. Nicklaus	277	Canterbury	$45,000	1996[†]	M. Brooks	277	Valhalla	$430,000
1974	L. Trevino	276	Tanglewood	$45,000					
1975	J. Nicklaus	276	Firestone	$45,000					
1976	D. Stockton	281	Congressional	$45,000					
1977[†]	L. Wadkins	287	Pebble Beach	$45,000					
1978[†]	J. Mahaffey	276	Oakmont	$50,000					
1979[†]	D. Graham (Aus.)	272	Oakland Hills	$60,000					
1980	J. Nicklaus	274	Oak Hill	$60,000					
1981	L. Nelson	273	Atlanta	$60,000					

All players are American unless otherwise stated
[†] denotes the winner won after a play-off
[1] The tournament format changed from match play to stroke play

THE RYDER CUP

1927 Played at Worcester Country Club (USA)

	Final Total
USA	9½
GB	3½

1929 Played at Moortown (GB)

	Final Total
USA	5
GB	7

1931 Played at Scioto Country Club (USA)

	Final Total
USA	9
GB	3

1933 Played at Southport (GB)

	Final Total
USA	5½
GB	6½

1935 Played at Rigdewood (USA)

	Final Total
USA	9
GB	3

1937 Played at Southport (GB)

	Final Total
USA	8
GB	4

The tournament was held in abeyance from 1939–46 due to World War II

1947 Played at Portland (USA)

	Final Total
USA	11
GB	1

1949 Played at Ganton (GB)

	Final Total
USA	7
GB	5

1951 Played at Pinehurst (USA)

	Final Total
USA	9½
GB	2½

1953 Played at Wentworth (GB)

	Final Total
USA	6½
GB	5½

1955 Played at Thunderbird (USA)

	Final Total
USA	8
GB	4

1957 Played at Lindrick (GB)

	Final Total
USA	4½
GB	7½

1959 Played at Palm Desert (USA)

	Final Total
USA	8½
GB	3½

1961 Played at Royal Lytham (GB)

	Final Total
USA	14½
GB	9½

1963 Played at East Lake (USA)

	Final Total
USA	23
GB	9

1965 Played at Royal Birkdale (GB)

	Final Total
USA	19½
GB	12½

1967 Played at Champions (USA)

	Final Total
USA	.23½
GB	.8½

1969 Played at Royal Birkdale (GB)

	Final Total
USA	.16
GB	.16

1971 Played at Old Warson (USA)

	Final Total
USA	.18½
GB	.13½

Irish players now became available for selection to the British side.

1973 Played at Muirfield (GB)

	Final Total
USA	.19
GB & I	.13

1975 Played at Laurel Valley (USA)

	Final Total
USA	.21
GB & I	.11

1977 Played at Royal Lytham (GB)

	Final Total
USA	.12½
GB & I	.7½

European players now became available for selection to the British and Irish side

1979 Played at Greenbrier (USA)

	Final Total
USA	.17
Europe	.11

1981 Played at Walton Heath (GB)

	Final Total
USA	.18½
Europe	.9½

1983 Played at PGA National (USA)

	Final Total
USA	.14½
Europe	.13½

1985 Played at the Belfry (GB)

	Final Total
USA	.11½
Europe	.16½

1987 Played at Muirfield Village (USA)

	Final Total
USA	.13
Europe	.15

1989 Played at the Belfry (GB)

	Final Total
USA	.14
Europe	.14

1991 Played at Kiawah Island (US)

	Final Total
USA	.14½
Europe	.13½

1993 Played at the Belfry (GB)

	Final Total
USA	.15
Europe	.13

1995 Played at Oak Hill (US)

	Final Total
USA	.13½
Europe	.14½

INDEX

PICTURE CREDITS

Michael Hobbs Picture Library

Pages 5, 8, 16, 18, 19, 20, 24, 25, 27, 28, 29, 31, 32, 34, 37, 39, 43, 44, 48, 53, 56, 69, 70, 71, 72, 76, 77, 79, 80, 81, 82, 84, 85, 86, 88, 89, 90, 91, 92, 93, 94, 95, 96, 97, 98, 99, 100, 101, 102, 104, 105, 106, 107, 108, 109, 110, 111, 112, 113, 115, 119, 120, 122, 123, 125, 127, 128, 132, 133, 134, 135, 137, 138, 140, 141, 143, 144, 145, 146, 147, 148, 149, 150, 151, 154, 156, 157, 158, 159, 160, 162, 164, 165, 166, 167, 168, 169, 170, 171, 172, 173, 174, 175, 176, 177, 192, 193, 194, 195, 196, 197, 200, 201, 202, 203, 204, 205, 206, 207, 208, 209, 212, 213, 220, 223, 236, 237, 238, 254, 259 and 294

David White

Pages 14, 15, 17, 18, 19, 23, 26, 32, 33, 45, 47, 49, 52, 73, 74, 80, 128, 131, 145, 152, 153, 155, 163, 198, 199, 219, 220, 222, 223, 224, 225, 239, 240, 241, 253, 255, 256 and 257

Sarah Fabbien Baddiel

Pages 50, 51, 55, 57, 124, 126, 129, 145, 161, 217, 220 and 221

Birdie Golf Ltd

Pages 191, 192, 193, 194, 195, 196, 197, 198, 199, 200, 201, 202, 203, 204, 205, 206, 207, 208 and 209

Anton Want

Pages 29, 224, 225, 226 and 227

Corbis UK

Pages 213 and 293

Alleghany Country Club

Pages 251 and 252

Hulton Getty Ltd

Page 216

Front cover images: Michael Hobbs Picture Library, Allsport UK Ltd, Sarah Fabbien Baddiel